T.L.S.

ESSAYS AND REVIEWS FROM
The Times Literary Supplement · 1963

2

T.L.S.

ESSAYS AND REVIEWS FROM
The Times Literary Supplement · 1963

2

London
OXFORD UNIVERSITY PRESS
NEW YORK   TORONTO
1964

Oxford University Press, Amen House, London E.C.4

GLASGOW   NEW YORK   TORONTO   MELBOURNE   WELLINGTON
BOMBAY   CALCUTTA   MADRAS   KARACHI   LAHORE   DACCA
CAPE TOWN   SALISBURY   NAIROBI   IBADAN   ACCRA
KUALA LUMPUR   HONG KONG

PRINTED IN GREAT BRITAIN IN THE CITY OF OXFORD
AT THE ALDEN PRESS

CONTENTS

NOTE

The present volume has been compiled on the same principle as *T.L.S. 1962*, though rather more has been done to give some coverage to the chief novels and books of poems published in the year. As before, articles written for special numbers have been omitted, with the exception of that on 'New Ways with Type', which appeared in the 'Book Production' number on 26 April. The other chief special numbers were on 'The Critical Moment' (26 July), 'Critics Abroad' (27 September) and 'The Art of Science' (25 October). The first two of these are expected to appear as a book from Messrs. Faber & Faber later in 1964; they will also be published in German translation as two booklets (by Verlag Günter Neske).

Articles from the previous year's special number 'A Language in Common' were republished during 1963 under the same title by *The Times* Publishing Company.

I

ANOTHER PRESIDENT

THE EISENHOWER MEMOIRS

THE ASSASSINATION OF President Kennedy has lent a graver interest to his predecessor's memoirs. The merits and defects of General Eisenhower's first volume are discussed below. But at a time when the whole world is shocked, in the strictest sense of the term, at the murder of President Kennedy, it is perhaps worth noting how, possibly unconsciously, General Eisenhower reveals to us not only the august character but also the immense burden of the presidential office. For quite a long time now the President of the United States has shared with the Chairman of the Soviet Council of Ministers the power of destroying the whole human race—a power that doubtless will sober even the most light-hearted and light-headed candidates for the White House or for the Kremlin. And it must be noted that President Eisenhower, like President Kennedy, steadily refused to be panicked into using or even threatening to use the power that science had, possibly unfortunately, given them.

*   *   *

The most famous of American political correspondents, Mr. James 'Scotty' Reston of the *New York Times*, is reported to have remarked of General Eisenhower's memoirs that General Eisenhower is too nice a man to be a good historian. One can see what Mr. Reston means. General Eisenhower is no Tacitus. There is no Swiftian *saeva indignatio*. The most that one can say is that there is a drop in the temperature when certain people are mentioned; but he never gets down to zero and hardly ever gets below 50° F.

Mandate for Change is a book of great charity and generosity. And if it must be wished that General Eisenhower had not pulled his punches so much, it must be admitted also that his astonishing popularity, as great in 1963, as the polls show, as it was when he left

DWIGHT D. EISENHOWER: *Mandate for Change, 1953–1956*. The White House Years. 650 pp. Heinemann. £3 3s.

1

office, is in part based on the public belief that General Eisenhower is a nice man, full of concern for the public weal and at the most inclined for brief moments to 'blow his top' and to display in no offensive fashion a harmless and often quite justified vanity.

There are, however, drawbacks to General Eisenhower's temperament when it comes to writing memoirs which are *documents pour servir*, and these drawbacks are no doubt what Mr. Reston had in mind. For, like a sundial, General Eisenhower tends to register only the serene hours. He makes it plain that he had great responsibilities and, as is sometimes forgotten, he again and again showed that sagacity which made him an admirable commander-in-chief of a coalition army. But there is a lack of edge to these memoirs which was not so visible in *Crusade in Europe*. It is hard indeed to think of any of the military memorialists of the last war who are less open to the charge of scoring off enemies or, what is even more tempting, allies, than is General Eisenhower. And although he glides over faults and failures in his administration and perhaps claims a little too much for it, there is none of that assumption of infallibility which has marked so many accounts of the late war from its leaders.

*   *   *

This amiability of temper in his writings, of course, detracts from the dramatic value of his memoirs. We know in fact a great deal more about the Eisenhower administration from the now quite numerous confidants of the President who have 'told all' than we learn from General Eisenhower himself. The General, in discussing the reasons which led him to campaign for the Republican nomination in 1952, puts very high indeed the desirability of rescuing the Republican Party from the self-destructive frustration to which it had been condemned by five terms of exclusion from the White House, an exclusion made all the more bitter as victory had seemed inevitable in 1948. Above all, General Eisenhower, head of Nato, had been alarmed at the signs of the resurgence of the 'fortress America' idea, a natural nostalgia for a day when it did not matter what happened outside the territory of the United States. General Eisenhower knew that this nostalgia was an illusion and a dangerous illusion, but he feared that it was an illusion very popular with a great section of the Republican Party (and not only of the Republican Party).

Revulsion from involvement in the affairs of the outer and wicked world had been reinforced by the unsatisfactory character of the post-war world. That hot war became the cold war was an immense deception for the mass of the American people. The Korean War, the fourth most bloody war ever fought by the United States, whose sacrifices in men and money it is fashionable to underestimate or ignore in Europe, was the last bitter ingredient in the cup. That after the most complete victory in history, with the Germans surrendering to General Eisenhower at Rheims and the Japanese to General MacArthur in Tokyo Bay, there should not have resulted *at once* an America free from any concern for the outer world and free from the pressures of war and preparation for war, was a wounding insult to American pride. And for many Americans the situation existing in 1952, with an uneasy truce in Korea, with a Europe which was very far from stable and very far from total commitment to the American side could only be the result of treason. For they suffered from what was, to quote a once well-known phrase, 'the illusion of American omnipotence'. General Eisenhower knew better, and there can be no reasonable doubt that his decision to enter politics, which he had refused to do earlier, was based, above all, on his desire to save the United States from the stultification of its victory, and, indeed, its possible ruin if some of the Republican politicians whom he mentions too kindly came into command.

*   *   *

That General Eisenhower is sincere in this description of his motives cannot be doubted. Just as Robert E. Lee is probably the only general in history who has taken command of one army after refusing the command of the opposing army, General Eisenhower is probably the only man in American history who could have run, and won, as the Democratic or the Republican candidate. Had he accepted President Truman's offer of support, he could have been nominated in 1952 and no doubt would have been triumphantly elected. He accepted the Republican nomination and was triumphantly elected as all competent observers of the American scene in 1952 realized was certain to happen.

General Eisenhower tells us candidly that the Republicans were in some doubt whether he was a Republican, and they had reasons for their doubts. The only other West Pointer ever to enter the White House, Ulysses S. Grant, voted only once before he entered the White House and he voted against the Republican candidate not because he was a Democrat but because he knew the Republican candidate, John C. Frémont. General Eisenhower was, in the Greek sense, almost as 'idiotic' as General Grant. From this political innocence came many of his troubles. With a generosity which is charming, but also regrettable, General Eisenhower pulls his punches when he comes to discuss his dealings with the Republican high command. He does, it is true, report his disgust when he discovered how narrow were the views of the Republicans whom he was carrying to victory, and how much their motives were local, personal, and even base: but he names no names, again a sign of amiability but of an amiability which makes his book less valuable than it might have been. One is led to hope that General Eisenhower has left, for the benefit of posterity, an unexpurgated version of his years in the White House.

*   *   *

It was widely reported in 1952 that General Eisenhower, when he consented to run, assumed that opposition to his nomination would cease. He soon discovered his mistake. He was opposed on two different grounds—the first the narrow and professional grounds that he was a 'Johnny-come-lately' not only to politics but also to the Republican Party. The labourers in the vineyard who had borne the burden of the day and the heat were not at all amused at the spectacle of the amateur going in and taking the prize without any contest. As it was, General Eisenhower and his party managers, like Senator Henry Cabot Lodge (now ambassador in Vietnam), had to fight hard to put the nomination over. There was a paradox in how this was done which General Eisenhower either failed to notice or has failed to comment on. In 1912 Senator Lodge's grandfather had organized the Republican Convention to secure the renomination of President Taft by the use of the Southern votes always given to the dispenser of patronage. In 1952 it was necessary to overthrow in the South, above all in Texas, the existing Republican machine in favour of the Eisenhower supporters, many of whom were very recent Democrats, and this was done in great part by Senator Henry Cabot Lodge, reversing the role of his grandfather in 1912.

One of the few really interesting human notes of this worthy book is not only the account of the distress of the Taft supporters when 'Mr. Republican' was again, as they thought, cheated of the nomination he had earned, but the account of the relationship which grew up between General Eisenhower and Senator Taft. Obviously, General Eisenhower resents the suggestion made at the time, and repeated often since, that he surrendered his principles to Senator Taft in order to get his support and there is no evidence that he did. Indeed, General Eisenhower reports his astonishment to learn how 'liberal' in the American sense Senator Taft was—much more liberal than General Eisenhower was in domestic matters. And indeed Senator Taft, the head of a great, wealthy, and patrician family with a long tradition of public service, was far more willing to use the power of the states and of the Union to heal social wounds than was the very self-made man from the wrong side of the tracks who was about to enter the White House. But Senator Taft was only slightly converted, if converted at all, to the Republican nominee's views on international affairs and was as devoted to budget balancing as most Republican and Democratic members of the Senate are in theory today.

General Eisenhower suggests, and it is not a baseless suggestion, that had Senator Taft lived he would have been an effective ally of the new President in his dealings with Congress. This is highly plausible because Senator Taft had very great weight in the Senate and was a man of very great ability and of great public spirit. He was succeeded by a senator whose political career had been largely accidental and who is now, as a result of vaulting ambition, editing a worthy provincial paper in California.

* * *

The Republicans had been out of office for more than twenty years; only one senator had ever served under a Republican President. Those Representatives who had known a Republican President in the White House were old, and, in some instances, very old men. The new President required a kind of leadership in each House which he did not get from the top brass of the Republican Party. In part, of course, President Eisenhower was to blame for his illusions. Used to the army chain of command system, he could not understand the very delicate relationship between the White House at one end of Pennsylvania Avenue and 'The Hill' at the other. He was at the beginning of his term at as great a loss in dealing with politicians as were the great businessmen he brought into his cabinet. Although he had been a kind of army lobbyist when serving on the staff under General MacArthur before the Second World War, he seems to have learnt no more about the handling of politicians than did General Grant, who had more excuse for his innocence.

The frustrations General Eisenhower faced in dealing with his party are reported, but not stressed. We have only an allusion to the project of leaving the Republican Party, of starting what would have been in effect a new party, cutting out those barnacle types who encrusted the ship of state. We have, in fact, learnt far more of this interesting if impractical project from Mr. Donovan's *Eisenhower: The Inside Story* which was published before President Eisenhower ran for his second term.

Without vanity, President Eisenhower knew that he was far stronger than the Republican Party. This lesson was reinforced by the Republican loss of control of Congress, very narrow even at the beginning of the first term in 1953. Indeed, President Eisenhower was to have the odd distinction of being the only President serving two terms with Congress in the hands of the opposition party for three-quarters of the time.

President Eisenhower knew that the American people had not turned against either the New Deal or the Fair Deal and that they had no desire to go back to 1932 or even to 1929. (It is worth noting that one of the people who supported President Eisenhower in this belief was ex-President Hoover.) President Eisenhower reasonably complains that his administration was given no credit for continuing and expanding the social service legislation of the Roosevelt and Truman administrations. This is true, and public ignorance of this fact was unjust, but President Eisenhower does not notice one cause of the injustice. Although most Americans voted in 1952 (and again in 1956) for 'Ike', a great many Republicans and a great many highly conservative Democrats came to interpret these personal tributes as a repudiation of the welfare state.

This was the attitude of many of President Eisenhower's most vociferous supporters and helped to spread the belief that the Eisenhower administration wanted to repudiate the New Deal and the Fair Deal.

President Eisenhower does not mention the odd effect produced by his nomination of a man who professed to want to abolish the income tax to head the Bureau of Internal Revenue, and he alludes only once to the curious career of Dr. Clarence Manion, quondam Dean of Notre Dame University Law School. He does not notice the nomination of a man who was an enemy of public housing to head public housing (actually, this nominee rapidly became a friend of public housing, but the public perhaps did not know this). Much more than President Eisenhower realizes, he has not appreciated what his appointees said and did.

* * *

For example, General Eisenhower reports his defence of the Civil Service system and in a sense his defence of his administration is valid. But no one who knew Washington in 1953 and 1954 can quite accept the defence, for there were plenty of enemies of the Civil Service in Washington, and some very odd things were attempted. The Republican appetite for office after twenty years' exclusion was ravenous, as the Democratic appetite had been in 1933, but it ran against the law and against an obstacle curiously neglected, 'Veterans Preference'; but not until a good deal of damage had been done to the morale of the Civil Service. This damage was especially noticeable in the State Department where Mr. Dulles displayed a contemptible disloyalty to his subordinates. It is perhaps worth noting that the name of Mr. Scott McLeod occurs only once. Yet he did nearly as much damage to the morale of the State Department and the Foreign Service as Senator McCarthy. When the damage had been done, he was sent off to the unfortunate Republic of Ireland where *teste* Mr. Claud Cockburn he was known as the 'copper's nark'.

In the same way, General Eisenhower's speech at Dartmouth College against book burning had little resonance when the public reflected on his silence in face of the antics of Messrs. Cohn and Shine and of what were worse than antics on the part of their great patron, Senator Joseph McCarthy. General Eisenhower does discuss briefly why, when he spoke in Wisconsin, he was induced to drop his tribute to General George Marshall, his great patron, lest it should offend the junior senator from that state; but he does not seem to realize the shock it gave to his admirers, a shock which has not totally disappeared even today.

President Eisenhower deserved better support than he got from the Congressional leaders, but he is probably wrong in thinking that his difficulties with Congress arose from the fact that for six years out of his eight in the White House he had a Democratic majority against him. President Kennedy did not do much better with a nominally very large Democratic majority in both Houses. With great charity, President Eisenhower passes over some of the actions of his appointees, like Secretary Weeks, who began his administration of the Commerce Department by an ignominious and doomed battle with the Bureau of Standards, an institution much more serious than Secretary Weeks appreciated. The very amiability and innocence which Mr. Reston commented on, if they have made President Eisenhower the most popular figure that America has known in the twentieth century, limited his efficacy as a President. His predecessor, Mr. Truman, is reported to have noted his successor's reluctance to engage in close in-fighting. 'If he doesn't like the heat, why didn't he stay out of the kitchen?' It is understood that ex-President Eisenhower and ex-President Truman are not on the best of terms; but Mr. Truman's comment had some validity.

On foreign affairs there are few or no revelations in this book. There are not many on domestic affairs either. And we know a good deal more about the external and internal history of the administration from insiders and semi-insiders than we are likely to learn from this remarkable book. Professor Oscar Handlin, of Harvard, has rightly raised the question of whether people like Mr. Emmet Hughes should be encouraged to quote from confidential documents and give an 'inside' view. Probably they should not, but they have done it and it is impossible to read this book without thinking that but for the work of Mr. Donovan, Mr. Hughes, and others we should be still very much in the dark about what went on in the White House and at Camp David. It is gratifying to note the obvious sincerity with which General Eisenhower recalls his wartime and post-wartime partnership with Sir Winston Churchill and the Earl of Avon. But it is odd to be told how anxious the American administration was over the political fate of that most sterile of Fourth Republic politicians, Joseph Laniel.

Mandate for Change, then, will be a valuable source for future historians and it will interest and inform *aficionados* of American politics and policy. In writing, it is clear but flat; it cannot for a moment compare with that masterpiece of American narrative, *The Personal Memoirs of U. S. Grant*. President Eisenhower mildly and delicately protests against the insinuation that he reads nothing but Westerns and that his grammar is peculiarly defective. As he points out, 'off the cuff' speeches often make very odd reading when taken down and shown to their author; and with what is an obvious allusion to his brother, Dr. Milton Eisenhower, the President of the Johns Hopkins University, he reports that a very experienced and highly erudite public speaker has often been horrified at the sight of his verbatim remarks. And even President Kennedy, who graduated *cum laude* at Harvard, sometimes produced very tangled paragraphs at his press conferences.

We should not forget that again and again President Eisenhower, like many distinguished soldiers profoundly pacific in temper, refused to pursue policies that might well have ended in an atomic war. He kept the peace and reinforced the general American position in Europe and to some extent in Asia at a time of great difficulty. This should be enough to give him respectable rank among the occupants of the White House, a much more respectable rank than that of a much better writer, President Grant. His greatest weakness was his inability to understand and either manage or intimidate the professional politicians. His reluctance to run for the Presidency perhaps came from an apprehension that he would be out of his depth. Of him it could be said in contemplating such figures as ex-Senator Bricker:

> He only in a general honest thought
> And common good to all made one of them.

2

ACQUAINTED WITH THE NIGHT

THE WORK OF ROBERT FROST

ROBERT FROST (whose death in his eighty-ninth year was announced on Tuesday of this week) has some claim to be the most patiently dedicated poet of this century. Born in 1874, he was eleven when his father died, and his schoolmistress mother took her two children from San Francisco to a Massachusetts mill town, Lawrence, where they came under the care of their paternal grandfather. Up to eleven Frost had had no formal schooling. He went to Lawrence High School in 1885, and during what in England would be called his grammar school years published four poems in the school magazine. After graduating from high school he went to Dartmouth College for three months, in 1893, and in the same year told his grandfather that he wanted to be a poet. His grandfather offered to support him for a year, while the young Frost discovered whether he was any good: the boy replied 'Give me twenty!'

It was just twenty years later, in 1913, that his first book, *A Boy's Will*, was published in England by a minor publisher, David Nutt. In the intervening years Frost had privately printed a tiny pamphlet of poems, worked as an artisan, a cobbler, a hired farmhand, tried independent farming not very successfully, married, spent two years at Harvard but not (in spite of his excellence in classics) taken a degree, and taught. He published poems very infrequently. For five years, between 1901 and 1906, no periodical accepted a poem, and his farming near West Derry, in Rockingham County, New Hampshire, was also unsuccessful. Between 1906 and 1912 eight poems were accepted. By 1912, when he was thirty-eight, he had published ten poems in magazines and no book. In that year he decided to leave America and settle for a time in England. Till he came to England he had never talked about poetry with another poet. In London, in 1913, he met Mr. Ezra Pound, who talked to him about the poetry of

JOHN ROBERT DOYLE, JR.: *The Poetry of Robert Frost*. 303 pp. Johannesburg: Witwatersrand University Press. 25s.

Edwin Arlington Robinson, and who was later to write a glowing review of Frost's first book, *A Boy's Will*. Harold Munro, F. S. Flint, and, rather strangely, Norman Douglas also recognized Frost's gifts.

A Boy's Will gave Frost a place. His next book, *North of Boston*, published in 1914, gave him a very high place. There would be no longer any question of any magazine rejecting any poem he chose to send it. But, apart from literary recognition, Frost's sojourn in England was his first experience of life in a literary community—his close friends included Edward Thomas, Rupert Brooke and Lascelles Abercrombie—which immediately accepted and liked both him and his poems. In the second half of his life, the rich years that remained to him, Frost became almost embarrassingly (but he was too proud and ironical to feel any embarrassment) the Poetic Voice of Sane Republican America: Mr. Randall Jarrell in a couple of excellent essays has made notes on this aspect of Frost's reputation:

Ordinary readers think Frost the greatest poet alive, and love some of his best poems as much as they love some of his worst ones. He seems to them a sensible, tender, humorous poet who knows all about trees and farms and folks in New England, and still has managed to get an individual, fairly optimistic, thoroughly American philosophy out of what he knows: there's something reassuring about his poetry, they feel—almost like prose.

And in his other essay Mr. Jarrell writes even more sharply:

Just as a star will have, sometimes, a dark companion, so Frost has a pig-headed one, a shadowy self that grows longer and darker as the sun gets lower. I am speaking of that other self that might be called the Grey Eminence of Robert Taft, or the Peter Pan of the National Association of Manufacturers, or any such thing—this public self incarnates all the institutionalized complacency that Frost once mocked at and fled from, and later pretended to become a part of and became a part of it.

Retrospectively, one can see that this was unfair to the poet whose grandest public appearance (Mr. Jarrell's book, in which this essay appears, came out in the middle 1950s) was to be at President Kennedy's inauguration, for which the tough old man had written a set of couplets saluting the daring, the independence, the gaiety of the new national leader. He had read, and approved of, President Kennedy's book on the brave odd men out, the intransigents, in American politics:

> There was a book of profile tales declaring
> For the emboldened politicians daring
> To break with followers when in the wrong,
> A healthy independence of the throng,

A democratic form of right divine
To rule first answerable to high design . . .
Less criticism of the field and court
And more preoccupation with the sport . . .
Firm in our free beliefs without dismay
In any game the nations want to play.

These lines do not represent Frost at his poetic best; but they do represent both a public tact and an imaginative political intelligence which are something more than the attitudes of what Mr. Jarrell described as 'the conservative editorialist and self-made apophthegm-joiner, full of dry wisdom and free, complacent, Yankee enterprise; the Farmer Poet . . . an imposing role perfected for public use, a sort of Olympian Will Rogers out of *Tanglewood Tales*'. Mr. Jarrell, of course, in both his essays on Frost, went on, with brilliant quotation and excellent close criticism, to make a claim for Frost at his best as being a great poet, as great as Hardy; though unlike Hardy's, he observes, Frost's 'tenderness, sadness, and humour are adulterated with vanity and self-complacency'. He praised Frost's power of organization, and noted that 'Frost's word-magic is generally of a quiet, sober, bewitching sort, though the contrasts he gets from his greyed or unsaturated shades are often more satisfying to a thoughtful rhetorician than some dazzling arrangements of prismatic colours'.

Mr. Jarrell's two essays on Frost are probably the best appreciative studies that have been written on him. The most intelligent, partly hostile, essay is by Professor Yvor Winters. Professor Winters objects to the manner of procedure of the poems; the lack of cogent moral argument, the evasiveness, the conversational elusiveness, or dodginess, as well as the conversational tone. This had been noticed earlier. In a richly and sanely appreciative new book on Frost, a friend of the poet, the Carolinian scholar Professor John Robert Doyle, quotes a description by Mark van Doren of how Frost digested a hostile response in his dark, unpublished Derry years. He had sent some of his poems for comment to a friend:

The friend's report was that they did not seem to him to be poetry. If he were asked what they did seem to be he would say: Conversation. Mr. Frost, far from being discouraged, knew that he had found out something. His poems had one quality at least. They sounded like something. There was something in them that could be named. So he said to himself: I will develop this quality until it becomes not my weakness but my strength; I will prove that conversation can *be* poetry.

The essence of Professor Winters's criticism is identical with that of Frost's early friend:

Conversation is the most careless and formless of human utterance; it is spontaneous and unrevised, and its vocabulary is commonly limited. Poetry is the most difficult form of human utterance; we revise poems carefully in order to make them more nearly perfect. The two forms of expression are extremes, they are not close to each other. We do not praise a violinist for playing as if he were improvising; we praise him for playing well. And when a man plays well or writes well, his audience must have intelligence, training, and patience in order to appreciate him. We do not understand difficult matters 'naturally'.

As Pater believed that all art aspires towards the condition of music, so Professor Winters seems to believe that all art aspires towards the condition of university lecturing. He is also hampered by his dogma that poetry is essentially expository rather than imitative. Real conversation taken down on a tape-recorder would not, of course, be art. But the imitation of the tones and transitions of conversation, by Donne, by Rochester, by Dryden, by Pope, by Swift, by Byron, by Browning, Eliot, Yeats, by Frost himself, can be very high art. Stiff formality is not the same thing as good manners, in literature any more than in life. Professor Doyle, in his detailed examination of a wide range of Frost's poems, notes the strength of Frost's 'frequent use of "direct statement"', and quotes some striking examples of this conversational directness. He would agree with Professor Winters that (in Professor Doyle's phrase) Frost's poems do not 'pretend to present a complete and coherent system of thought'. But even Milton's *Paradise Lost* will not 'stand the analysis of a philosopher'; yet there can be no doubt that Frost, like Milton, thought.

Man's mind, according to Professor Doyle, is one of the two things Frost most admired; the other is the earth, or the earth as man loves it. Other things that Frost admired were the acceptance of contrasts and contradictions; a refusal to give absolute answers; neighbourliness and concern; courage in the face of adversity; a belief, nevertheless, that goodness is not merely a reaction against adversity but something with its own independent roots; moral independence combined with a respect for the ultimate, but not immediate judgement of the market-place; 'the belief that man's goal should be effort and accomplishment, not happiness'; the awareness of life as always a point of balance between opposite tugs or stresses; and some sort of balance, in life at its best, between 'reason and desire—seeking, respectively, justice and mercy'.

This is a set of ideas more massive and coherent, more variously relevant to ordinary human experience, than the set of ideas of many good poets. It is not a set which justifies Professor Winters's definition of Frost as 'the spiritual drifter as poet'. It may be in a way a local set of ideas; behind it one can sense both the puritan and the pioneer traditions of New England, and there are also touches in it of later American traditions: pragmatism, that mixture of extreme scepticism and the need for practical faiths; and the peculiar, and unique, American mixture of a sweetness like candy, a hardness like hickory:

> Something there is that doesn't love a wall . . .
> He only says, 'Good fences make good neighbours'.

The total impression that one gets from Frost is certainly not Professor Winters's impression of an evasion of tragedy—it may be an impression of a decent reticence about tragedy—and of a treatment of major topics in a manner that is 'usually whimsical, sentimental, and evasive'.

In a sense, this is a memorial article on a very great, though unobtrusively great, modern poet. It might be well to end it with a full citation, and some comments on a shorter poem which Professor Winters himself, Mr. Jarrell, and Professor Doyle all recognize to be great, the poem 'Acquainted with the Night'. Professor Winters, who can praise as firmly as he can sharply condemn, says this about it:

There is one poem . . . the sonnet entitled 'Acquainted with the Night', which surpasses any poem thus far mentioned and which seems to be one of the two or three best poems that Frost has written. Superficially, the poem deals with the feeling of loneliness which one has when walking late at night in a strange city; but symbolically it deals with the poet's loneliness in a strange and obscure world, and the clock which tells him that the time is neither wrong nor right is a symbol of the relativism which causes his melancholy. The understanding of his predicament seems to be greater in this poem than in most of the others; he knows, at least, that it is a predicament and realizes the state of mind to which it has brought him.

Mr. Randall Jarrell, an emotional, an impressionistic critic, utterly different in temperament and method from Professor Winters, expresses himself to a different purpose but with equal enthusiasm:

I think that Dante would have read with nothing but admiration for its calm universal precision the wonderful 'Acquainted with the Night', a poem in Dante's own form and with some of Dante's own qualities. . . . Is this a 'classical' poem? If *it* isn't, what is? Yet doesn't the poem itself make the question seem ignominious, a question with a fatal lack of magnanimity of true comprehension and concern? The things in themselves, the poem itself, abide neither our questions nor our categories; they are free.

Professor Doyle, with an excellent thoroughness typical of him, notes technically that 'while maintaining an illusion of artlessness, the author has not only used the difficult Italian terza rima but has made the form more difficult than need be by adding characteristics of the French set forms and of the sonnet', and had, in addition, 'imposed upon himself a rigid relationship between stanza and sentence pattern'. He analyses details of the diction and the structure lovingly, and relates the symbolic meaning of some of the images and episodes, the night, late walking, to other poems by Frost. This poem is perhaps the poem which would most immediately win over an imaginary reader, an admirer of Yeats and Pound and Eliot, who had been accustomed to think of Frost as mainly a combination of the ideal Georgian poet the English Georgians ought to have been and a somewhat too loquacious cracker-barrel Yankee wit:

> I have been one acquainted with the night.
> I have walked out in rain—and back in rain.
> I have outwalked the furthest city light.
> I have looked down the saddest city lane.
> I have passed by the watchman on his beat
> And dropped my eyes, unwilling to explain.
> I have stood still and stopped the sound of feet
> While far away an interrupted cry
> Came over houses from another street,
> But not to call me back or say goodbye;
> And further still at an unearthly height,
> One luminary clock against the sky
> Proclaimed the time was neither wrong nor right.
> I have been one acquainted with the night.

There is the hardness of iron there under the suavity of movement and diction; and yet with the hardness the sense also of an extraordinary sad gentleness of spirit. Few poets quite, on meeting, live up to the impression made by their best poems; vanities, touchinesses, sentimentalities, nobly suppressed or transcended in the work, come out, too often, with frightening intensity in the social self. Professor Doyle's fine book brings out (though in passing and not as a major topic) how Frost's being rang as true as his verse. Frost visited England in the 1950s and, old and tired as he was, devoted much time in talking and listening to young English poets and lovers of poetry. They will remember his tall gangling form, his great granitic kindly landslide of a face, his unaffected dry warmth; man and poet have rarely been so much at one with each other.

3

BLACK MAN'S BURDEN

JAMES BALDWIN AS MAN AND WRITER

'SOMETIMES I FEEL like a motherless child', 'Nobody knows the trouble I've seen', 'A man born of a dark woman sees dark days', &c.— from all the folk sources comes the same tortured cry as is nowadays rammed home by statistics, economic analyses and the reports of prison committees and public health inquiries. Coloured people remain coloured throughout their lives and theirs is not a happy lot. No sane person, it would seem, given the choice, would prefer to be born black rather than white. There are precious few examples of white people trying to 'pass for' black in coloured quarters of the great cities, yet millions of coloured men and women, day in and day out, abjure the coloured part of their ancestry and try to 'pass for' white in the new communities to which they have moved, communities where no one knows about or is interested in their forebears. Among writers, only Pushkin has celebrated, with proper filial reverence, the name of a black grandfather, and though Pushkin may be numbered among the world's greatest writers, it remains true that, for a variety of reasons, he is the least well known of these great writers in the English-speaking world.

It is as a writer that Mr. James Baldwin would undoubtedly prefer to be evaluated and yet there are few living authors whose creative work is more closely linked with the intellectual and sociological formulations which he has coined elsewhere. Thus, there is a strict correlation between the embittered, hate-ridden father of *Go Tell it on the Mountain* (one of his two early novels which have now been re-issued) and such a sentence as the following, which must have been written about the same time:

And there is, I should think, no Negro living in America who has not felt,

---

JAMES BALDWIN: *Go Tell it on the Mountain*. 256 pp. *Giovanni's Room*. 248 pp. Michael Joseph. 21s. each. W. HAYWOOD BURNS: *The Voices of Negro Protest in America*. 88 pp. Oxford University Press, for the Institute of Race Relations. 8s. 6d.

briefly or for long periods, with anguish sharp or dull, in varying degrees and to varying effects, simple, naked, and unanswerable hatred.

And yet, there are and have been very few writers of any period whose social commitment has less relevance to the appraisal of their books as works of art. His true forte is not that of a social protester on either racial or sexual grounds but lies rather in the concocting of beautifully elaborate sentences and thoughts and stories which give off an aromatic hint of decadence like an overblown rose. He has, in a recent television interview, claimed that his literary progenitors are Dickens, Dostoevsky, and Henry James. Since he is totally innocent of anything approaching humour, one can only imagine that he means the late Dickens of *Bleak House* and *Our Mutual Friend* rather than the chap who disported with Mr. Pickwick. Similarly, one imagines that his reading of Dostoevsky is selective and that he prefers the self-conscious self-inquisitor to the dealer in grotesqueries and buffooneries who is only now beginning to be recognized in this country. On the whole, therefore, one feels that he is best qualified to appreciate Henry James, that he would respond almost equally to *The Bostonians* and *The Turn of the Screw* and that such a story as *The Real Thing* would come nearer than almost any literary production we can think of to making him laugh.

But what Dickens and Dostoevsky share with Henry James is a capacity for elaboration, the elaboration of syntax and story which best expresses the psychological subtleties with which they are concerned. And Mr. Baldwin too is, above all else, an elaborate novelist. Even in the simple outlines of his career we can see hints of the elaborateness which informs all his work. His first book, *Go Tell it on the Mountain*, was the usual first novel—though unusually well written and unusually mature—the largely autobiographical description of a difficult adolescence. Almost all its characters are coloured. The central crisis is sexual in essence and religous in expression, and to anyone who has read a few pages of Freud it is obvious that the hero, John, is going to develop into a homosexual. Surely enough, the next book *Giovanni's Room*, is largely about homosexuality but in every other way it is completely different from *Go Tell it on the Mountain* and, indeed, were it not for the beautifully intricate yet simple-seeming style, might easily have been the work of a different hand. To begin with, it contains no coloured characters at all. There is no mention of the Negro from its opening sentence to its final one. Whereas, in his first book, Mr. Baldwin had created a whole community which, in spite of its strangeness, carried conviction, in this second he records a portrait in depth of one or two individuals who, though society finally does erupt into their lives and destroy them, might otherwise have been living on the other side of the moon.

*   *   *

Now Mr. Baldwin is far too intelligent a man and too self-conscious an artist to make a renunciation of this magnitude and in this direction by accident. Nor is it likely that money entered into his speculations since he could more easily have cashed in on his reputation as a story-teller of the Negro American community than invest himself with a totally new reputation as a clinician in depth of homosexuality. No. One feels rather that he wished to prove that he was quite as capable of appreciating the emotional problems of white people as any of their own race. And he did so triumphantly. *Giovanni's Room* is a technical *tour de force*. Only Mr. Joseph Heller among living American writers has played such consummate tricks with time, putting a hint of the future here, a suspicion of the past there, and in the present an idyll, so that the whole disgusting truth formulates itself slowly among a myriad of imprecisions and the occasional clarities enforced by desultory honesty. And it is at precisely this point where he has best shown his sympathy for the white man and his numerous dilemmas that Mr. Baldwin makes his most telling criticism of the white ethos. None of the characters is particularly admirable—not even poor Giovanni, who as an underprivileged white may be thought of as having the worst of all possible worlds. In him love has turned to hate. In the others it had never really existed. Neither David nor his girl-friend, Hella, is capable of love. She resents her dependence on men: he fears to lose his independence in her, and so he takes Giovanni who is 'so beautiful' and who is presumed to be less demanding. When he proves in fact to be more so, he is hastily deserted and thrown to the wolves. He kills one of them before they get him, but in any case, he has to die. That was, after all, why he was born.

There is something about the savagery of the white rat race, its strict division into winners and losers, killers and victims, saints and sinners, which would appear to be almost incomprehensible to a civilized African and, in so far as he retains his African heritage, to the American Negro. His own concepts of good and bad are not absolute, but relative. That may, to some extent, account for what is often referred to as the 'political genius' of Africans. 'It's an ill wind that blows no good' is perhaps the nearest one comes in English folklore to the underlying attitude of almost all Africans to whatever phenomena confront them. They feel as Herskowitz has pointed out, that what is bad for one person will undoubtedly be good and useful for somebody else. And in the writings of Mr. Baldwin one can feel the shock administered to such an attitude by the *complete* waste of talent, of emotion and of action which is such a feature of our present civilization. From Giovanni's death nobody gains anything—not even an insight into their own true nature for, to tell the truth, their very natures have become lies, fighting for what they least want.

That Mr. Baldwin's attitude toward white civilization is very different from that of any other Negro leader has recently been emphasized by the publication of Mr. W. Haywood Burns's *The Voices of Negro Protest in America*. What Mr. Burns tries to do is give a dispassionate account of how Negroes have protested against their living conditions in America. He starts from the quite simple moral premise that white Americans should at last redeem their promises and give their black brethren a voice in the country equivalent to their numbers. He seems to think that white society will do this if the Negroes protest long enough and hard enough and he chronicles the vehicles through which Negroes have expressed their dissatisfaction, organizations like the National Association for the Advancement of Coloured People and the Congress for Racial Equality, demonstrations like those of the Freedom Riders and, his ultimate condemnation of white society, the carryings-on of the Black Muslim Movement.

Historically, his account is barely adequate and certainly not brilliant. He does not mention, for example, that Negro slaves were the first people to 'vote with their feet' and leave the plantations for the North. At a deeper emotional or philosophical level, moreover, his whole inquiry would seem to be falsely oriented. He seems to think that even the Black Muslims are motivated by 'what they see as white deceit in matters of equality, and not a compulsive racism'. This implies that, as soon as blacks are given equality with whites, the problems of the world will be solved and everything will be all right. Mr. Baldwin, however, who knows a good deal more about the world than Mr. Burns, would certainly enter a caveat here. The white world, he would say, is itself so corrupt, so incapable of loving, so entangled in an historical nullity of its own making, that only

black insights, black sympathy and black heroism can possibly keep
it from suicide. For Mr. Baldwin is that rare human being who is
proud of being what he is, in all its littleness and nastiness, its stupidity
and fright—who has totally accepted not only his own limitations
but those of his fathers before him and who is able to look on all this
hurried and fumbling misunderstanding and see that it is good. He is
able to do this without a trace of the kind of racial arrogance in which
the Black Muslims specialize because he is as aware as any English
aristocrat that other families have skeletons in their cupboards and
that no life can be without episodes which its liver would prefer to
forget about. It is interesting to speculate on the sociological background of this confrontation of Mr. Burns with Mr. Baldwin. Mr.
Burns is a Negro gentleman, Harvard educated, with the gloss of a
Cambridge finish. He is infinitely at ease in any company, modest,
intelligent and able, if pressed, to bring forth remarks of suitable
acerbity. Mr. Baldwin on the other hand is little better than a gutter-
snipe. He was brought up in one of the toughest sections of Harlem
and, since he is not a large man physically, one can imagine that he
had to suffer his fair portion of indignities. His education, as far as
can be ascertained, stopped at high school level, which means really
that he had to teach himself to write. If he belongs to any aristocracy
at all it is that which includes Villon and Oliver Goldsmith. It has
nothing to do with what, for want of a better term, we can call the
American Negro establishment of which Mr. Burns is a bright
luminary. And yet it was to Mr. Baldwin that Mr. Robert Kennedy,
in what was surely his most inspired moment, went for advice about
the legal status of American Negroes rather than to Mr. Burns or any
other American Negro leader.

Only a man who has been repeatedly taken off the street and
gratuitously beaten up by white thugs, most of them in uniform, can
gauge the depths of the white man's hatred of the Negro. And only
one who is able to guess, at any rate, at its depth will even begin to
think about why it should exist. Mr. Baldwin, indeed, would seem to
be almost the only American Negro who has succeeded in learning
the white man's language without losing some portion of his racial
integrity in the process. Just how much of his racial attitudes and
characteristics he has managed to retain can best be appreciated by
the study of his most recent novel, *Another Country*. There, for example, we find an account of a funeral, the funeral of Rufus, a boy
who committed suicide by throwing himself off Brooklyn Bridge.

This is a Christian funeral, yet many of the speeches would be more at home in Dahomey or in pre-settlement Liberia. The minister, while preaching over the deceased, is able to say things like:

I ain't going to stand here and tell you a whole lot of lies about Rufus. I used to know Rufus, I knew him all his life. He was a bright kid and he was full of the devil and weren't no way in the world of keeping up with him. He got into a lot of trouble, all you know that. A lot of our boys get into trouble and some of you know why.

Such an address would be unthinkable in this country where all denominations agree that panegyric must be panegyric and no word of criticism is allowed to break the spell. Our dead are universally good. They are better than the kindest, strongest, cleanest, neatest, nicest people we shall ever meet. They can do no wrong now and they never did any before. They are all, so far as officialdom is concerned, wrapped up in haloes and very different from anybody we ever actually met. But African religion takes a different view of the dead. They allow the mourners to have one last fling at what displeased them in the conduct of the deceased. They are afraid that unless they do so their unspoken animosities may wake him in his grave and cause him to come and trouble their sleep at night. It becomes a matter of loyalty to be truthful, something very different from anything that ever happens in a white community.

It is not only about Rufus that Mr. Baldwin feels he must be truthful. Every situation in his life must be evaluated by his own honesty, and every situation in our lives, too, every situation, that is, which he feels competent to judge. For Mr. Baldwin admits, as every artist must do, that everyone has his secrets where it is not only bad manners but blazing *dishonesty* to trespass. And by 'everyone' he naturally means both black and white, male and female, child and adult. Among humanity Mr. Baldwin makes no distinctions, because he is on very good terms with humanity. Only the inhuman annoys him. He has a contempt for it.

4

A COLD SPRING

(a) THE LONG TALK

THE FULL TEXT of Mr. Khrushchev's speech of 8 March to 'a meeting of party and Government leaders with writers and artists in the Kremlin' has been published in English under the modest title *The Great Strength of Soviet Literature and Art*. It runs to thirty-eight pages or about 20,000 words, and is available from the official *Soviet News* (3 Rosary Gardens, London, S.W.7) for sixpence. It is, to put it mildly, a document that everyone interested in the future of the arts should read.

The highlights (if that is the right word for anything so obscurantist) were widely reported at the time. Mr. Khrushchev defended Stalin against too complete condemnation ('those were bright, happy years'); he attacked the writers Ehrenburg, Yevtushenko, Victor Nekrasov, Paustovsky and Voznesensky, the artists Zhutovsky and Neizvestny, the films *Ilyitch Zastava* and *The Young Guard*, 'abstractionism and formalism' in art, dodecaphony in music, 'so-called modern dances' and 'the obsession with jazz'. He let fall the usual thudding aphorisms:

There is no Jewish question in our country. . . .
When I listen to Glinka's music, tears of joy always come into my eyes. . . .
A revolution of workers and peasants to overthrow the capitalist class is the supreme manifestation of humanity. . . .

He drew the usual ('peaceloving'?) military-aesthetic analogies: culture as a 'sharp ideological weapon', the artist with his 'arms in complete readiness, prepared for battle', music 'mobilizing' people,

---

(*b*) *Novy Mir*, No. 11. Moscow: Izd. 'Izvyestiya sovyetov deputatov Trudya-shchikhsya SSSR'. 70 kopecks.

(*c*) *Novy Mir*, No. 7. ALEKSANDER SOLZHENITSYN: *Dlya polzy dyela*. Rasskaz. 33 pp. Moscow. 70 kopecks.

(*d*) *Vasya Konakov: Rasskazy*. 224 pp. Moscow: Voyen. Izdat. Min. Oborony SSSR. 35 kopecks.

(*e*) *Mozaika*. 72 pp. Vladimir: Vladimirskoye knizhnoye izdatelstvo. 10 kopecks. *Treugolnaya Grusha*. 114 pp. Moscow: Sov. Pisatel. 12 kopecks.

(*f*) *A Precocious Autobiography*. Translated by Andrew R. MacAndrew. 126 pp. Collins and Harvill. 16s.

  Autobiographie Précoce. Translated by K. S. Karol. 173 pp. Paris: Julliard. 9 fr.

the writer's duty 'to be in the ranks', the speech itself as a 'review of the forces' of literature and art.

The real essence of the speech lies in its insistence that there can be no common ground between Soviet writers and artists and their capitalist colleagues abroad or between the official Socialist Realist aesthetic and any other possible communist approach to the arts.

Art belongs to the sphere of ideology. Those who think that both socialist realism and formalist and abstractionist trends can peacefully live together in Soviet art inevitably backslide into positions of peaceful coexistence in the sphere of ideology, which are alien to us.

Peaceful coexistence of this kind—in other words, agreement to differ in the field of ideas, to lay off the propaganda and respect one another's cultural aims—is 'treason to Marxism-Leninism'. This is a blank snub to those distinguished and, it might be thought, impeccably communist 'people working in literature and the arts' who had argued that a variety of different styles was essential if Soviet art was to survive. Picking on Mr. Ehrenburg as one of them, Mr. Khrushchev told him he was guilty of 'a gross ideological mistake'.

A lot follows from this cold-war view of the arts. Success abroad becomes automatically suspicious: 'If the enemies of our cause start to praise you . . . ', said Mr. Khrushchev to Mr. Yevtushenko, 'the people will justly criticize you. So choose which suits you best.' The poet's proposed trip to the United States has been cancelled; so has the meeting of the British-Soviet Society, and no doubt other instances of artistic isolationism will follow. The implication of Mr. Khrushchev's whole attitude is that it is best for Soviet culture to be thoroughly disliked abroad (except by a few dutiful foreign communists) and that in this campaign the art of Socialist Realism is a weapon that makes us capitalists tremble. In fact, it makes most of us yawn, and if we went in for ideological war there is nothing we should like better than to see a Soviet Premier laying down his own tastes with a vulgarity and an incomprehension that will alienate every left-wing artist and intellectual outside Russia and a good many in.

One reason why such things alienate them is that unlike Mr. Khrushchev himself (apparently) and the Soviet Communist Party, and indeed the whole carefully sheltered Russian public, they have vivid memories of the art policies of those supposed *ur*-capitalists the Nazis. Long before Mr. Khrushchev was in a position to tell us authoritatively that military bands are 'a source of inspiration' or that modern art can never rival a beautiful Russian winter's day, there used to be two quite incompatible schools of thought in the western world: the aesthetic-free-for-all of the democracies (where the Soviet works of the 1920s had a considerable influence), and the tightly disciplined Victorian-based conservatism of the Third Reich. Now which of the two is Mr. Khrushchev aligning himself with? Here he is on page 25:

Formalist and abstractionist vagaries are alien to and not understood by the people . . . it makes you sick to look at such a filthy mess.

Exactly the same sentiments about

their unnatural smearings and daubings which . . . have always been alien to the healthy instincts of the German people, indeed seemed horrible to it

were expressed by Hitler opening the Haus der Deutschen Kunst in 1937. Take these remarks:

1. Only outstanding works of a great revolutionary and creative character reach a man's heart and mind, arouse high civic feelings in him and the resolution to devote himself to the struggle for these people's happiness.

2. Art education is popular education in the loftiest sense, for it arouses that which is most valuable in man; it makes him say 'yes' to life. It is not by dinning the stuff of learning into our comrades that we improve their social and sociological position, but by calling on them to throw their spiritual energies into the struggle.

3. Any art which cannot count on the deepest and most joyful approval of the broad healthy mass of the people . . . is intolerable. It is trying to confuse the healthy, instinctively certain feelings of a people instead of joyfully supporting it.

It is doubtful if Mr. Khrushchev himself, the author of 1, would recognize that 2 was from *Das Schwarze Korps* of 25 February 1937 and 3 from the same Hitler speech. They are so perfectly in line with his own views.

For some reason painting brings out all that is worst in politicians; they charge blindly in when they would do better to stop and think; and the result is a set of rulings which necessarily apply to literature and music too. Fired by his dislike of the unfortunate Moscow abstract artists in the Manège exhibition last December—the heat of his reaction and the squalor of his language on this occasion can be gauged from the entirely credible transcript in the current *Encounter* —Mr. Khrushchev has made perhaps the longest and most pernicious speech on the arts to come from any twentieth-century politician. It is longer than any of Zhdanov's and quite as bad, far more comprehensive than Hitler's; it puts Mr. Ilyichev's speech of 17 December (which was already a nasty enough shock) in the shade. Stalin, of course, never orated on this subject, and in Lenin's time just because the leading politicians knew so much more about the arts they were prepared to say much less.

Perhaps it may not be a mortal blow. The present Soviet leadership seems disinclined to persecute its citizens, despite certain lapses, and Mr. Ilyichev originally pooh-poohed the idea that it might be starting 'a crusade against people who are searching for new forms'. All the same, it is very doubtful whether even Stalin's own campaign to enforce the standards of Socialist Realism was intended to have quite the effects it did. That did not stop men like Babel, Tretiakoff and Meyerhold from losing their lives. Given the right atmosphere of hysterical suspicion and 'vigilance' all these accusations of ideological unorthodoxy, 'betrayal of the cause', 'instability' and so on might quite well be taken seriously by some literal-minded official. Fortunately the atmosphere is not there at the moment, but it is still a very dangerous game to play. There are already artists and writers who are threatened with losing their jobs or their membership of the all-important official organizations, and the restoration of normal cultural relations with the outside world has been postponed yet again.

(b) A SOVIET LANDMARK

Novy Mir, No. 11, November 1962

In the Soviet Union it is in the literary periodicals that signs of change, innovation, or originality are most often detected, but it is rare indeed to find together two works of such interest as those in the November number of *Novy Mir*.

One Day in the Life of Ivan Denisovich by Aleksander Solzhenitsyn is a sixty-three page novella, written apparently some time ago and stored away in a bottom drawer in the hope that one day it could be printed. As Mr. Tvardovsky, in a combined introduction and apologia for the story, somewhat unnecessarily tells us 'the subject matter on which A. Solzhenitsyn's novel is based is unusual in Soviet literature'. Unusual it certainly is, being an account of life in a post-war 'corrective labour camp' in Siberia. Apart from its literary merit the documentary interest of the story must be immense; these camps have been much discussed and much described, but hitherto the truth

C

has been dulled in most westerners' minds by a feeling that everybody
has some axe to grind. It has been assumed that the Russian refugee
will exaggerate and that the Russian communist will minimize.
Now, incredibly, these two are on common ground and it turns
out that there has been little exaggeration. It would, in this case, be
almost impossible.

The narrative, which covers exactly one day in the camp from
reveille to lights-out, is mostly straight eye-witness description.
There is little reflection, either philosophical or political, and no
conclusions are drawn. Thoughts would stand out ridiculously in
this account of a way of life where the characters have hardly a
minute to themselves. Just occasionally the author takes time off
for a few lines of pity and bitterness, as when he catches the Baptist
Alyosha reading his Bible and thinks how silly it was to imprison
the whole sect, since they were doing no harm. Greater interest is to
be found in the ghoulish yet fascinating details of camp life: the
convict number painted on the left knee; the little formal announce-
ment made every day before the march to the work compound,
warning prisoners that they will be shot if they try to escape; the
private enterprise conducted in the currency of parcels from relatives; and above all the cold and hunger—with happiness measured
in grammes and in degrees, in grammes of bread and in degrees
centigrade.

Yet for every hell there is an inner circle, and here it is the detention block, of which we read:

The walls there are of stone, the floor of cement; there is no window. They
heat the stove just enough so that the ice on the wall should melt and lie on
the floor in puddles. You sleep on naked planks. Daily bread ration—300
grammes, and soup only on the third, sixth, and ninth day.

Ten days! Ten days of detention here, if you sit them out right to the end,
mean that you lose your health for the rest of your life. Tuberculosis, and
you'll never get out of hospital.

And anybody who has done fifteen days is already under the damp earth.

The style of writing is most unusual: staccato sentences of clipped,
colloquial Russian full of obscure camp jargon. The language is
often on the coarse side, with words and expressions not often
printed in Soviet books. Mr. Tvardovsky apologizes for these but
acknowledges that in the circumstances they are understandable.

The printing of Mr. Solzhenitsyn's book (an English version was
subsequently published by Gollancz, and another by Pall Mall

Press) is indeed an event, but perhaps a predictable one, a continuation of the 'uprooting of the personality cult'. More striking, possibly, is the article by Viktor Nekrasov, author of the novels *Kira Georgievna* and *The Trenches of Stalingrad*, called 'On Both Sides of the Ocean'. This is an account of his visit to Italy last March to attend the Congress of the European Confederation of Writers. While he was there he met a number of Italian communists and was impressed by their frankness and vitality. 'They are not dogmatists but neither are they revisionists', he writes. They explain to him some of their difficulties as campaigners for communism:

Every Italian—worker, official or peasant—has to choose. In order to choose he has to know what is better. He reads newspapers and he can buy any of them; the Vatican *Osservatore Romano* costs just the same as *Unità*. One says one thing, the other the opposite. In one he reads that everything in the Soviet Union is bad; in the other than everything is good. At any rate that is what we used to write, that *everything* is good. Then it was explained that not everything, far from everything. . . . We used to write that Stalin was great, wise, and infallible, and they believed us, many people believed us. Now we are no longer writing about his infallibility, rather about his sins, and people are asking us, 'What were you thinking about before?'

He was also asked about the selectiveness of Soviet publishing houses, and recalls a visit to Leningrad by Alberto Moravia. The Italian asked Mr. Nekrasov and some other Russians what they thought of Kafka: 'We looked at each other in silence and were unable to reply; at that time we had not even heard of him.' He finds it hard to explain the Soviet reluctance to publish Faulkner, Camus, and Mlle. Sagan.

Mr. Nekrasov is, of course, a committed communist. His criticisms are constructive and are aimed at the improvement and enlargement of the communist movement. What is unique in the whole tone and content of the article is a desire to be fair, to give credit where credit is due, even to one's ideological enemies. With a few exceptions British journalists can justly claim that, however anti-communist they may be, when they visit Russia they do not ignore the good and report the bad. No attempt is made to underplay the Soviet achievements in industry, science, construction, and general education. These achievements are undeniably great and must be reported as such. But articles about the West in the Soviet press seem hardly ever to avoid such subjects as unemployment, colour prejudice, evictions of tenants, or general moral degeneracy. One does not often find the outright lie; it is simply that the attentions of Soviet correspondents are confined to the dark side of the picture. This irritates westerners and it seems, Mr. Nekrasov, too; he writes:

I am reminded of the remarks of a certain not very clever journalist of ours, with whom I was travelling in America. On the third or fourth day he began to complain, 'When are they going to show us some slums? There's nothing for me to write about here, everything smooth, clean, comfortable.' ... When I see slums I am sorry for the people who live in them, and I am not at all glad that these frightful houses and barracks still exist, even though this is in the capitalist world, which is alien to me. The same journalist said to me again. 'What the devil! Did you see, there are Negroes staying in our hotel! There were even a pair of them sitting in the restaurant today.' It seemed to me that he was sorry that those two Negroes were not thrown noisily out of the restaurant, so keen was he to get material for an article!

And this is why Mr. Nekrasov, while he gives a balanced account of the poverty of the Italian south and of the strikes and labour movements of the north, gives his readers, too, a glimpse of the unseen bright side of the capitalist world. He writes that Italy is now going through a period of economic boom, that the standard of living has sharply risen, that unemployment has decreased and that new homes are being built on a large scale.

The western press is criticized by Russians for making too much of 'liberal movements' in Soviet literature. As Mr. A. Dementiev writes in this same number of *Novy Mir*, and as Mr. Ilyichev stated repeatedly in his speech of 17 December, Soviet writers may have their small differences, but they are united in their main purpose, which is the attainment of communism. But these differences are not small. Oceans separate Mr. Nekrasov, who realizes it is possible to be fair and objective without prejudicing his beliefs, from, say, Mr. Kochetov, who counts capitalist misery his greatest joy.

(c) FOLLOW UP

Novy Mir, No. 7, July 1963

Last year Aleksander Solzhenitsyn, a forty-four-year-old Russian, astounded the world with his first novel, which described life in a Stalinist corrective labour camp. Since then he has published three novella-length stories, all in *Novy Mir*. The first two, which appeared in the January number, were 'Krechetovka Station', the story of a young lieutenant at the time of the German advance on Moscow who denounces a probably innocent man to the NKVD, and 'Matrena's Homestead', an account of life in the backwood *glush*.

The third story, 'For the Sake of Efficiency', which appeared in July, is about a secondary school in a small town. For some years the children, who specialize in wireless technology, have had to make do with cramped classrooms, lack of recreation ground, and remote sleeping accommodation. They are assigned a site and a sum of money for a new building, and in order to improve their lot as quickly as possible they spend all their free time for a year doing the unskilled labour themselves. At the start of the story the children are just preparing for the move, waiting for the building to be certified as serviceable by the factory director. They are a bolshie lot, though, of course, basically loyal and constructive, and quip merrily with their teachers. Suddenly two Volgas draw up to the school, containing a faceless 'comrade from the ministry', his staff, and, strangely, the factory director. After a lightning tour of the old building, which they regard as entirely adequate, they announce to the appalled headmaster that the new building is being requisitioned for a research institute and that the lowly technical school will have to muddle along as before.

The rest of the story deals with the vain efforts of the headmaster to fight heartless bureaucracy. Both he and his pupils toy with the ultimate resort, the 'telegram to Moscow', but this would be probably useless and possibly dangerous. Going through the usual channels the headmaster finds some allies; the secretary of the town council takes the matter up at district level. 'We should build communism not with stones but with people', he claims. He is coldly advised to consider the broader national interest. When all is lost the headmaster is left darkly suspicious of graft on the part of the factory director and vowing to construct another, and better, building.

Mr. Solzhenitsyn teaches mathematics and physics in Ryazan, south-east of Moscow, and so in this story he is on his home ground. (He was, of course, equally writing from personal experience in *Ivan Denisovich*.) He is, perhaps, generally more of a recorder than of a creator. His heroes—the quite ordinary Shukhov in the labour camp, the panicky Zotov in 'Krechetovka Station', the religious and backward *tyomnaya baba* of 'Matrena's Homestead', the nervous and unambitious headmaster—are far from the normal 'positive' ideal. The man who shunned the publicity of his best-seller, paid a brief visit to Moscow, and then returned to his mathematics class, seems to be emulating his characters in humility. It may be that he is the first of a new type of Russian writer, not given to speech-making or aggressive sermonizing.

But the aim of the Soviet writer remains primarily to educate and inspire his reader with the right ideas. As the reader becomes more sophisticated he is less attracted by the saintlike 'good Soviet man'; he needs more of the constructive grumbling and credible characterization of Mr. Solzhenitsyn. This new brand of 'realism' is, of course, far more readable from the westerner's point of view— and this story in particular is impressively entertaining—but this is a purely incidental advantage.

(d) A QUESTION OF INTEGRITY

Viktor Nekrasov: *Vasya Konakov*

Viktor Nekrasov, now 52, the son of a Kiev doctor, is one of the few Russian novelists who were bona fide soldiers throughout the four years of war, from 1941 to 1945. He did not begin to write until it was all over, and his first book, *The Trenches of Stalingrad*, published in 1946 and based on his own experiences as a lieutenant in that fearful battle was an immediate success. Since then he has written a play and three or four other books, including *Kira Georgievna*, which is, in a sense, a forerunner of Aleksander Solzhenitsyn's famous concentration camp story; its action revolves round the arbitrary arrest in 1937 of the heroine's husband, and his return to his wife after many years of exile. But perhaps the most significant of all his books is this small collection of short war-time stories, written over a period of years, only a few of which have so far been translated.

Mr. Nekrasov's position as a writer of (by Soviet standards) unusual intellectual integrity was described recently in this journal with reference to his article in last November's *Novy Mir*. During a recent visit to France he was interviewed and explained, as it were, his artistic credo. He was not interested, he said, in describing in his books 'exceptionally heroic' characters, paragons of all civic and patriotic virtues. He liked to write about 'the people', and by this he meant 'just ordinary chaps' each of whom acted when it came to the point, in his own personal way, rather than in accordance with any rigid party or propaganda line. Life, he said, was extremely *nuancé*, whether under capitalism or under communism, and there was nothing he hated more than 'ham' writing and 'prefabricated' characters—an obvious dig at the more primitive didactic canons of socialist realism.

This book of nine short stories illustrates admirably this gentle and subtle approach to people. Except for one gentle satirical story about the former King of Saxony, who opens a ladies' hat shop in the ruins of Dresden and inflicts upon the narrator, a Russian captain (whom he obsequiously addresses as 'Herr Oberst'), a hideous and very expensive hat, all the stories deal with very 'ordinary chaps' in the Red Army; but the main point of Mr. Nekrasov's beautifully told stories is perhaps precisely the fact that no 'chap' is ever quite 'ordinary'. Thus a man nicknamed 'Pike', an ichthyologist in private life and at first despised by the soldiers under him for his awkward, clumsy, and hopelessly civilian behaviour, turns out to be a much cleverer soldier than his highly professional captain during a particularly tricky night operation. In 'Senka' he tells the story of a soldier who, panicking during an air raid, and thinking he can 'stand it no longer', fires a bullet through his left hand; he is about to be court-martialled when he suddenly finds himself faced with three advancing German tanks; and the 'coward' behaves like a perfect hero.

More striking still is 'The Second Night', in which a naïve young conscript is sent on a reconnaissance job at night. He passionately hates the Germans, especially since, the day before, he had seen a gallows in a liberated town, with several men and women whom they had hanged. In the course of the operation he kills a German in single combat. There are then found in the dead man's pockets a number of photographs: a picture of the dead German, a handsome eighteen-year-old boy, together with his girl on the sea-shore, both radiant with happiness, and another picture of the same boy with his father and mother. Looking at these snapshots, he is suddenly bitterly upset and almost weeps.

As Mr. Nekrasov commented on this story: 'Of course, it makes no sense; if my chap hadn't killed the German, the German would have killed him; but then the human heart doesn't always act according to any set pattern, such as Ehrenburg's admittedly brilliant "Nothing is jollier-than-German-corpses" kind of propaganda.' To Mr. Nekrasov men, communist or not, seldom, if ever, act like robots; it would be no exaggeration to say that a story like 'The Second Night' comes perhaps closer than anything else in Soviet literature (apart, perhaps, from a few Kazakevich stories) to Tolstoy's 'ordinary' soldiers in *Sebastopol* or *War and Peace*. A big question is whether this gentle humanist tradition, so typical of Russia, will inevitably come into conflict (as it has done in the past) with the official concept of 'Soviet Man', or whether the two can, somehow, go on coexisting.

(e) THE INDIVIDUAL POET

ANDREI VOZNESENSKY: *Mozaika, Treugolnaya Grusha*

Is it only a coincidence? In September 1946 thousands of young people in Moscow attending a 'Poets' Evening' in the crowded Dom Soyuzov staged a great demonstration in favour of Boris Pasternak and Anna Akhmatova, and treated with deliberate indifference, if not downright hostility, all the approved poets of the Stalin régime who had also come there to recite their verses. 'This will lead to no good', Anna Akhmatova remarked when the meeting was over. Sure enough, less than a fortnight later Zhdanov, on behalf of the Central Committee, started on his pernicious series of 'conferences' in which all the arts, one after another, were ordered back to the socialist-realist fold. Akhmatova and Zoshchenko were promptly expelled from the Writers' Union, and many others were to be victimized and boycotted in various ways for years afterwards.

On 30 November 1962 a similar 'Poets' Evening' was held in the even vaster Luzhniki sports stadium in Moscow, and the hall was packed with 14,000 people. This time the greatest ovation of all was given to twenty-nine-year-old Andrei Voznesensky. Did the party regard this, too, as an 'unhealthy sign'? For, oddly enough, a fortnight later Mr. Khrushchev visited the large exhibition of Russian paintings in Moscow, and his somewhat obvious witticisms on abstract painting have since then acted as the green light to the conservatives, not only in painting but also in literature. This time the role of Zhdanov was performed by Mr. L. F. Ilyichev, Secretary of the Central Committee (an all-out Stalinist in the past), whose remarks were quoted in *The Times Literary Supplement* of 4 January. He was followed by others. On New Year's Day space was given in

Pravda to Mr. Vsevolod Kochetov, often regarded as head of the crypto-Stalinist faction in literature, so that he could revive once again all the old Zhdanov clichés on 'people's art'. A few days later, Mr. Laktionov, that by-word of ultra-academic 'ham' painting, was given even more space in the same paper to attack 'modernist' painting and those who were encouraging it, in the first place Mr. Ilya Ehrenburg.

Paradoxically, the publication of Aleksander Solzhenitsyn's anti-Stalinist concentration-camp story has been followed by an almost Stalinist reaction against 'formalism' in art and literature. And it should not be surprising if in this new atmosphere a poet like Mr. Voznesensky—who makes no secret of his views on 'formalism'—were to be given some rough treatment by his critics after his return from France where, for the past month, he has been mixing with *avant-garde* poets and with dangerous characters like Chagall and Picasso.

In a recent interview with *The Times* he attributed his great popularity with the young Soviet generation to the simple fact that these young people were sophisticated. The 'technical intelligentsia' —which ran into millions—worked on highly complicated industrial processes, and that was partly why they liked poetry, too, to be 'complicated' and not childishly obvious.

Nothing, indeed, is less obvious than Voznesensky's poetry, as represented by the two remarkable little volumes under review. It is rich in the most unexpected images, sounds, and rhythms, ranging from the rock 'n roll and Negro-jazz rhythms of his American cycle of poems, with their beatnik themes, to the exquisitely elegiac and *pianissimo* 'Autumn in Sigurda', or to this strange little poem dedicated to J.-P. Sartre:

> I am a family and, as in a spectrum,
> There are in me seven 'I's'.
> Unbearable like seven beasts,
> But the bluest of them plays a pipe.
> [A sámy síni svistít v svizél.]
> And in springtime I dream
> That I am
> An eighth one.

To a good Socialist Realist this may sound like pure gibberish; but is it? The old guard (with a few exceptions, like Mayakovsky's friend, Mr. N. Aseyev) have attacked him for this poem, and for much else, and have even accused him of 'double-think', and of writing beatnik poems under the guise of anti-beatnik poems, such as his 'Beatnik Monologue' in his latest book:

> Roaring from its rocket-sites
> Sprinkling the world with atomic dust,
> Time spits on me,
> Just as I spit on Time. . . .
> We are beatniks, and amidst all their insults,
> We are like little wolves and beasts
> Dragging clanging scandal with us like convict chains. . . .

Some have even accused him of 'atomic catastrophism'; only, as he has himself said: 'I am no pessimist. But even when, lying on the grass, I kiss a girl, I still remember at the back of my mind that the grass is poisonous with atomic fall-out.'

Mr. Voznesensky loves Russia, but he is non-conformist, and even rebellious at times. In *Mozaika*, his second book, published in 1960, there is one poem beginning:

> You try to frighten me with formalism,
> How divorced you are from life,
> You experts stinking of mothballs and incense!

And in the newly published *Treugolnaya Grusha* (*The Triangular Pear*—'the triangle', he has explained, 'is the geometrical essence of a pear, and is also the shape of the New York Subway lamps') he simply sticks out his tongue:

> How I love my critics!
> Perched on the neck of one of them
> There shines a fragrant naked anti-head.

He is not afraid of 'formalism' or even of surrealism: every painter, he argues in *The Triangular Pear*, seems to have his opposite number in poetry; thus, 'Picasso explains Lorca better than a thousand translations':

As for me, something much more than mere interest makes me gaze for hours at the hypnotizing paintings of Joan Miró. I feel strangely close to his restless fantasy.

Poetry, he also says, is revolution; and Mayakovsky is much nearer to Pushkin than 'all those iambic-mumbling nonentities'. But the poet's fate, he says, can be tragic, and he sees a symbol in Eluard being choked by poison gas in the trenches of the First World War. Mr. Voznesensky's future career may well prove a test case. Will his experimentalism, his originality, his youthful, disrespectful verve survive the gas being generated now?

(*f*) ANGER AND HOPE

YEVGENY YEVTUSHENKO: *A Precocious Autobiography*
EUGÈNE EVTOUCHENKO: *Autobiographie Précoce*

'A poet's autobiography is his poetry. Anything else can only be a footnote.' But poetry can seldom leap the language barrier and so Mr. Yevtushenko has sensibly put down some of his memories and ideas in a simple and universally accessible prose. He wrote his little book last winter during a visit to France and, most rashly, allowed it to be serialized in the 'Paris bourgeois weekly' *L'Express* without submitting it for official Soviet approval. Retribution has been swift; he has been called a 'malcontent', a 'blower of his own trumpet' and accused of 'capitulating to our ideological opponents'. He has been forced to add his own voice to those of his disparagers, to confess that his autobiography contains 'much that is superficial and much that is indiscreet. . . . I committed an irreparable mistake. I feel a heavy burden of guilt on my shoulders.' As so often, though oppositely, happens, the reviewer is unable to agree with the author's assessment of the present work.

Mr. Yevtushenko is thirty and comes from the region of Lake Baikal. As a *sibiryak* he has many of the qualities that we associate more readily with Texans. The spaciousness of ranchland or *taiga* seems to give their people an air of ownership and bombast; it makes them unamenable to discipline. From many of the stories he tells Mr. Yevtushenko himself comes out unashamedly heroically. It seems that when he was a child he was beaten up by a street bully; Tom Brown fashion, he studied ju-jitsu in secret and floored the bully ignominiously in front of his cronies. He also tells how he jumped into a racing river to save a drowning man even though he could not himself swim.

This lack of inhibition, though, is a great help when it comes to communicating the workings of the author's and his compatriots' minds: how, for instance, as a child whose grandfather had just been arrested by the NKVD, he could still trust and adore Stalin and gaze with wide-eyed envy at the children selected to take him flowers on May Day. In his first teenage poems it seemed as normal to write of Stalin as to write of the moon or a lover: brilliant public relations work had made him the Russian people's kind Uncle Joe.

Mr. Yevtushenko admits that he was taken in like the others, though he feels that his youth excuses him in part—he was twenty when Stalin died. In an impressive purple passage he tells how the scales first fell from his eyes. A vast crowd was gathered in Trubnaya Square to see Stalin lying in state. Hemmed in and funnelled by militia lorries the crowd got out of control and was thrown about in hysterical waves. Those who fell were trampled underfoot. The militia refused to move the imprisoning lorries so long as they had no orders. In this blind, gullible obedience and chaotic sheep-mindedness the poet caught his first glimpse of the true causes of Stalinism.

Mr. Yevtushenko's opinion of Stalin is the same as that of most westerners: 'Stalin's theory that people were the cogwheels of communism was put into practice with horrifying results.' He sees little connexion, though, between Stalinism and his high communist ideal. The Revolution may have been betrayed but it is now emerging from the winter of suffering into the spring (he rejects Mr. Ehrenburg's term 'thaw') of progress and happiness. One wonders what he now thinks of his little personal cold spell that has resulted from this book. Still, he argues, just as it is unfair to judge Christianity by the Inquisition and the sellers of indulgences, so it is unfair to condemn communism on account of a few million liquidations. The Russian people has brought its socialism into being in suffering and labour, but just as a mother loves especially a child whom she has suffered much to bear, so the Russian people must love its socialism.

Mr. Yevtushenko does not shrink from a full revelation of the 'mistakes of the past'. About the 'literature of tractors', for instance, he writes:

The heroes of novels smelted steel, built houses, sowed wheat, but never thought or loved—or if they did it was as woodenly as puppets. . . . Poets visited factories and building sites but wrote more about the machines than about the men who worked them. If machines could read, they would have read such poems with interest. People did not.

He rails against the Stalin-Prize grubbers, the privileged bureaucratic _élite_ and the enforced hypocrisy of that unhappy time. He tells of his first severe brush with Marxist conservatism in 1957 when, for defending Vladimir Dudintsev's book _Not by Bread Alone_, he was expelled from the Writers' Union and from the Komsomol. Two years later, like a pilgrim to a shrine, he visited Pasternak in his _dacha_:

He was a man of complete integrity—all the more criminal then were the actions of those in the West who, against his will, used his name in the cold war, and the more deplorable the actions of some of our writers who used this pretext to try to strike his name from the pages of our literature.

In Russia far more than in the West poetry has the power to move mountains and masses. Mr. Yevtushenko knows what he wants and he intends to use his poetry, which is topical and journalistic, as a tool to get it. He is a convinced communist but a hater of dogma: 'An ideology moulded into final shape cannot be Marxist, because genuine Marxism is for ever moulding itself.' These views are still slightly heretical, but at least they have caused him only a setback in his career and not a bullet through the back of the head.

The book has not yet appeared in Russian and there are considerable differences between the Collins and Julliard translations, the English being more sober and needing fewer exclamation marks. It looks as if either the English editors have toned down the literal version or the French have jazzed it up. Somehow one suspects the latter. This is a pity because it is a compact and pleasantly written story. It is not Sunday-newspaper stuff and should not be sensationalized as a political document. Anyway, whether one views the writer as a bourgeois revisionist or as a new, more insidious type of red, it is hard to doubt his sincerity. The more rational reader would surely find it easy to coexist with Mr. Yevtushenko even if, together with Mr. Khrushchev, he found his Siberian trumpet-blowing a little infuriating.

(g) INTO THE OPEN

Last March was a bad time for Russian writers. For some months before then a number of good, readable, and unstylized works had come from the Soviet Union. Apart from Aleksander Solzhenitsyn's belated concentration-camp exposé there had been Ilya Ehrenburg's memoirs, Viktor Nekrasov's travel notes, a book of poems by Andrei Voznesensky called *The Triangular Pear* and, issued outside Russia, Yevgeny Yevtushenko's *Precocious Autobiography*. Then on 8 March, a few weeks after he had made some naïve and, reportedly, lavatorial remarks at a Moscow art exhibition, Mr. Khrushchev delivered a speech attacking Ehrenburg, Yevtushenko, Nekrasov and Vasili Aksenov; there was talk of a return to the darkest days of narrow-mindedness and dogma.

The attacked writers, of course, went through the usual motions: Yevgeny Yevtushenko humbled himself upon the rostrum and Vasili Aksenov made good resolutions in the magazine *Yunost*. People analysed themselves and each other. Young writers departed far from the capital on penitential journeys.

One of Mr. Khrushchev's more engaging traits is his readiness to admit, albeit tacitly, that he is wrong. He must realize that every word he utters, be it pondered or unguarded, is seized upon by the men around him, many of whom are still stern dogmatists, and he has not forgotten how they let him down in the Pasternak affair. In this case he quickly called the hunt off, at the beginning of May, probably by some remarks he made at the première of the East German film *The Russian Miracle*. On 8 March he was proclaiming that 'it would be wrong to overlook the serious faults that exist in the work of our writers, artists, film makers and composers'; on 19 May *Pravda's* more encouraging words were 'the Party calls our literary masters to creative boldness and independence'.

A small voice of calm in the storm was provided by Aleksander Tvardovsky's *Novy Mir*. It published Mr. Khrushchev's speech but continued to print the memoirs of Ilya Ehrenburg, the man Mr. Khrushchev attacked most bitterly. Then during August the magazine, which has been running behind schedule all this year, printed in its seventh number another story by Aleksander Solzhenitsyn called *For the Sake of Efficiency*. It was a simple story of good against bad, the heartless Stalinist bureaucracy against the new 'humane' officialdom but it was most efficiently written and cast a new light on the world of Russian schoolchildren, one which the author presumably knows well. The story was at once attacked by Vsevolod Kochetov's diehard *Oktyabr* and by *Literaturnaya Gazeta*. The criticism ran along the usual lines: the positive heroes were not positive enough, the writer's knowledge of Soviet society was out of date, he was suggesting that the interest of the individual be put before that of the state and, perhaps most importantly, there was a pernicious irony in the story's title *For the Sake of Efficiency*.

Unusually, *Novy Mir* has not allowed the matter to rest. In its tenth issue, printed only four weeks ago, it included three lengthy 'letters from readers' which take Yuri Barabash, the *Literaturnaya Gazeta* assistant editor, to task for his review. (It is noteworthy that

when a Russian disagrees with a review he writes to the criticized
publisher, not to the critic.) They answer Mr. Barabash in his own
Socialist Realist language—Mr. Solzhenitsyn's first concern *is* the
state, his positive heroes *are* positive—but they leave no doubt as to
their dislike of dogma:

Regarding the two different styles of Party rule, we are against the 'iron'
method of [the villain] which reeks of the methods used by Stalin. We support the methods used by [the hero] and are not afraid of his excessive
goodness and genuinely Lenin-like love of the people.

They consider that articles such as Mr. Barabash's 'disorientate the
general reader and especially our youth'.

It rarely happens that a literary argument of this fierceness is conducted openly in the press. One would have expected spasms of
jockeying, plotting and cutting behind the scenes, with finally
nothing being printed at all. A probably authentic 'Letter from a
Soviet Writer' in the American magazine *The New Leader* on 9
December recently pointed out that the sheer mechanics of censorship, the armies of clerks for ever putting question marks in the
margins of manuscripts, are so immense that many influential men
must now have a personal interest in the literary *status quo*. The
article claims that 'about a dozen people read every manuscript in the
office of *Foreign Literature* and for each it is a matter of prestige to
find something questionable in what is submitted'. The editorial
readers are only the first hurdle.

A writer in Russia nowadays has to decide: either he writes with
one part of his brain and inspiration concentrated on the censors,
men whom he probably knows personally, or else he writes for the
desk drawer, hoping that one day some civil servant will give the
imprimatur. No wonder he is taking refuge in the irony of Mr.
Solzhenitsyn's title. The playwright, Edward Albee, who has just
completed a thirty-day exchange visit to Moscow, remarked of his
recent hosts, 'I keep coming back to the work "ironic" '. They have
presumably experienced so much triumph and disaster that they are
seeking an attitude of mind that can embrace anything, however
unexpected. This insecurity of livelihood, which even established
Russian writers still feel, cannot be conducive to good and original
writing. It will disappear only when literary controversy and dis-
agreements can be carried on normally and in the open. With luck,
this is what many Russians are now trying to achieve.

5

VINDICATION: 'YES, BUT–'

DR. LEAVIS'S MONUMENT

'A JUDGEMENT IS PERSONAL or it is nothing; you cannot take over someone else's. The implicit form of a judgement is: "This is so, isn't it?" The question is an appeal for confirmation that the thing *is* so; implicitly that, though expecting, characteristically, an answer in the form. "Yes, but–," the "but" standing for qualifications, reserves, corrections.' Thus Dr. F. R. Leavis in his Richmond Lecture for 1962, describing 'a diagram for the collaborative-creative process in which the poem comes to be established as something "out there", of common access in what is in some sense a public world'.

*　　*　　*

There are two reasons for taking this quotation from the Richmond Lecture as a starting point for a consideration of *Scrutiny*, an occasion offered by the republication, by the Cambridge University Press, of the whole run of that famous quarterly in nineteen volumes (1932–53) plus a twentieth volume containing Dr. Leavis's own 'Retrospect' (also available separately as a pamphlet) and a comprehensive index, the work of Mr. Maurice Hussey. The first reason is that the passage illustrates very clearly the continuity of what many readers may consider the main and most attractive factor in Dr. Leavis's own principles and practice as a critic. Some thirty years earlier, when *Scrutiny* was completing its first year of publication (Volume 1, No. 4, March 1933), Dr. Leavis wrote an editorial commenting on a critic's jejune remarks on the implications of the titles of the two quarterlies *The Criterion* and *Scrutiny*. Meeting the complaint that his own quarterly had not shown its colours, was not—

Scrutiny. Reissued in twenty volumes with an Index by Maurice Hussey and Retrospect by F. R. Leavis. Cambridge University Press. Twenty-volume set, £45. Single volume, £2 10s. F. R. LEAVIS: *Scrutiny*. A Retrospect. 24 pp. Cambridge University Press. 3s. 6d.

in the ideologically mixed-up days of the 1930s—'committed', he replied: 'But judgement is not a matter of abstraction; it involves particular immediate acts of choice, and these do not advance the business of judgement in any serious sense unless there has been real and appropriate responsiveness to the thing offered.' That editorial contained other eloquent passages which will call for a later reference; the sentence just quoted will be seen to proclaim in essence the same sturdy *credo* embodied thirty years later in the more positive paragraphs of his farewell set-piece on his retirement from his official teaching post at Cambridge.

The second reason for using the quotation from the Richmond Lecture as an epigraph is, of course, that it should arm any truly converted reader or rereader of *Scrutiny* with the courage to adopt this same admirable stance when confronted with the volumes themselves and the whole movement to which they gave impetus. One obvious use of the precept, for example, would be to employ it in a consideration of the quality of the criticism of the 1933 editorial, contrasted with that of most of the 1962 Richmond Lecture—but that would lead one away from *Scrutiny* itself, and a more handy example of the later criticism will be provided by the 'Retrospect', issued as a tailpiece to the volumes.

'Particular immediate acts of choice': that, above all, was what each particular issue of *Scrutiny* itself demanded from its readers; and was what it so rarely received. Now that the whole set has been made available there is no further excuse for the blanket dismissals or the blanket acceptances which demonstrated how little the partisans had understood the journal's very watchword of discrimination.

*   *   *

Looking back, it seems clear that the varied nature of the impact of *Scrutiny* arose from the fact that its chief editor, Dr. Leavis, was unusually well equipped to play two roles. In his first role he was a social critic of the radical missionary tradition vigilant against such things as the excesses of advertising and other forms of deception, political or journalistic or literary. This side of his campaign may be seen in its most concentrated form in such associated work as the book *Culture and Environment* (1933), written with Mr. Denys Thompson, which has the revealing subtitle 'The Training of Critical Awareness'. Naturally enough, such concern also involved a study of the social effects of current reading matter (e.g. snobbishness in novels or in publishers' advertisements); the link here is with Mrs. Q. D. Leavis's book *Fiction and the Reading Public* (1932). But at the same time, Dr. Leavis happened also to be a first-class critical historian of English literature. When in this role he was dealing with topics lacking any very obvious contemporary application, he could excite wholehearted admiration from readers who opposed, or were simply not interested in, his social views. Such work as the essays on Swift, Pope, Keats, has been acclaimed and used by teachers of literature who can find it in a collection like *Revaluation* (1936, subtitle 'Tradition and Development in English Poetry') without the products of the 'other' Dr. Leavis.

*   *   *

Yet the vigour in both types of criticism, social and literary, is the vigour of the same editorial mind—and it has been very difficult for *Scrutiny* readers to pick and choose, even when the titles of individual essays looked 'harmless' enough. Hence, for instance, all the pother about the essay on Milton, which opened with the now famous words: 'Milton's dislodgement, in the past decade, after his two centuries of predominance, was effected with remarkably little fuss.' The content of the essay was that of the literary critic; the tone of voice was that of the engaged social critic. In this instance, as in so many *Scrutiny* essays (not all by Leavis), the same radical missionary zeal marks—some people would say disfigures—the literary-historical articles as marks the social-contemporary commentaries. From this complex, all sorts of muddled responses took their origin. This was why, for example, there was a continuous tone of righteous protest in *Scrutiny* even when the main fare offered in some of the later issues would turn out, as will be seen, to consist of revaluations of medieval poems or seminar-like commentaries on earlier papers on Hawthorne. This was why less committed readers, who felt no passionate involvement in the *Scrutiny* movement as a whole, were glad enough to accept, use or 'steal' a high percentage of the offerings in 'straight' literary-critical history. They felt no more guilt or obligation than if they had found a good piece of work in, say, *Essays in Criticism* or *The Virginia Quarterly Review*. The unnamed 'advanced Cambridge intellectual', mentioned in the 'Retrospect', who confessed '*I* am not a moral hero', may not have been an admirable figure; but one can spare some sympathy for him if all *he* wanted to do, as a presumed subscriber to *Scrutiny*, was to acknowledge the excellence, shall we say, of Dr. Leavis on Dr. Johnson or L. C. Knights on Ben Jonson. Your confirmed *Scrutiny* supporter can no doubt see that all these things are inextricably involved with the shortcomings of weekly reviewing or the work of the British Council; yet those who do not feel combative about it are not necessarily stupid or even unsympathetic readers.

*   *   *

It is natural that the name of *Scrutiny* should be linked with that of Dr. Leavis, the author of its guiding 'political' editorials and also its most illustrious and constant contributor. But *Scrutiny* was also, from the beginning, the co-operative enterprise of a group of dedicated people. The first two numbers bear the editorial names of L. C. Knights and Donald Culver. They were joined in Volume I, No. 3, by F. R. Leavis and Denys Thompson. The one editor whose name appears in every number of the nineteen volumes is L. C. Knights, now Professor of English at Bristol University. Mr. Culver's name was replaced in Volume II by that of D. W. Harding, now Professor of Social Psychology at London. Mr. Thompson's name stayed until Volume VIII, No. 2, and midway through Volume IX the editorial team was joined by W. H. Mellers, later Professor of Music at Pittsburgh. In the last number of Volume XIV Mr. Harding gave place to Mr. H. A. Mason; in the last number of Volume XV Mr. Mellers dropped out, leaving the last four volumes under the triumvirate Leavis-Knights-Mason. And it would be unjust not to add that Mrs. Q. D. Leavis, whose book *Fiction and the Reading Public* is quoted as an important document in the broad campaign, was closely associated throughout the life of the quarterly.

There may well have been good reasons for the growing concentration on specifically literary matters; it is certainly undeniable that over the years the original broad front of the *Scrutiny* battle-front narrowed as one sector after another was evacuated and the troops were recalled, so to say, to the central literary-critical bastion. Volume I (1932–33) contains among its main articles such things as Lowes Dickinson on the political background, Dr. I. A. Richards on the Chinese Renaissance, Mr. Michael Oakeshott on Bentham, Professor Henri Fluchère on *Surréalisme*, Mr. L. C. Knights on the Training Colleges and, as earnest of the admirable intention that contributors themselves should not be immune from assessment, an evaluation of I. A. Richards by Mr. D. W. Harding. There were poems by Mr. Ronald Bottrall, Mr. Selden Rodman and Mr. C. H. Peacock, who also contributed some pages from a novel. There is no such variety in the final Volume XIX (1952–53), the main features of which are (No. 1) articles on the Milton Controversy, Graham Greene, Dr. Leavis on Lawrence's *The Rainbow*, Dr. D. A. Traversi on *King Lear* (the first of three articles); (No. 2) articles on the American literary historian, Miss Rosemond Tuve, *King Lear* (II), Fenimore Cooper, and Dr. Leavis's stimulating exercise in the practical criticism of three poems; (No. 3) an editorial on criticism, *King Lear* (III), an article on Cowley, Marvell, and Restoration art; (No. 4) the editor's 'Valedictory' and essay on Lawrence's *The Captain's Doll*, plus pieces on Crashaw and *Much Ado About Nothing*.

With the contraction of subject-matter went an increasing unanimity of tone. In the earlier numbers there was room for an occasional lightness of touch, a freedom of reference such as makes vivid, even now, Mr. W. H. Auden's hilarious yet grimly serious review of the then Mr. Winston Churchill's *Thoughts and Adventures*. Rereading it thirty years later, one is transported back to those vigorous pre-war days when a Churchillian paragraph on Foch and Clemenceau could be described as 'this account of senile homicidal maniacs' and the reviewer could ask himself how to relate 'the utterly humourless face which confronts us in the frontispiece to the savage, vivid farce of the pages which follow'—even though he allows the author the tribute: 'The old humbug can write.' Perhaps by the post-war years it was assumed that the most conscientious readers of *Scrutiny* would be drawn from those generations of undergraduates who had passed through the English Tripos into the country's schools and colleges as teachers. By the autumn of 1950, anyway, Volume XVII, No. 3 (to cite but one example) carried as its main offerings articles on medieval idiom in Shakespeare, *Wynnere and Wastoure*, a section of Dr. Leavis's study of Lawrence's *Women in Love*, and a 'rejoinder' to a 'disagreement' about a previous comment on Henry James's *What Maisie Knew*—all difficult stuff, one would suppose, for any but the most devoted specialist in literature, and a rather narrow interpretation, certainly, of that Volume I editorial which promised: '. . . one of the functions of *Scrutiny* is to provide criteria, from the world of general intelligence, for determining which specialists can be trusted, and how far. . . .'

With nineteen volumes to survey, however, it is hopeless (as it might even be misleading) to attempt too close a documentation of 'trends'. When *Scrutiny* was in its full stride any representative issue could show (to be crude about it) quite extraordinary value for money in its main articles—as witness the long essays in Volume VII, No. 2 (September, 1938) covering the philosophy of Marxism, Baudelaire, E. M. Forster (Leavis) and the French composer Roussel (Mellers). Equally good was the chance of finding among the book reviews an unsurpassed rigour of judgement on new writers combined with assessments of scholarly work which were themselves short essays of real value. Mrs. Leavis on 'The Case of Dorothy Sayers' (Volume VI, page 334) was devastating not simply because of her tart observations (e.g. 'Lord Peter is not only of ducal stock and all that a Ouida hero was plus modern sophistication and modern accomplishments—such as being adored by his men during the Great War and able to talk like a P. G. Wodehouse moron . . .') but also because she had room, and cared enough, to be fair, allusive and sensibly persuasive in her 'placing'. This exercise in up-to-the-minute judgement was immediately followed (Volume VI, page 341) by a sympathetic review by L. C. Knights of Dr. Louis B. Wright's *Middle Class Culture in Elizabethan England* which, while remaining admirably scholarly in tone, yet placed a sensitive finger upon one matter, for example, which has recently been much aired in the columns of this paper but not, perhaps with such simple aptness:

'The real merit of the book, however, is not that it is rich in out-of-the-way information, but that it continually forces the question: What is the relation between this mass of popular reading matter, which served the various needs of the day, and those books and plays which proved themselves of permanent importance?' The range of authority represented by these two random cheek-by-jowl reviews may illustrate, even if baldly, the range of *Scrutiny* at its most confident best.

*   *   *

After all, there must have been *some* reason for the fact that many readers interested in literature, and aware of the high value of a large proportion of the essays in *Scrutiny*, nevertheless shrank from the intemperance of much of its reviewing. The 'senior' contributors —Dr. Leavis himself, Professor Knights, Mr. J. C. Smith and a dozen others—were often enough severe to the point of scorn; but there was always some sort of sense and some sort of critical authority behind their strictures. This was not always true of the 'juniors'.

Scanning again these well-remembered volumes, one cannot absolve all contributors from the charge of unnecessary offensiveness. It was one of the later editors, Mr. H. A. Mason, who wrote, of a poem by Mr. Ronald Bottrall, 'If these lines were composed before Mr. Bottrall had read *Little Gidding* he should in self-defence have mentioned the fact' (Volume XIV, page 221). The rejoinder of the poet (himself, let us recall, represented in earlier numbers of *Scrutiny* and generously praised by the chief editor) was mild enough: 'It would be very trying, anyhow, if a poet had always to list at the bottom of each of his poems works he had *not* read, particularly if, as in this case, the other work had not, at the time of writing, been published' (Volume XIV, page 294). Again, the occasional head-strong charges come oddly from writers who pride themselves on their ability, as critics, to distinguish the finest shades of meaning. It was Mrs. Leavis herself, for instance, who wrote of 'the serious, the vicious aspect of this assimilation of James to Proust and Pater'. One does not necessarily have to be a lover of Proust or Pater, but merely a *Scrutiny*-trained reader, to feel obliged to reply (in the spirit of 'yes, but—'), ' "serious", maybe; but "*vicious*"—?'

It may be considered a naïve point, but a rereading does revive one's sense of nagging contradiction, in many *Scrutiny* editorials and related documents, between the high claims made for a minority culture with impeccably high standards and, on the other hand, a violent reaction to any sign of opposition or indifference within that majority culture from which members of this sensitive *élite* are to hold themselves immaculate. Let us allow that such a reader may be convinced by the splendid passion giving life to Dr. Leavis's own pronouncements—a passion reminiscent, at times, of the best passages of Milton's pamphleteering. Surely he may then be genuinely baffled at discovering how much he is expected to *mind* having to adopt the very attitude of defensive stoicism which is recommended to him. 'Of course we gratefully recognize', such a reader may be imagined to agree, 'how important it is for literary scholars to recognize the value, for example, of the *Scrutiny* demonstration of the most intelligent and rewarding way to read English poetry. This is magnificent—but there will always exist less sensitive readers eager to demonstrate (in the Sunday newspapers and *The Times Literary Supplement*, perhaps?) how inferior is *their* equipment. Does a man gather figs from thistles?'

Is this perhaps a clumsy way of saying that the tone of *Scrutiny* was marked throughout by its editors' resolute discounting of Original Sin (or, to steer clear of theological implications, Original Stupidity)? If so, it was at once magnificent and hurtful. Magnificent because a belief in human perfectibility is the pedagogue's one resource against despair. Hurtful because in the absence of a clearly defined enemy (even so melodramatic a villain as the Old Adam), benevolent neutrals and even wishful allies could often draw, and waste, a lot of precious ammunition.

* * *

To readers and rereaders who remember the first impact of *Scrutiny*, the intellectual excitement of those early volumes, when viewed from the still more parlous days in which we now find ourselves, has something of the nostalgic bite of the political excitement of the days of the Spanish Civil War. They have in retrospect, those days, the same sense that *this* was the time when vital issues were confronted, *this* was the time when men stood up to be counted; so that, intellectually at any rate, the more momentous events of succeeding years have had a strange flavour of anti-climax about them. Young men so stirred went out to teach not only English literature but also (so the 'Retrospect' reminds us) such subjects as anthropology, with a missionary zeal not easily discernible among a new generation of recruits confronting more horrendous possibilities. It is difficult to convey this feeling of 'something must and *can* be done' to a new generation which can now contemplate many of the major scrutineers on their individual platforms of deserved professional or personal authority. They are still separately active, most of them, but the loss of the common impact has been significantly felt. One way of indicating the place once filled by *Scrutiny* is to confess how much nowadays one still misses it. One current example must serve for illustration. Professor L. C. Knights has recently reviewed in *The Guardian* Dr. A. L. Rowse's biography of Shakespeare. The distance between that brief but pungent comment, hit upon by chance, and the full-blown demonstration one would have looked to find, in *Scrutiny*, from the pen of the author of 'How Many Children had Lady Macbeth?' and 'Drama and Society in the Age of Jonson', is a measure of our loss.

* * *

To piece together the editorial accounts of the sad and often shameful history of the reception of *Scrutiny*, both at Cambridge and in the wider literary world, would make depressing work for a political moralist. Yet if there is truth in the accusation that 'official' Cambridge was so consistently inimical to all that *Scrutiny* stood for, it is certainly true also that 'official' Cambridge, in the personification of its University Press, has made handsome amends by this un-precedented tribute of a complete reissue of a literary magazine first privately published. This act of restitution is rather sourly acknowledged. In the 'Valediction' of 1953 Dr. Leavis wrote: 'But, in the university that produced *Scrutiny*, overt recognition of its exist-ence (the conclusion is unavoidable) is still bad form, the existence itself being so deplorable.' Now he writes that although *Scrutiny* was 'essentially Cambridge's achievement' it was so in spite of every discouragement, since 'if you are interested in vindicating the Idea of a University . . . you will know that the academic spirit may smile upon and offer to take up the causes of your advocacy, but that it will none the less remain what it is and be, in the academic world, always a present enemy'. Alas, the problem of power seems to bedevil Establishment and Anti-Establishment alike. Dr. Leavis's 'Retrospect' tells us that Mr. Eliot, in the days of the 'Criterion Miscellanies', first invited and then rejected his essay on criticism, presumably because its 'pamphleteering strength' would have incurred 'unforgiving hostility in the dominant literary world'. Before long, we are told also of the 'embarrassment' caused when 'animus was incurred' by the rejection by the editors of *Scrutiny* itself of contributions from 'known and established names we didn't want'. Shall we, some day, be reading the retrospective complaints of *these* rejected prophets? One has only to phrase the question to hear in one's mind's ear the imagined explanation that the cases are in no way comparable; and one confronts again that sense of mission which gave *Scrutiny* its character and makes it so difficult for un-committed readers to pick and choose as they will among its offerings.

For committed readers, of course, there is a clear consistency in *Scrutiny* policy throughout its valorous twenty-one years. Young men in the 1930s, for whom the quarterly's viewpoint was not so much an interesting cultural phenomenon as something approaching a religious article of faith, may well have been deeply stirred, for instance, by the reference to D. H. Lawrence in the editorial of March 1933, quoted above: 'In him the human spirit explored, with un-surpassed courage, resource and endurance, the representative, the radical and central problems of our time.' And if one believes resolutely that all Lawrence's writing 'exhibits reverence as a fact, a fact of honesty, strength, and sensitiveness', then presumably the long sequence of Dr. Leavis's essays on Lawrence between Spring 1950 and October 1953 would seem to be in proportion. Some other readers, perhaps, recalling that the same editorial had spoken out eloquently for an educational movement fostering 'an anti-acquisitive and anti-competitive moral bent', may have regretted that towards the end of their subscriptions *Scrutiny* was able to find less room for articles in the straight political-educational field. Yet even they must have recognized an underlying seriousness of purpose so unrelieved, so wonderfully unrelaxing through periods of immense difficulties for editors and readers alike, that a *Scrutiny* article on, say, James Fenimore Cooper or Abraham Cowley somehow had more in common with the original *intention* of the 'movement' than a quite serious essay on a contemporary problem in some other paper. It was, and is, a remarkable feat of group purpose and editorial integrity.

*   *   *

Dr. Leavis has said many harsh things about *The Times Literary Supplement* as, at other times, he has said harsh things about the British Council, the B.B.C., the English Association, and other bodies from which he may well have felt entitled to expect a more courageous encouragement than, in his 'great' years, he received. Against all this should be set the extraordinary influence of *Scrutiny*, to which the present reprint is sufficient testimony. It may throw a sidelong light on one curious facet of English cultural life (the 'gentleman-scholar' facet which *Scrutiny* itself did not often emphasize) if the reviewer confesses that the only other possessor of an original set who is personally known to him is a high officer of one of the 'Big Five' joint-stock banks. (He once indignantly rejected an invitation to sell them for a handsome sum to an American university—thus proving himself, unlike the resident Cambridge intellectual, a 'moral hero'.)

Be that as it may, *Scrutiny* is now available again for the libraries of the English-speaking world. It is unlikely, this time, that 'the academic spirit' will bar it from the shelves. Has the wheel come full circle? Maybe, but only if our tributes, seeking to sweeten a little a history so marked by grievance, may show that we have learnt at least one of *Scrutiny's* lessons by keeping open the crucial judgement:

'Yes, but—.' It was and was meant to be, an uncomfortable organ. It dealt wounds and received them. That self-applauding quality of English 'urbanity' which shrank from contact with it was itself a major object of attack. Some present-day 'urbane' readers, looking back over these revived volumes, may even acknowledge with hindsight that those summary dismissals, those relentless applications of high standards, have more often than not been justified by later slower assessments. Yet *Scrutiny's* lasting legacy will consist not of those topical and deliberately provocative demonstrations, but the brilliant series of literary assessments by a handful of hardworking critics which in effect presented an entirely fresh approach to the history of English literature.

6

BY CAPE WRATH TO EDEN

THE CRITICISM OF W. H. AUDEN

IF WE COULD suppose that poets chose their names themselves, we should have to acknowledge that Wordsworth had made a sublime scoop. But in a subtler way, with his famous flair for effect, we might feel that one twentieth-century poet had done almost as well. The name is 'Auden': a blunt, unmusical sound, redolent less of Arden than of ordinary hours and places, yet still, lingeringly, a poet's name. Such associations would be right, anyway, for the image of the man many English readers have, the image left by his poems of the 1930s. The Auden of those distant years shows in the mind now as a kind of Yorkshire Shelley, outspoken, not notably introspective, with a keen eye for all that was old, mad, blind, despicable and, especially, dying in pre-war England; but a man at the same time full of romantic self-concern and wild hope, the strangers and leaders who haunted his poems all suspiciously like projections of himself, the telegraphic instructions they received— 'Leave for Cape Wrath tonight'—confidently implying cataclysmic changes for the better. Marx and Freud had come to stay, it seemed, and he could say, rejoicing,

all pasts
Are single old past now.

The language of this poetry, meanwhile, was the language of a man in a hurry: metaphors here as elsewhere could be distinguished as having vehicle and tenor, but in this verse every vehicle was driven frantically for no more than a foot or two before being crashed in a ditch and abandoned for another. The contents of these early volumes came at their readers as thick and humming as showers of arrows. Yet a poem like 'A Bride in the Thirties'—ardent, pleading, witty, horrifying—still quivers where it fell, on the target.

That poet vanished before the 1930s were out. Mr. Auden, now an

---

W. H. AUDEN: *The Dyer's Hand.* 527 pp. Faber & Faber. 42s.

American citizen, is still in the 1960s a prolific and dazzling writer. But his poetry today—except that some favourite sources of imagery remain—reads like the work of a different man. England has perhaps not quite followed the change, although in 1947 Mr. Edmund Wilson could already speak of him as an 'American family poet'. The uncertainty in England about Mr. Auden's character as a writer now is not only to be explained, however, by his distance from our literary scene. The comparatively unsuccessful quality of his work during the 1940s contributed; and it did not help that the *Collected Shorter Poems, 1930-1944* (1950), though containing many new poems, was arranged alphabetically, not chronologically. (The one advantage seemed to be that Mr. Auden could put one of his best poems first.)

The new Auden only emerged, a superb lyric poet of a quite new kind, in the 1950s. He had found a quite new attitude to poetry in the meanwhile: a new attitude which sprang directly from his conversion to Christianity.

The first point, in this new and typically individual way of his of thinking about poetry, is a doubt about the serious value of poetry at all. He writes in *Homage to Clio* (1960) that he is:

> one of those
> Who feel a Christian ought to write in Prose
> For Poetry is Magic. . . .

But the impulse has remained, nevertheless, to try to write a kind of poetry that is acceptably Christian, and he has evidently decided that in his case this might take the form of celebrating with appropriate vividness and ritual beauty such perceptions of the happiness in the Just City, or of the nature of Eden, or of the possible experience of undivided being, as his Christianity and his temperament have endowed him with. The result, paradoxically, is that his uncertainty about the utility of poetry has been accompanied by a new care—on the evidence, indeed, a new mastery—in the composing of varied and exquisite forms to suit his delectable subjects. This poetry dwells largely on moments when perfect unity of being seems to be attained, or more often when the play of imagination may make believe it has: the moment of waking, or a stay in Ischia, or an instant of repose in a first-class restaurant after an excellent meal, as in *Nones* (1952)—or scenes chosen by a more idiosyncratic fancy as in *The Shield of Achilles* (1955):

a lawn over which
The first thing after breakfast,
A paterfamilias
Hurries to inspect his rain-gauge.

But Mr. Auden perceives one great danger in such a course: the danger that such work may make writer and reader forget that they live in the imperfect, fallen world, where choice is obligatory on us, and most often wrongly made. Consequently, to recall us from the glamour of his images of Eden, Mr. Auden sometimes plays a trick which no poet can surely have ever done with quite the same purpose before: he deliberately introduces a vulgar or clumsy word into some delicate portrayal, as at the end of 'Lakes':

Moraine, pot, oxbow, glint, sink,
crater, piedmont, dimple . . . ?
Just reeling off their names is ever so
comfy.

Alternatively he lets words from the Prayer Book end a poem, taking over from him, as in 'At the Grave of Henry James' or 'Atlantis'.

This thought leads, however, to the other main theme in Mr. Auden's new poetry: the glory of man's freedom to choose, poor success though he may have in making his choices. This is the prevailing theme of *Homage to Clio*, where most of the poems belong quite properly under the title, and Clio is revered as the muse of the 'unique historical fact'. This theme inspires the satire in the volumes, too: satire directed against tyrants and tyrannical societies which try to deprive man of his freedom to choose. In all this work Mr. Auden's tone would be unrecognizable to those who only knew his pre-war poetry: it is bland, charmingly witty, confident, leisured (one is obliged frequently to take down the dictionary, but the poem can always wait); the intimate, reassuring 'Of course' that flecks the poems gives the note even of the most publicly addressed, a phrase you could search his early volumes for in vain.

The Dyer's Hand, Mr. Auden's new volume of essays and addresses, musings and aphorisms, has to be seen against this background. It is a fat, fascinating book that could well be described, in a phrase of Mr. Auden's own from *The Age of Anxiety*, as a 'Think-Fest'. It is full of the gaiety and the fine varied flavour of ingenious thought. The old looseness of his verse, banished now from his lyrical poetry, reappears in this book's ebullient darting from idea to idea. Even thoughts once composed into articles and reviews have been broken up again into notes, to emphasize Mr. Auden's belief that while a 'closed system' is necessary in poetry, allusive, untidy thought gets nearer to the truth in prose.

A certain amount of personal reflection has its interest. We learn something of his first impulses to write. One remark seems almost certainly to describe his opinion of his own early work:

The young writer . . . finds himself obsessed by certain ways of thinking and feeling. . . . As a rule the disease is some spiritual malaise of his generation. . . . Time passes. Having gotten the poison out of his system, the writer turns to his true interests, which are not and never were those of his early admirers, who now pursue him with cries of 'Traitor!'

His reluctance to write about his more intimate religious experience —evident enough in his recent volumes—gets commented on: 'Is there not something a little odd about making an admirable public object out of one's feelings of guilt and penitence before God?' (There is one fine exception in his case, a poem about his conversion called 'The Prophets'.)

But *The Dyer's Hand* is mainly concerned with just the same ideas and feelings as the newer poetry, which it both illuminates and is illuminated by. Many of the essays and comments are on works of literature. But they are not literary criticism proper. They are original quests for further images of Eden lurking in other men's works, further solutions to the problem of how to create such images.

Mr. Auden is ruthless in this turning of books to his own purpose. (The first words of *The Dyer's Hand* are 'The interests of a writer and of his readers are never the same and if, on occasion, they happen to coincide, this is a lucky accident'.) The most striking example is his essay on Falstaff. Starting from the point that Falstaff is really like a baby, for whom all fact is subjective fact, 'what I am actually feeling and thinking at this moment', he goes on to argue that every fat drinker has set out 'to combine mother and child in his own person', getting his big belly from his desire for it and from drink, not from eating, since 'solid food is to the drunkard a symbolic reminder of his loss of the mother's breast and his ejection from Eden'. Then with a splendid bravura challenge he claims that for this very reason the spectacle of Falstaff should make us question our motives for *accepting* the world, offers Falstaff as a comic symbol of a man living as one would live under 'the supernatural order of Charity' and presents Prince Hal as none other than the 'Prince of this world'.

By the end of the essay Falstaff has taken on the lineaments of Christ himself.

This is the forceful way in which Mr. Auden approaches nearly all the works he discusses. He constantly finds a mythopoeic imagination at work in them, or brings it to them himself. He discerns in Mr. Pickwick another Eden-dweller, an Eden-dweller forced to take account of the fallen world when he finds himself in the Fleet. Don Quixote, in Mr. Auden's eyes, is an indirect portrayal of a saint—he speaks the language of Eros 'but its real meaning is the Christian agape'. He hears the voice of Agape, too, in the exchanges between Bertie Wooster, blessed in his humility, and the godlike Jeeves:

'All the other great men of the age are simply in the crowd, watching you go by'.

'Thank you very much, sir. I endeavour to give satisfaction.'

And the detective story, he claims, appeals to us because it offers a picture of a seemingly innocent society to identify ourselves with, all suddenly threatened by the possibility of guilt and all (save one who may be forgotten) finally restored to confidence in their innocence and deserved happiness.

But he reverts often to the theme found in the poems that these perceptions of Eden, even at their finest, must not blind us to our fallen state: this will involve us in irresponsibility and sin, as much as the equally understandable attempt to create Utopias and New Jerusalems in reality. (There is a superb poem on just this point in *The Shield of Achilles*.) Cervantes, therefore, Mr. Auden argues, was obliged to restore Don Quixote to sense and let him die, for even Don Quixote would be guilty of a sin if he went on being for ever interesting. (We may recall, here, too, Caliban's words from *The Sea and the Mirror*; only 'amongst the ruins and bones' of a work that is in the end imperfect may we 'rejoice in the perfect Work which is not ours'.) In another essay in *The Dyer's Hand* Mr. Auden's Graham Greene-ish remark on his liking for America seems to strike the same spark from a different anvil. He lists, among other aspects of the American scene,

the unspeakable juke-boxes, the horrible Rockettes, the insane salads . . . without which perhaps . . . the immigrant would never understand by contrast the nature of the Good Place nor desire it with sufficient desperation to stand a chance of arriving.

The really deadly danger, here as in the poetry, is seen as coming from those people who seek to exercise power over the mind. The best example again comes from one of the Shakespeare essays, a free-flying interpretation of Iago's character, who is seen, in the way he manipulates the destinies of all those about him, as a 'parabolic figure for the autonomous pursuit of scientific knowledge through experiment'—the treatment of human beings not as individuals but interchangeable units.

There are many other striking and intriguing observations on literature in *The Dyer's Hand*: on symbolist poetry ('like tea-table conversation, in which the meaning of the banalities uttered depends almost entirely on vocal inflection'), on American poetry, on Byron's poetic technique and Lawrence's doggerel, on Ibsen and his problems. An extremely fascinating essay is concerned with the technical problems of translating opera libretti. But even when he is making a more usual and particular kind of literary comment, Mr. Auden will fly back at the slightest cue to the themes that dominate the book.

For Christian and non-Christian alike, in short, Mr. Auden goes on producing a wealth of ideas and delights. But, in perspective, *The Dyer's Hand* and his recent poetry both seem to have one disturbing limitation. In their very assurance and charm they both have the constant air of brilliant play about them, the air of the top-class liar-dice player, the air even of Bishop Blougram himself. Mr. Auden is well armed against this possible criticism. First, there is his repeated insistence that all art is after all a kind of play:

> When
> We consciously pretend to
> Own the earth, or play at
> Being Gods, we thereby
> Own that we are men—

which seems to make Mr. Auden a twentieth-century Dr. Arnold, recommending intellectual sports for young Christians. Secondly there is the insistence, implicit, it must be acknowledged, in the first point, that the aim of such play is to remind us of the lamentable difference of the world we are actually obliged to live in.

Nevertheless, even when speaking of recalcitrant nature—ours and the world's—Mr. Auden always seems seriously to pare its claws. Dame Nature herself, as

> that old grim She
> Who makes the blind dates for the hatless genera

is superbly portrayed—but not really very grim. What Mr. Auden speaks of as the limitation of opera seems frequently applicable to his own work.

The singer may be playing the role of a deserted bride who is about to kill herself, but we feel quite certain as we listen that not only we, but also she, is having a wonderful time. . . . Consequently the pleasure we and [she] are obviously enjoying strikes the conscience as frivolous.

We cannot but be grateful to Mr. Auden for the abundant and distinctive pleasure he gives. But he must have become used, since living in America, to hearing himself actually addressed *as* 'Mr. Arden'. It seems to be another scene that he should let his splendid mythopoeic imagination play on.

E

7

KARL JASPERS

A PHILOSOPHER OF HUMANITY

DEATH, SUFFERING, CHANCE, guilt, conflict: only in such boundary situations do human beings come to awareness of what they are. But if we can approach the understanding of what we are only in these lonely limits of existence, it is in communication, in the rich and rare togetherness of persons who love in honesty and openness, that we become truly human. Only in another's being have I my being, only in another's freedom my freedom.

These two thoughts of the boundary situation, and of personal communication, are constant themes throughout the writings of Karl Jaspers, and, seen from this year of his eightieth birthday, throughout his life. That they are constant themes in his voluminous publications he himself said, ten years ago, in his 'Philosophical Autobiography'. But that is to say, at the same time, that they are constant themes in his life: for it is yet another constant theme of his that there is no Philosophy as such, no once-for-all system of Ideas or clever technique for dispelling paradoxes. There is only philosophizing, reflective thought absorbing the whole person of the thinker: thought directed first and last to that most puzzling and most urgent of questions, the Socratic question: what is it to be a man?

Even in this sense of philosophy, moreover, Jaspers hesitates to count himself a philosopher. Philosophy being literally the love of wisdom, he, as a lover of philosophy, is, he says, at two removes from

Karl Jaspers: Werk und Wirkung. 217 pp. Munich: Piper. KARL JASPERS: *The Great Philosophers: The Foundations.* Edited by Hannah Arendt. Translated by Ralph Manheim. 396 pp. Rupert Hart-Davis. 42s. *Philosophie und Welt.* Reden und Aufsätze. 408 pp. Munich: Piper. DM. 22. *General Psychopathology.* Translated by J. Hoenig and Marian W. Hamilton. 922 pp. Manchester University Press. £3 15s. *Der philosophische Glaube angesichts der Offenbarung.* 540 pp. Munich: Piper. DM.32. *Lebensfragen der deutschen Politik.* 315 pp. Munich: Deutscher Taschenbuch Verlag. DM. 3.60. *Die Atombombe und die Zukunft des Menschen.* Politisches Bewusstsein in unserer Zeit. 506 pp. Munich: Piper Paperback. DM. 9.80. Abridged paperback: 369 pp. Munich: Deutscher Taschenbuch Verlag. DM. 3.60.

the possession of wisdom itself. He would guide us, as in his *Great Philosophers*, to fructifying contact with their vision; he does not count himself among them.

*   *   *

Yet if we look back at the panorama of his career we must feel that it is something not unlike wisdom that marks his life and work, one as they are. Or if wisdom must be reserved for the giants of philosophy, perhaps the right word is: humanity. Jaspers's philosophical works, indeed, are long, long-winded, repetitive in the extreme, as it seems to English readers only German professors know how to be. And the dead earnest of his philosophizing, unleavened by the slightest spark of lightness or humour, is often too solid and too vaporous at once, if that be possible, for English stomachs to digest. Looking at it as so very many words making over and over the same solemn pronouncements, we *want* to find it pompous nonsense. But give Jaspers a concrete issue, a moral issue with intellectual implications, or an intellectual issue in a moral context, give him, in short, a boundary situation, and you find an integrity, a moral rightness of argument and decision, a luminous clarity, sometimes even economy, of expression that can only evoke our unqualified assent and respect. So, over the years, he has spoken, for example, on the nature of mental illness, on the intellectual crisis of our time, on academic freedom, on the 'total falsehood' of National Socialism, on the responsibility of all Germans, and all men, for that calamity, on the bomb, on the meaning and prospects of German unity, on the role of the churches in the modern world—and there may be more such themes to come.

*   *   *

Shall we then in our reading of Jaspers stick to his treatment of limited issues and leave the broader sweep of his philosophy alone? In a sense translators and publishers have done this, for although there have been a surprising number of his works published here and in America, no one has produced an English version of his three-volume *Philosophie* or of his 1,100-page work on truth, itself the first volume of a projected Philosophical Logic. Yet if his work and his life are one, so, *a fortiori*, is his work itself a unity, and in the particular judgements that command our admiration his fundamental philosophical concepts, Truth, Freedom, 'Vernunft', transcendence, are never far removed. The best guiding line, perhaps, for trying to understand him is the philosophical autobiography, recently re-published in an eightieth birthday Festschrift (*Karl Jaspers: Werk und Wirkung*), as well as in the collection *Philosophie und Welt*. (It was originally written for *The Philosophy of Karl Jaspers*, a volume in an American series, where it was, unfortunately, badly translated.)

Karl Jaspers has lived since boyhood in and with a boundary situation of his own. He suffers from an organic bronchial and heart condition which was diagnosed when he was eighteen, the prognosis being death in the thirties at the latest. His life has been organized around his illness, but—as is plain from his activity as writer and teacher—in such a way as to control it rather than let it have control of him. The impact of his personality derives partly from the courage and discipline necessary to such a life. Seeking within these limits for the greatest possible contact with human reality, he chose medicine and in particular psychiatry as a career.

Although his active clinical work had perforce to be restricted his pioneering achievements in this first profession were of such importance that his *General Psychopathology*, first published in 1913 and now in its seventh edition, is still in use, and, happily, has now been made available to the English-speaking public by Manchester University Press. Here, as ever after, it was the respect for human beings as such which basically motivated Jaspers's reform of psychiatry. The Heidelberg school, when he joined it, interpreted mental illness almost wholly as physically caused. Jaspers approached each patient, instead, as an unfathomable human person, to be encountered, and understood, as such.

*   *   *

After the *Psychopathology* his next major work, *Die Psychologie der Weltanschauungen*, was transitional to his future, more speculative interests. It has the philosophical importance of introducing the concept of the boundary situation. But it was not until December 1931 that his first considerable philosophical work, the three-volume *Philosophie*, was published, and as he says himself his own understanding of and critical reflection on the great philosophers was even then and has been ever since in process of development. Contributing to this development, and central to all his thought, as he repeatedly says, was the influence of his wife, formerly Gertrud Mayer, whom he had married in 1910. His emphasis on communication is often explicitly, always implicitly, bound to this nearby instance of what he calls 'loving conflict in total honesty'. His interest in biblical religion, in particular, he owes to his wife's Jewish upbringing.

The other major influence which must be mentioned in any account of Jaspers's work is that of Max Weber. Jaspers's conception of the objectivity of science and its abstractness—that is, its necessary confinement to selected, almost artificially limited, problems—is deeply Weberian. And as his stress on human togetherness is linked to his own marriage so, one suspects, his deep reverence for human greatness reflects his feeling for Weber, the great man whom he himself in his youth knew and revered.

*　　*　　*

In the *Philosophie* it is the first of the three volumes, *Weltorientierung*, which clearly shows Weber's mark. Jaspers's conception of natural science is an almost positivist one, plainly stamped with the ideal of 'wertfreie Wissenschaft'. The other two volumes show how his scientific naturalism is supplemented by concern for the other essential, and deeper lying, aspects of human experience, *personal existence* and *transcendence*. The concept of *existence* derives from Kierkegaard, but the stress on communication is scarcely Kierkegaardian. Nor is the almost Kantian emphasis on 'Vernunft', that more than ratiocinating German Reason, which has moved more and more to the centre of Jaspers's thought, as for example in the lectures on *Vernunft und Existenz* (1935; *Reason and Existence*, Routledge, 1955).

Transcendence for Jaspers, in contrast to the use of that term by Heidegger, retains its traditional meaning. It is ultimate mystery, which we can grasp only through image and symbol, through deciphering, 'das Chiffrelesen'. It is not, however, the faith of any church to which Jaspers is turning here, but what he calls 'philosophical faith', a concept which again he has continued to develop in his later writings. In his most recent book, *Der philosophische Glaube angesichts der Offenbarung*, he contrasts the self-closing circle of revelation with the circle of philosophical faith, which by its very nature remains open for and beyond failure and suffering. But these later elaborations retain, as it were, the shape already adumbrated in the three volumes of 1931–32.

Jaspers was Professor of Philosophy at Heidelberg from 1921. As a philosopher, as an active participant in the administration of a great university, dedicated by its nature to the free pursuit of truth, as the husband of a Jewish wife, as a German thinker steeped in the humanism of Goethe and of Kant, he stood from 1933 to 1945 in the second great boundary situation of his life. He was deprived of his chair in 1937; working patiently but, of course, quite privately, and without hope of a future, at his 'philosophical logic', he heard in 1945 that he and his wife would be taken away on 14 April. The Americans occupied Heidelberg on 1 April, and so rescued, if not the greatest, certainly the best of living German philosophers from destruction at the hands of his fellow-Germans. Quickly reinstated by the occupying forces to lead the resuscitation of the university, he accepted three years later a call to the University of Basle and there retired from active lecturing in 1961.

*　　　*　　　*

Hitler, it has been said, made Jaspers a political thinker. This is not quite true, for politics had long concerned him, and his well-known *Geistige Situation der Zeit* (1931; *Man in the Modern Age*, Routledge, 1933, 1951) is not without its political implications. But it is since the Second World War that he has produced his most important political works: *Die Schuldfrage* (reprinted in the DTV volume *Lebensfragen der deutschen Politik*; *The Question of German Guilt*, New York: Dial 1947) and *Die Atombombe und die Zukunft des Menschen* (Piper, 1958; *The Future of Mankind*, Chicago, 1961). In both these works the philosopher of the boundary situation shows his power.

In everyday circumstances, in a reasonably fortunate life, ordinary 'rule-bound behaviour' goes smoothly on its way. We may pride ourselves on subjecting to enlightened criticism the rules of our society, but in the main we follow them without undue concern, and follow by implication the ultimate ideals on which in turn they rest. But most of us do come some few times, even in such a cushioned life, to turning points at which we must go one way or the other, yet on neither course can we say serenely, that was what the rules prescribed. At places where the rules massively collapse and our freedom stands glaringly alone in all its peril and ambiguity: there we stand at a boundary. Life in the French Resistance, as Sartre expounded its meaning in the 'Republic of Silence' and dramatized it in *Morts sans Sépultures*, was life at such a boundary. For every decent and sensitive German life under National Socialism was life at such a boundary, and Jaspers in *Die Schuldfrage* probes the complex levels of responsibility implicit in such an existence. This little work can stand alongside the *Crito* for its illumination of the human condition as such, arising out of reflection on a concrete situation.

Germans under Hitler lived at a boundary, and so did we all indirectly. So *do* we all when the threat of total injustice, the boundary situation of tyranny as Thucydides and Plato first pictured it for us, has been transmuted by the power of technology to its radical totalitarian form. The total threat to freedom is with us constantly and for ever. But the threat to life itself, in the nuclear age, has been similarly magnified. Not only each of us singly must learn, in Kierkegaard's phrase, to 'rejoice over 70,000 fathoms'. The human race itself stands in every moment at the verge of annihilation.

*   *   *

This global boundary situation, where freedom and life are equally imperilled, Jaspers turns to in the 'bomb book'. Originally a broadcast, this shorter version is also reprinted in the *Lebensfragen*. Published in much expanded book form, it became a bestseller in Germany, gained for its author the German publishers' peace prize (Friedenspreis des deutschen Buchhandels) and is now out in two paperback editions as well as in an American edition. The book contains, again, much practical wisdom on such topics as colonialism or the United Nations, or such figures as Roosevelt or Gandhi. And yet the concluding part of the argument brings us once more into the quagmire of 'Vernunft' and 'Wahrheit'.

This is distressing. When Jaspers speaks, for example, in an address called 'Volk und Universität' in the DTV *Lebensfragen* about the nature of the university as the place of the untrammelled pursuit of truth, we know what he means by freedom, by truth; his thesis is brilliantly clear, his argument impeccable: the whole piece is a classic. Why, then, when 'truth' and 'freedom' and 'reason' get out on their own do we find ourselves floundering? Why are the particular consequences so plain and so true, yet the general premises so formless and so cloudy? Can it be the case, as so many German speakers have believed, that the English tongue is unsuited to philosophizing? Or can it be that even the profoundest insights, left too much scope for expansion, tend to dissipate themselves, somehow, out of sheer bulk.

Jaspers writes by accumulating jottings on slips of paper, which gradually work themselves into a book. The leading ideas, he believes, are less important than the detailed expositions they were meant to stitch together. These accumulated musings, in the case of his first book, his great text on psychopathology, took on their final shape *un*revised! Since then, he says, he has always read through his manuscripts and corrected them; and his publisher and friend Klaus Piper pays tribute to the beautifully finished state in which the manuscripts are received. Yet one cannot help feeling that in this revision there is little pruning. Perhaps it is not so much a limited subject-matter as a limiting occasion, like a broadcast or a public lecture, that is needed to make Jaspers intelligible to those not used to the diffuseness of German thought and speech.

Be that as it may, not only his political pronouncements but also his vast philosophical projects have still continued to proliferate. Three of these later projects should be mentioned in a general survey of Jaspers's work. First, there was *Vom Ursprung und Ziel der Geschichte* (1949; *Origin and Goal of History*, Routledge, 1953), a massive work singling out the 'axial period' in which the roots of our culture were laid down. Related to this view of history, with its emphasis on the significance of biblical Christianity, is, secondly, the recent work already mentioned on philosophical faith in relation to revelation. Jaspers recognizes frankly the impotence of the churches as a force in contemporary culture, and he has no easy prescription for rethinking the traditional image of God to suit the secular disposition of modern man. Rather it is, as so often in his thought, a fundamental tension in our nature which he hopes to illuminate.

The philosopher, he believes, comes inevitably to awareness of a transcendent medium which for ever draws but for ever eludes his knowledge. This endless code-reading, groping through and beyond symbols for the ultimate, the philosophical thinker knows to be his task, but he knows it to be in principle incapable of fulfilment. The person who believes out of piety, on the ground of revelation, though not, it is to be hoped, in conflict with the philosopher, does stand on a different foundation in his relation to the being that surrounds us. And Jaspers doubts whether these two, the way of broad philosophical vision, and the way of prayer and worship, can be united in a single life. Again we come to the boundary, and take one path or the other. Those who go the two ways are to be honoured each by the other, but there is no ultimate synthesis, no one human way that can assimilate all differences.

*   *   *

Last, and perhaps the best avenue of approach to Jaspers for English readers, is his grand project for a study of *The Great Philosophers*. Volume I, which was published in 1956, has now appeared in an excellent English version. The framework of the whole work, announced in the introduction, is, once more, alarmingly elaborate and over-schematic. The philosphers are sorted out into such groups as 'the seminal thinkers, the great disturbers, the creative orderers'. No such classification, Jaspers would be the first to admit, is fixed and final, but the sheer complexity of it, and the air with which it is announced, might make one hesitate to embark on the first leg of the journey—for this should be the first of numerous volumes.

The work itself, however, is intended not as a formidable work of categorization but as an introduction for the ordinary reader, to the great thinkers of the world. It is just that. In this volume there are, first, four chapters on what Jaspers calls the four 'paradigmatic individuals', not philosophers, but men who have served as models to hosts of others: Socrates, Jesus, Buddha, and Confucius. Then follow three studies of as many 'seminal thinkers': Plato, Augustine and Kant. These are the thinkers who, Jasper believes, best help men in their own thoughts. His own thinking is closest to Kant, and perhaps for that reason his exposition of Kant is less accurate as a tendering of his original. In particular he is too eager to make the sage of Königsberg wise in the knowledge of 'life'. But there is still much to be learnt from his exposition. And the introductions to Plato and Augustine are magnificent.

* * *

For precisely what Jaspers hopes to do here he succeeds in doing: that is, to bring the reader to an enriching *encounter* with a great mind. This kind of 'introduction' is out of fashion in Great Britain. It is more usual to dissect particular passages for their 'logic' or lack of it than to attempt to understand the mind that conceived the passage, or better, conceived the work from which the zealous analyst has extracted it. What frequently emerges from such logical exercises is not an understanding of the philosopher in question but an admiration for one's own cleverness. For most of us, however, it is more rewarding to listen to Plato or Augustine or Kant than to ourselves.

Not that Jaspers presents these thinkers as authorities we ought blindly to follow: quite the contrary. But if we are to wrestle with the perennial problems of philosophy—to ask who we are, what kin 'mind' is to body, what it is to live justly, what 'time' and 'history' mean, how general concepts are related to the particulars of sense— if we are to ask these questions, responsibly, in and of ourselves, we must ask them when and where we stand within a long tradition of such asking. So out of our own reflective seeking we should turn to confront the great minds who in the past have asked these same root questions and by their answers, or even sometimes their reasons for not answering, have helped to shape our questioning and our answers. In this sense it is at least as basic for our education to 'live in the company of the great philosophers' as it is to live with the great poets or composers or discoverers. To read *The Great Philosophers* would be an excellent way to begin, both to meet the great thinkers of the past and to meet the contemporary philosophizing of Karl Jaspers.

8

NOVELS OF 1963

(a) GÜNTER GRASS

Hundejahre, Cat and Mouse

The Tin Drum was so extraordinary a *tour de force* that it might easily have exhausted Herr Grass's powers of invention and recollection. Moreover it was a poet's novel which, if not autobiographical, drew liberally on the circumstances of the author's early years; and according to the rules and precedents, the retrospective novels of poets neither permit nor demand a sequel. Few readers, in fact, can have expected another novel on the same scale to follow after only four years, least of all another novel covering much the same historical period and set for the most part in the same localities.

Yet Herr Grass's talent has always been prodigious and unpredictable. Already his next work of fiction, the small-scale *Katz und Maus* (now available in a paperback edition and in an excellent English version by the translator of *The Tin Drum*) showed that he had other, and very different, capacities. *Cat and Mouse*, it is now apparent, was a chip off the block of Herr Grass's new long novel *Hundejahre*. His decision to work it separately, on its own terms, may have helped him to acquire the new skill and the new discipline also remarkable in the longer work, which is much more controlled, much more clearly and purposefully wrought, than *The Tin Drum*. Since Herr Grass, above all, is an artist, he has been able to write an essentially different kind of novel, though *Hundejahre* draws on the same personal experiences as *The Tin Drum*.

The Tin Drum was dominated by a single character, and much of its ultimate ambiguity even was due to the extent of Herr Grass's

---

(a) *Hundejahre.* 684 pp. Neuwied: Luchterhand. DM. 24.50.
    Cat and Mouse. Translated by Ralph Manheim. 191 pp. Secker & Warburg. 18s.
  (b) *Le Chaos et la Nuit.* 280 pp. Paris: Gallimard. 12 fr.
  (c) *La cognizione del dolore.* 223 pp. Turin: Einaudi. L. 1,500.
  (d) *Mr. Stone and the Knights Companion.* 160 pp. André Deutsch. 16s.
  (e) *The Secret Ladder.* 127 pp. Faber & Faber. 16s.

imaginative self-identification with that character. *Hundejahre* has two main characters, Matern and Amsel, to whom one could add the alsatian dogs Harras and Prinz (alias Pluto), but Herr Grass does not identify himself to any comparable extent with any character in the book, human or canine. This in itself is a major difference. Certain readers and critics, indeed, may regret that Herr Grass has denied himself some of the sheer rumbustious playfulness of the earlier work—some, but by no means all of it; but Herr Grass would not have succeeded in writing an essentially different novel if he had not subordinated some of his picaresque and fairytale inventions to a more consistently realistic concern. In the same way it may be regretted that Matern and even Amsel—for all those exploits with scarecrows which correspond to Oscar's magical and artistic faculties—lack the tin drummer's heroic monstrosity, without a compensating gain in finely differentiated sensibility. In *Hundejahre*, too, personal relations remain somewhat crude and infantile, and it is characteristic that both Matern and Amsel devote a great deal of energy in their mature years to the business of coming to terms with their youth. Just as the diminutive Oscar of the earlier episodes was more vivid than the adult hunchback, both Matern and Amsel become more shadowy as they grow older, their exploits less individual than representative, if not allegorical. This peculiarity is more striking in *Hundejahre* because more weight falls on the later years, and because Oscar's arrested development has no parallel in the basic conception of the new novel. It seems that Herr Grass's imagination remains fixed on the early years, as it remains fixed on the lost environment of his own childhood and adolescence.

Much of *Hundejahre*, therefore, is sustained less by the exploration in depth and by the interaction of the principal characters than by their exploits and external configuration; but though the action is not unified by a single agent, and even the narrative is attributed to a staff of writers employed by Amsel (alias Brauxel) to compile the diverse evidence, all the seeming deficiencies of *Hundejahre* are only the reverse side of Herr Grass's minutely documented recapitulation of the past and of his devastating assault on the present. Among other things Herr Grass has written by far the fullest and most convincing critique of Nazism yet achieved in fiction. He has done so by deliberately de-mythologizing, de-heroizing and, as he puts it, de-demonizing that phenomenon, whereas Thomas Mann, who had no direct experience of its everyday drabness, chose to demonize it in

Dr. Faustus and so paid a paradoxical tribute to its perverse appeal. Only a writer of Herr Grass's generation could accomplish the more difficult and more effective task of exposing its vulgar shoddiness from the inside.

This tone and medium, of course, were anticipated in *The Tin Drum*, except that both the exuberant fantasy and the essential ambiguity of that work tended to blur the general issues. In *Hundejahre* Herr Grass has managed to combine his humorous, often farcical, impartiality with the systematic deflation of Nazism. The ambiguities are still there. Matern is at once a Nazi and an anti-Nazi. Amsel, though half-Jewish and a victim of the régime, corrects the excesses of Matern's condemnation of the German character. Yet these complexities can no longer be mistaken for an ambivalence on the author's part; they are facets of a reality which he has made more palpable than any writer before him. Again, it is impossible to enumerate all the means used to attain this end; but the interweaving of the dog motif with the lives of Matern, Amsel, Tulla, Harry and many minor characters is at once the most subtle and the most powerful. Tulla (also prominent in *Cat and Mouse*) at one time chooses to share the kennel of Harras, the sire of Prinz who becomes Hitler's favourite dog; and it is Tulla who does her best to ruin the non-Nazi Amsel and Brunies. When Matern decides to poison Harras, what he has come to see in the dog is nothing less than the embodiment of Nazism. More layers are added to this complex when Hitler, just before the end of the war, initiates a vast military action to recapture his dog Prinz, and this action is both conducted and reported in a vacuously mystifying code which parodies the abstract terminology of Professor Martin Heidegger. Prinz runs away to the West; and ironically it is Matern who becomes his new master, though he gives him the name Pluto.

The scarecrow motif is another that unifies the whole book, though its final elaboration in Amsel's post-war factory, a kind of modern inferno, is almost too deliberately allegorical. Like the dog motif and the prophetic meal-worms of Matern's father, the miller, Amsel's animated scarecrows link the early Danzig chapters to the west Germany of the *Wirtschaftswunder*, which is shown to depend on the miller's financial predictions—and, ultimately, on worms. Matern's frustrated attempts to avenge himself on his former Nazi mentor and bosses after the war, with the help of the names and addresses that appear miraculously in the public lavatory of the Cologne railway station, have the scurrilous abandon of many episodes in *The Tin Drum*, but their relevance to the larger satirical scheme is never left in doubt.

A particularly gruesome form of revenge is to be practised during confession on a Roman Catholic priest, but abandoned when the priest proves to turn a literally deaf ear to those who confess to him. The same confessional, however, serves Matern for an act of adultery with the wife of another 'war criminal', and Herr Grass's love-hatred for the Church has lost little of its vehemence. Professor Heidegger, whom Matern also wishes to confront, completely evades him in the funniest and most metaphysical of all these 'Materniads'.

The great Nazi atrocities are only hinted at, not described, for Herr Grass is tactful enough to keep his de-demonologizing within its proper limits. The brutal beating up and rolling into a snowball of Amsel by a gang of masked S.A. men, one of whom is his best friend and 'blood brother' Matern, only cost him all his teeth and changed him from a fat boy into a thin man (an instance of those fairy-tale transformations which Herr Grass can still reconcile with the most astringent realism elsewhere). Herr Grass was wise to confine himself to what he knows and understands, the latent cruelty, malevolence and moral cowardice of children, which can so easily be fostered and exploited by an adult world for ostensibly adult purposes. Mahlke, the hero of *Cat and Mouse*, differs from Matern in his exceptional resistance to such pressures. Amsel does not resist them, but neutralizes them by parody, and this is his way—perhaps Herr Grass's also, in *The Tin Drum* at least—of preserving his independence and integrity. The fact that Matern is at once a 'good' and a 'bad' German not only makes his early relationship with Amsel all the more convincing and significant but is vital to the design of the whole novel. Matern has to be saved from his self-hatred and self-disgust as a German by his half-Jewish friend; but Amsel's Jewish father had been deeply influenced by the self-hatred and the self-disgust of Otto Weininger who claimed that 'the Jew has no soul. The Jew does not sing. The Jew does not play games'. The eagerness of Amsel's father to prove that the second and third rules, at least, do not hold good for him is a valid reflection on tendencies widespread among the assimilated German Jews. Eddi Amsel himself sings in the church choir and, with Matern's help, learns to hold his own in a fierce German ball game.

These few threads may suffice to show that the *Hundejahre* is not only the rambling, episodic and richly inventive novel which is to be expected of the author of *The Tin Drum*, though this is suggested both by its length and its seemingly heterogeneous narrative structure. Little has been said of Herr Grass's admirable re-creation of a whole community and way of life, his retracing of the topography, folklore and idiom of his native region in Book I of the new novel; but every reader of the two earlier books must be aware of this distinction, as of his incomparable verbal ingenuity and zest. Nor is it necessary to stress Herr Grass's related ability to enter into the psychology of children and adolescents, and to present their barbarous rituals and codes as though they had been his only yesterday. What makes *Hundejahre* an essentially different book, and one that promises further developments of Herr Grass's capacities as a novelist, is his success in combining comic spontaneity with a serious and ambitious design.

(b) HENRY DE MONTHERLANT
Le Chaos et la Nuit

This latest novel by M. de Montherlant is not one of those he wrote years ago and still, for mysterious reasons, keeps locked up in his drawers. It bear the date 1961–62, and so was composed in the author's sixty-fifth year. A preface warns us that we should not read into it any autobiographical implications, but M. de Montherlant has always been the hero, or anti-hero, of his works and his new main character, a Spanish Republican called Don Celestino Marcilla Hernandez, is closely related to all his other creations. Also, any reader of the author's *Carnets* will recognize a great many of Celestino's reactions as being those of M. de Montherlant himself.

There are at least two Montherlants: the positive figure, imperious, contemptuous, sexually assertive, rather posturing and pugnacious, and the negative *pauvre type*, a worrier rather than a warrior, sombre, bleak and inconsolable. Celestino corresponds mainly to the second and, in spite of his preface, the author does not always manage, or even try, to keep himself distinct from the character. More than once he breaks into the narrative to announce, in the same voice as that used by the hero, that he will continue with the story in the next chapter, if he does not die in the meantime. M. de Montherlant is clearly satirizing himself, and sympathizing with himself, under the shadow of dissolution.

A Spanish Republican may seem an unlikely choice as a vehicle for M. de Montherlant's self-projection. Actually M. de Montherlant's consciousness of aristocratic tradition has always made him an unconventional reactionary, capable at times of coming out with very radical statements. Besides, his Spaniard is not much of a Republican; he is an Anarchist, a traditionalist with a very keen sense of honour; an enemy of the Church rather than a lover of the people, and his whole political philosophy, such as it is, is little more than a system of hatreds.

The plot is slight. Celestino has been living in France with his daughter, Pascualita, since the end of the Civil War, and he has been able to do so in comfort, since he has a go-between who has arranged for him to receive the income from his Spanish property. He spends his time writing bad, passionate political articles, which are never published. He has only two or three friends, exiles like himself, and, having reached the last stages of irritation because of his sense of the imminence of death, he deliberately alienates them. He feels guilty about his daughter, who knows no one and has no future, and at the same time he is exasperated by her feminine lack of interest in the things that concern him.

An opportunity to return to Spain occurs when his sister dies and he has to settle matters arising out of her will. He goes back largely for the pleasure of watching a bull-fight, and this is the final disenchantment. Everything now appears vulgar and tawdry to him: the ritual costume, the gestures of the matadors, the reactions of the crowd. He returns to his hotel, ill, and dies in painful stages like a bull, intensely aware, in his moments of lucidity, of the meaninglessness of life.

The whole book seems to have been written to serve as an introduction to the long, destructive account of the *corrida*, as if M. de Montherlant, true to his principle of ringing the changes on opposites, wanted to demolish the bull-fighting myth, which he extolled in his youthful documentary novel, *Les Bestiaires*. This episode is, in fact, a very impressive piece of writing. M. de Montherlant has lost none of his cunning as a stylist and happily, the only effect of age has been to reduce the passages of windy rhetoric. Few living French writers can equal him in crisp delineation of essential detail, and his most prejudiced, or even silly, remarks are minted by a perfect linguistic sensibility.

The 'message' of this novel is one that M. de Montherlant has long been expressing: nothing in the universe makes any sense; any human existence is a short period of chaos between two stretches of eternal night; therefore the individual temperament may as well be a law unto itself. However, he takes out a small insurance policy against the possibility of Roman Catholicism being true after all. When Celestino is found dead in his room in a pool of blood, he has four sharp wounds in his back and neck, corresponding to the blows that killed the bull. Since he died alone, these can only be a proof of supernatural martyrdom. The miracle is grim, yet a miracle it is, and the first one M. de Montherlant has ever allowed himself. He also ends his book with the words inscribed on Celestino's tomb: Laus Deo.

(c) CARLO EMILIO GADDA

La cognizione del dolore

The richness and freedom, the past ragbag eclecticism and present polyglot pervasiveness about the globe, the sheer (and apparently inexhaustible) bounce and elasticity of our language—its casualness over rules, its high-handedness with syntax, its whole unacademic, far-fetched metaphorical bias that loves the concrete palpable image, and avoids the abstract and highflown—all tend to make current Italian appear by comparison staid, uninventive, unused and unsuited to the somersaults and baroqueness of the kind of linguistic acrobat so easily bred on English. Admittedly, in the hands of an average literate Italian his language is probably less plastic than English is in the hands of his English-speaking counterpart (Welshman or West Indian, Texan or Tristanian), and the everyday acquisitiveness of our spoken language, our way of standing habit on its head, making up new words when we want them, interchanging the function of verbs, nouns, adverbs and almost everything else, tend to seem, to the same average Italian (who is likely to be more academic in training and attitude than his equivalent here), heretical, barbarous or enviable, depending on temperament.

But Italian is not confined to its average or everyday uses, and in the hands of a master of language it can be used with as much freedom as ours is, can stretch in as many directions, can defy rule and custom as ours does, and above all can bring the compactness and

F

allusiveness of poetry into prose. And, apart from the obvious linguistic elasticity that diminutives, augmentatives and superlatives can provide (a form of elasticity English almost entirely lacks), Italian has a subterranean hoard of riches little known abroad, because untranslatable: the familiar riches, the entire sub-culture, of dialect.

That Carlo Emilio Gadda is a master of language is not disputed; the most common comparison—and it is not far-fetched—is with Joyce. But the claim, sometimes made, that he is Italy's foremost living writer can mean little in this country, one way or the other, because the very qualities that make his language, in a sense, so un-Italian (so unacademically Italian, at least)—the whole baroqueness with which he is inevitably labelled, and even more so his free and remarkable use of dialect—make it hard for him to be translated into English: a language that, ironically, would seem to have special affinities and sympathies with his.

The Formentor group recently awarded him the Prix des Éditeurs, given yearly to a writer who seems to deserve more international acclaim than he has had so far. Specifically, the prize this year went to *La cognizione del dolore*, an unfinished first novel published chapter by chapter between 1938 and 1941, then abandoned, and now reprinted in full; but it recognized too Gadda's whole body of work, which includes a number of *novelle* collected under the title *La Madonna dei Filosofi, Il castello di Udine, L'Adalgisia* and *Accoppiamenti giudiziosi:* essays, short stories, poetry; and the best known of them all, the extraordinary novel that first appeared, like *La cognizione del dolore*, chapter by chapter in a literary review, and was published in its complete form in 1957, *Quer pasticciaccio brutto de via Merulana*.

This last, within the framework of a detective story, takes Gadda's linguistic experiments about as far, perhaps, as they will go, not simply in the eccentricity of syntax and vocabulary, and the enormously complex and exciting effects this achieves, but in the use of dialect as an integral, though not overwhelming, part of the narrative. Gadda does not (like Pasolini, for instance) use dialect throughout his narrative, nor does he stick (again like Pasolini) to the one dialect: in *Quer pasticciaccio* it is Roman, with more southern additions, in other works it is Milanese, or even (in so far as it can be called dialect) Tuscan. From using it in dialogue he slides, sometimes still using it, into interior monologue, the hero's observations, or the narrative itself, then abandons it for paragraphs or pages, using it rather as the main characters might—with some people and not others, for some occasions and not others. The difficulties of translating such writing into English seem insuperable, particularly as the concept of dialect in the sense Italians use it does not exist in this country (or anywhere else in the English-speaking world, for that matter). The horrific effect of translating Pasolini's Roman speech into cockney has been seen in the sub-titling of his first film, *Accattone*; and Gadda's Romans, who are mostly not even proletarian like Pasolini's, would find themselves in even greater difficulties.

Gadda is seventy, an untypical literary figure who, as an engineer, worked in France, Germany, and Argentina as well as in Italy, and was a prisoner of war in Germany during the First World War. In a country where the self-consciousness of intellectuals is matched by the frequent literariness of much current writing, he stands out as refreshingly unprovincial, large-minded, and (in spite of the intensely difficult and allusive language) non-national, non-local. Above all he avoids the abstractions (even, as it were, the syntactical abstractions, the sentence structure that divides so much written Italian entirely from the spoken, ruminative, everyday language) that in others seem unavoidable; his writing is solid, present, tangible, intensely pre-occupied with the moment, intensely readable because one is there, one is part of it. He is also extremely funny at moments, with a desperate, throwaway humour that seems to include all sorts of moods and humours. Vladimir Nabokov comes to mind, with his linguistic brilliance and his dark grey jokes, but Gadda is darker and denser; or the Argentinian writer admired by Graham Greene and Camus, Ernesto Sábato, with his nightmare world of guilt and hallucination, described with cinematic lucidity.

La cognizione del dolore betrays the painful circumstances of its birth, and like much (perhaps most) fiction written under tyranny it transfers the problems, horrors and secrets of the present to another time and place: an imaginary South American country, Maradagàl, where Gonzalo Pirobutirro d'Eltino, an engineer, is consumed with an infinite though indefinable sorrow, a sickness the doctor tries in vain to find, which bursts out in rancour, hatred and bitterness against the world in general and in particular against the only person in it he might possibly love—his mother. Parallels with Italy are clear and painful, and Gadda found himself unable to bring the story to the murderous conclusion he had planned for it; and so simply stopped.

It makes strange reading at this distance, although it is much more than an historical document or period piece; and although in boldness and freedom its language has probably not been equalled in Italy since, except perhaps by Gadda's own writing, which has grown more bizarre though not necessarily more remarkable than it was in this tormented and obliquely autobiographical work. What explodes from it, not least in its wild, far-fetched humour, is a spiritual frustration so intense that (because unadmitted) it can be embodied only in the hero's spleen: a blackness of the spirit that is not the usual Italian melancholy, which is altogether milder and more diffused; but a concentration of suffering that in a sense seems unmotivated (that the doctor cannot diagnose or outward circumstances, even, justify), yet we know exists, makes sense, has a meaning, for the sheer force and ferocity of the language can persuade us of it. Gadda would seem to have planned a long, or rather large, book, much bulkier than this, for he approaches his central theme in all sorts of tentative, sidelong ways, and spreads himself on externals, minor incidents and characters, a rich life of *things* (objects he likes to list and justify, an 'outside' world of facts and realities) that accumulates, rather than immediately presents what he has to say. The result seems like the opening chapters of something enormous, much larger than Gadda in fact accomplished, a commentary not specifically on repression, or Italy, or the sufferings of any particular place and time, but on man and the mystery of his pain.

(d) V. S. NAIPAUL

Mr. Stone and the Knights Companion

With his new novel V. S. Naipaul has moved from the Caribbean to England. And what a surprising England it is: the respectable self-important suburban people with their 'positions', maidservants and obsessive self-effacement; their timid imitations of the moneyed or upper classes which they think so advanced and distinguishing (the *wine* at the dinner party but only a single bottle and sipped like a liqueur, the men left at table by the ladies but without the ability to talk politics or the courage to tell dirty stories); most typically the pretence and misunderstanding which affects their contact with one another at every level.

Mr. Stone (£1,000-a-year head librarian after life service with the firm of Excal) epitomizes these. He watches his neighbours: the Male who continually redecorates his nest, and the Monster 'an enormous fat woman who hibernated in winter and in the spring tripped out daintily among her flowers in what looked like a gym slip, wielding a watering can like a choric figure'. He resents knowing the names of those who have moved into his street within the past decade and has fantasies about the damage their cats do to his garden. For half the book one seems to be back in the world of *The Diary of a Nobody*. Mr. Stone is almost as ridiculous-accident prone as Mr. Pooter and his house might well have been called 'The Laurels'.

Gradually the story edges into a more modern setting, though Mr. Stone—and this is its skill—remains an Edwardian figure in a world he does not understand. He becomes a victim of his own brain-child: a scheme, born of the sense of his life running out, to bring back the companionship of their office days into the lonely old age of retired members of his company. They shall visit one another, carrying small presents. Miraculously, Mr. Stone is transferred to 'Welfare', and a Public Relations Officer, Mr. Whymper, is employed to help him.

Whymper is magnificent and the best character, among many good ones, in the book. His brand of seedy brashness is exactly recognizable at every fresh piece of corny slickness. Whymper gives life to Mr. Stone's idea or 'licks it into shape', and in the process it is subtly but irretrievably damaged. In spite of this we feel pity not anger, which reaches a climax when he confides in Stone about his mistress, a little-known radio actress with no bust to speak of and a bottom 'long rather than broad, hung very low':

And Whymper said: 'I can put my head between her legs and stay there for hours.'
He spoke with an earnestness that was like sadness. And thereafter the sight of Whymper rolling a cigarette between his lips always brought back this unexpected, frightening, joyless sentence.

But, delicious as such social satire is, it is only a part of Mr. Naipaul's purpose. Nor is this a study of the problems of retirement and old age except in so far as he makes us realize that the phrase is a cliché of sociological journalism because they are only the problems of life in an acute form. What he has done is to give Mr. Stone success and, by giving it to someone whose weakness is so apparent, shown us the impermanence of all success. Beyond this we see its non-existence in any form we recognize. Mr. Stone's triumphant creation of his Knights Companion in part collapses around him, in part is taken from him by people who have found it useful but never understood it. To himself he remains the person he always was and to him comes the realization that 'nothing that came out of the heart, nothing that was pure ought to be exposed'.

Mr. Naipaul writes with an exactness of word and phrase which is delightful and makes the efforts of many contemporary humorists seem ponderous and crude. But funny as he is about his characters, and he is very funny, he never ceases to give the sense that he is handling them very gently. His story is a short one and perhaps lacks the nicely rounded finish one hopes for from a novel of this length; there is a sense that the perfect conclusion escaped him. It remains a comic, touching, and original book.

(e) WILSON HARRIS

The Secret Ladder

When Mr. Wilson Harris's first novel appeared there was no suggestion from the publisher that it formed part of a more ambitious work, and indeed the second and third novels also appeared without any reference being made to the grand design. However, his fourth novel, *The Secret Ladder*, is announced as the last volume of his 'Guiana Quartet'.

Those who know the previous novels may have detected the multiple nature of the work for themselves, but this would not have been easy. In fact even now it would not be difficult to read the quartet as a whole and remain unaware of anything so much as the proof offered once again that a novelist makes technical progress from his first book on, and remains obsessed by the same ideas throughout his working life. Perhaps Mr. Harris's fifth novel will be the test to which the description of his first four as a quartet will have to be put, before it can truly stand. But for the moment, elusive as the design may be, and unknown as it may be when Mr. Harris himself first realized where his creative impulse was leading him, the fourth novel is without a doubt to be recognized not only as a work of great authority and power but also as one whose inner life is illuminated and intensified by all that has gone before.

The Secret Ladder is the easiest of the four, the only book in the quartet with a straightforward narrative line. It has a close resemblance to the first novel, of which it is a restatement and a clarification. The parts played by the two middle books are not so easily defined.

In the first novel, *Palace of the Peacock*, a man called Donne is going up-river to collect labour for his estate, but the reader must soon relinquish his grasp on such a workaday circumstance and commit himself, as it were, to the poetry of motion through a dark interior where words like *death* and *dream* are almost synonymous, where Donne and his crew exist in a limbo compounded of myth and reality. The disastrous journey becomes a struggle not so much to survive, one feels, as actually to re-create a world 'a window on to the universe'—by which perhaps is meant a vantage point from which to watch the rest of the quartet unfold. Or the reader may wonder, perhaps there has simply been laid the first of the four biblical cornerstones of Creation, Fall, Flood and Messiah? If so, to what particular Guianan purpose? Is one in the end to come to nothing more enlivening than a parable of political emergence?

The task that faces the reader who is unfamiliar with West Indian myth and symbol is enormous, but for a time the biblical connotation seems to hold out promise of guidance on the journey through savannah and jungle, through 'the doom of the river and the waterfall'. In the second novel, *Far Journey of Oudin*, part-titles like The Covenant, and The Second Birth, are made to the expected measure, and the title of the third novel, *The Whole Armour* (a quotation from Ephesians, vi, 13: 'Wherefore take unto you the whole armour of God'), suggests a point of total comprehension not far ahead. But in spite of these signposts, and others within the novels themselves, it is upon a growing sense of being borne up by forces no longer alien in a landscape increasingly imaginable that the reader eventually depends.

The comparatively greater clarity of the second and third novels helps. In *Far Journey of Oudin* the story of the moneylender and the heir to a fragmented estate can be followed with less uncertainty about what is dreamt or felt or believed and what actually happens.

The same, and a bit more, can be said of the story in *The Whole Armour* about a young man called Cristo who is accused of murder, helped to escape by his mother, and exchanges clothes with a dead man. If a first reading of the quartet does not uncover anything like the whole of the relationship the two middle novels need to bear to the first and last to rank as *structurally* indispensable, it does show them as indispensable in the business of conditioning the mind to immediate recognition of the fact that in the end of the quartet is its beginning.

The story in *The Secret Ladder* which we might have taken at its face value—of Fenwick, the young West Indian land-surveyor, charting the upper reaches of the Canje river and falling foul of a settlement ruled by an old African—we take instead in a mood corresponding to Fenwick's, of 'inner rhapsody and grotesque meditation'. We have an understanding, if not exactly the measure, of what is really at stake: not the destruction of the settlement by flooding as a result of a new irrigation scheme but the destruction of a 'perception of depth more lasting than time', and of the moral privilege and right of a place that has acquired 'the stamp of a multiple tradition and heritage'.

But what does this *mean*? Fenwick, in whom there is African, English, French, and Amerindian blood, says of his confrontation with the old African (Poseidon): 'I wish I could truly grasp the importance of this meeting. If I do not—if my generation do not—leviathan will swallow us.' Is this a plea for the preservation of something that is being lost in Guiana, something purely African? If so, is it a political or a cultural loss? Or is Poseidon, this descendant of a runaway slave whose lips do not seem to Fenwick to move in unison with his speech, to be seen as the repository of an 'emotional dynamic of liberation' that no longer guides a nation's conscience or consciousness?

In a final paragraph epitomizing the quartet Mr. Harris leaves Fenwick in a doubt we no longer really feel ourselves because the concept of that lost dynamic reaches beyond poetic Guianan imagery into our own human and national awareness. The quartet has been an inquiry into 'the dramatic role of time and being, the dangers of mortal ascent and immortal descent'. The one chosen to descend (Poseidon) is 'crying something' Fenwick is 'unable to fathom . . . but the echoes of annunciation grew on every hand and became resonant with life'.

Quartet or no, the four novels culminating in *The Secret Ladder* are clearly the work of a man who should not be described as a West Indian writer in the narrow, restrictive sense of the words. He is a novelist of already distinguished talent writing in English out of a common perception, a particular experience, and a unique vision.

9

THE VATICAN COUNCIL

(a) ROBERT KAISER

Inside the Council

THE CONCILIAR MOVEMENT which issued in the Council of Constance in 1414 was primarily concerned with closing the Great Schism; it was an attempt to find some way of controlling the appointment to the Papacy so that ecclesiastical and national factions could no longer produce the scandal of competing Popes. It ended the Schism but did little more, and it is one of the odd facts of history that one of the three Popes of the moment, the one who called the Council and was deposed with the other two, was a John XXIII. The dream of governing the Church by Council faded and the Vatican officials remained in control. Their position was immensely strengthened by Trent, the Council called to deal with the problem of the vast Reformation revolt against the medieval Church. It dragged on for nearly twenty years, and the sum of its effect, with its definitions and anathemas against the Protestants, was to turn the Roman Church in upon itself as a highly organized defensive body looking back forlornly to the lost medieval world. That siege mentality was further strengthened when, in 1870, Vatican I promulgated the infallibility decree which, with the elaborate apparatus of the Holy Office, the Index of prohibited books, and the like, set the Curia firmly in control.

The whole story was an unhappy one, for the world, not necessarily unchristian or unorthodox, was moving away from the authoritarianism of the past. If on the one hand there was the remarkable spread of Protestantism which, now out of control, was taking many forms, on the other hand there was developing a whole world of new ideas in culture and government upon which the Roman Church was left to

(a) The Story of Vatican II. 250 pp. Burns & Oates. 25s.
(b) Vatican Council II (first session): Background and Debates. 289 pp. Faber & Faber. 30s.

frown unavailingly. In many areas of that modern world Rome and its old-world ceremonies seemed as remote as Tibet. That huge divorce between the Roman Church and the world of every-day was something that the late Pope, having lived and worked in Milan, knew much better than the men in the Vatican, who saw its facts only in books, printed stuff that could be banned in the process of defence. Mr. Kaiser very appositely quotes *The Times*'s reference to the Roman Church at the time of the infallibility decree as 'a great institution in its day'. It was a hard saying, but it was uncomfortably near the truth. There is an opposition between Christianity and the world in which it has to function, but if Christianity regards itself as a besieged city it could find itself unable to function.

That was one side of the problem which confronted the Roman Church when just 400 years after Trent John XXIII became Pope. The Church was far from dead, but there was about it an air of implacable opposition to the world of freedom of thought in which it was called upon to do its work, and in the Vatican the curialists looked fondly towards the vanished authoritarian past. But there was another side. Protestantism for some fifty years had been acutely conscious of the culpable folly of its divisions, and the Ecumenical Movement, from its small beginnings as a conference about missionary work, had grown into a widespread stirring towards unity between the churches. It was seriously examining the causes of the divisions, and here and there was achieving unions. Barriers were being breached, and churches, long almost completely separated, were anxiously working towards understanding. The Orthodox Church, at first almost as suspicious as Rome, had been drawn in and was beginning to contribute to the world-wide discussion.

The Roman Church had been placed by Trent and Vatican I in an extremely difficult position. *Roma locuta est* closed discussion, and while the Tridentine definitions seemed so complete as to leave nothing to talk about, Protestantism had been firmly anathematized, with the result that the curialists were understandably uneasy lest even to send observers to the conferences of a Protestant movement might seem the abandonment of Rome's absolute claims. It was The Church, and there was nothing for Protestants to do except return from the desert. But outside the Vatican the climate of opinion was changing, and on recent occasions observers have been allowed to attend ecumenical conferences. Pope John, who was

seriously concerned that the Church in the new age should be
equipped to deal with the difficulties of the time, saw that a fresh
approach should be made to Protestantism, and the Council that he
had in mind must discuss the exposition of the Faith in the world
of modern biblical scholarship and thought and social upheavals.

The fundamental difference between the world of the Tridentine
fathers and the world of Pope John is not that the Protestant revolt
had widely succeeded, or that Protestants in many respects had made
good their criticisms of the medieval Church; nor is it even that
thought and scholarship have developed far beyond what might have
seemed conceivable 400 years ago. Such considerations obviously
present an immensely difficult problem to the backward-looking
elements in the Roman Church. But the much more serious change
has been in the position of Christianity itself. In the sixteenth
century the western world in which the Church mainly operated was
Christian. The Protestants were revolting not from Christianity but
from the expression of it centred at Rome. The disagreement was
entirely theological. If Trent spoke largely to theologians, at least it
spoke in a Christian world where the essential Christian ideas were
still valid currency. It was mistaken in thinking that its anathemas
still carried their former weight or that excommunications and
interdicts would still be effective; but Europe was still Christian.
That is no longer true.

Further, during that interval the Church, from Rome and from
Protestantism, has spread into a world that at the time of Trent was
to all intents and purposes unknown. It has been a period of extraordinary missionary activity in which the spirit of sincere Christian
evangelism had behind it the additional impetus of western culture.
The missionaries were welcomed for a variety of reasons, but among
them was the prestige of the West, its education and its technical
skills. What the missionaries were doing was part of what came to be
called colonialism, so that they were protected and encouraged by
the commercial and power politics of the West from which they drew
their staff and their finance. They worked in what was a willing world,
and almost everywhere Christianity was successfully established in
all its forms in areas where the old religions seldom proved difficult
to displace. In our own time that picture has completely changed.
Everywhere local nationalism has reacted, sometimes violently,
against western colonialism, and Christianity is often seen as no
more than the West in another form, while religions that had once

been regarded as moribund have in many great areas of the mission-ary world suddenly come to fresh and vigorous life. If the West is no longer Christendom, in the sphere of missionary activity Christianity itself is suddenly suspect, and the Roman missionary bishops are as aware of the change as are the Protestants.

It was to deal with this strange and difficult situation that Pope John suggested a Council, which on the one hand should attempt to end the ancient schisms by looking freshly both at the Orthodox Church and the Protestants, and on the other should consider how the Church should meet its new situation in a world that was largely non-Christian or even hostile. He had probably no idea of the immense interest that the project would arouse. If it matched the stirrings towards unity among Protestants, it met also the amorphous but widespread feeling that the world was drifting, without knowing how to escape, to what could be complete destruction. Could this venerable Church with its tremendous claims break out from its traditional isolation, mend the divisions between the churches, and really speak in an understandable voice to the condition of the age? And would the conservative Curia allow it to do so?

All the circumstances of modern publicity combined at once to fasten attention upon the Council, its significance, and its outcome. Press, television and wireless commentators, as so often in recent years, correctly interpreted the mind of the people. In their anxiety about the world's future, about the conflict between the great Powers, about the lack of serious purpose among statesmen, they turned to this Council of the Roman Church in the hope that out of it might come something more than the pronouncements of ecclesi-astics defending an intransigent theology. The press quite correctly saw its own function as more than the mere reporting of prepared statements. It knew the current anxiety. It knew that Pope John XXIII, with his genial friendliness to all and sundry, his obviously deep Christian outlook on men and events, his willingness to find some good even in communism, had caught the public imagination as had no other Pope in modern times. And of course the press knew of the attempts to stop and then to frustrate the Council and Pope John; such knowledge was not something that in the circumstances of the time it could suppress. It is not an exaggeration to say that the press was, as it were, the principal 'observer', the world attending the Council.

It is this fact that helps to make Robert Kaiser's book so absorb-ingly interesting. He is a highly accomplished man, a Latinist and a linguist, one of the most distinguished American journalists. His account of the issues involved, of the great events and of the personalities engaged, is first-class writing and always fair, but there emerges from it a strange picture of press frustration and an equally frustrated lack of understanding by the Vatican officials. To them the press representatives were intruders, laymen who lacked the theological knowledge to appreciate the issues and therefore needed instruction. The instruction was extremely inept, consisting often of extracts from pamphlets or articles which Mr. Kaiser had read, or from encyclopedias which he quickly identified. He was anything but an uninstructed layman. His account of his efforts to get at hard news, at real reports of what had taken place makes astonishing reading. Sometimes what were issued apparently as reports of a session proved to have been written before the session took place.

Yet it is understandable. What the theologian does not see is that his work, the careful logical processes of his thought, can seem incredibly remote from reality to men who live in a world where events are happening, a world where they are not abstractions for discussion. Behind the curialists is an immense intellectual structure, a defence mechanism that from the premise of complete truth revealed to the Church proceeds step by logical step to what in the real world may be a completely frustrating conclusion. It is that conclusion, for example the scandal of divided Christendom, with which people like Mr. Kaiser are concerned, and through him the eyes of the world watch the Council, whose second session began on 29 September. People are uneasy lest the logic of the theologians will prove that nothing can be done, and the divisions remain unhealed. They see the policy of rigid defence turning the Church into a besieged city whose besiegers want to become friends. They are impatient with the logic. But behind the ramparts the curialists look out at enemies and dangers, so that they are afraid even to allow the worship of the Church to be wholly in the vernacular, as though Latin were not only somehow sacred, but had its place in the logic of theology.

Mr. Kaiser writes as the representative of an anxious and would-be friendly world, and his book, always searching and sometimes caustic, might do something to bring home to the members and officials of Vatican II that the world would like to see a dove bringing an olive branch from the ark. The Roman Church has been afraid of the world for too long, and in its fear has come near to forgetting the realities of its mission. That is the challenge of the moment. Mr. Kaiser sees that the world looks to the Roman Church not for a fresh display of remorseless theological arguing but for charity, for a confidence in its mission that can accept freedom of thought and varieties of method. Certainly it is charged with the eternal unchanging Gospel, but it has somehow to express that Gospel in a world that has changed completely since the Council of Trent closed the gates. It would be a very great tragedy if Vatican II confirmed that intransigent authoritarianism.

(b) XAVIER RYNNE

Letters from Vatican City

The best kept secret of the first session of the Vatican Council, it seems, is the identity of the author of these *Letters* which, first as articles in *The New Yorker*, and now much expanded into a lively book, give a blow-by-blow account of the conciliar debates as well as an informed, if edged, commentary on their background. Xavier Rynne writes with the insider's awareness of what was going on— and of what was left unsaid. He is evidently a man of parts—if he is one man at all—and the hand of the rewrite expert can be discerned in reports of theological discussions which at first sight seem hardly to lend themselves to such a Manhattan glossiness.

But this is altogether a serious book, a proof of Xavier Rynne's simple statement that 'the Council was essentially a religious experience; it can only be understood as such'. Its hero—as, surely of the Council itself—is Pope John, who, against all probability, called the Council in the first place and unflinchingly kept its purpose firm. His address at the solemn opening of the Council on 11 October 1962 is a magisterial definition of its aims, with the generous recognition that the Church 'prefers to make use of the medicine of mercy rather than of severity. She meets the needs of the present day by demonstrating the validity of her teaching rather than by condemnations.' The task, then, was to be a pastoral one: to acknowledge the need for renewal within the Church as a prerequisite for the restoration of Christian unity. The Pope's serene dismissal of 'those prophets of doom who are always forecasting disaster' set the tone for the essential optimism that was to mark the Council's proceedings, however deep the divisions sometimes seemed to be.

With such a lead, the Fathers of the Council were able from the outset to realize, in the Pope's words, that 'everything, even human differences, leads to the greater good of the Church'. The prolonged debate on the Liturgy, with which the Council opened, revealed how wide was the support for reforms which were wholly designed to make the Church's worship not only more intelligible but in accord with the larger pastoral purpose which Pope John had so often stressed during the two years of preparation. The later, and more crucial, discussion on the sources of Christian revelation reflected the same emphasis. It is altogether too naïve to present the debates in terms of liberals and conservatives, and Xavier Rynne, in the interests of a lively narrative, sometimes seems to envisage the Council in terms of an American party convention, with Cardinal Ottaviani and the Roman Curia as an entrenched caucus determined to resist all change. The differences were real, but it was the special value of the Council to have made the discussion really free and to have destroyed the fiction of a monolithic structure that left no room for honest questions and a variety of answers. If the first session achieved nothing else it at least revealed a candour and a concern for the Church's true mission in the modern world, and it was this, more than anything else, which impressed the observers from other Christian Churches who were given every opportunity to follow the Council's work and to appreciate the sincerity of its debates.

It was the presence in such large numbers of bishops from the new nations of Asia and Africa that above all stressed the urgency of the council's work. They, together with such Eastern Catholics as the Melkite Patriarch Maximos, bore colourful witness to the true dimensions of the Church. In their very persons they were a reproach to the Latin and legalistic categories so habitual to the Curia and their Italian, Spanish and—perhaps ironically—English speaking supporters. The impressive contributions of such cardinals as Suenens, Liénart, Léger and Bea, and of such bishops as De Smedt of Bruges, were not merely 'liberal': they spoke for the significant majority of the Fathers of the Council whose concern was not with the niceties of theological debate but with the daily problems of presenting the Church's true function to millions for whom the inherited attitudes of so many European prelates were meaningless.

The contribution of the Fathers from English-speaking countries was hardly impressive. Cardinals Spellman and MacIntyre were constant in their defence of the *status quo*, but it certainly seems true that many who remained silent were profoundly impressed by the discussions as they proceeded. The Council was above all else an education for the bishops themselves, learning as they did at first hand of problems that had hitherto seemed remote from their experience but which were now revealed as crucial for the whole Church.

It might seem that the Council in its first session achieved very little. In fact, despite some defects of organization and a notable failure in official relations with the press, it provided the opportunity for the sort of self-examination which is indispensable for reform. Xavier Rynne's book, with its careful documentation (which in- cludes a summary of each day's proceedings, with a list of subjects and speakers, as well as a digest of the main speeches) and its alert sense of what was at issue, is an encouraging introduction to the remainder of the Council's work. For, now that the ground has been so thoroughly cleared of many initial obstacles—and it has to be remembered that nearly a century had elapsed since the first Vatican Council was suspended—it may be supposed that Pope John's hopes for the Council may in fact be realized by his successor, so that

bringing together the Church's best energies and striving to have men welcome more favourably the good tidings of salvation, it prepares, as it were, and consolidates the path towards that unity of mankind which is required as a necessary foundation in order that the earthly city may be like that heavenly city 'where truth reigns, charity is the law, and whose extent is eternity'.

G

10
DRAMATIZING THE POPE

The Representative

THIS IS, WITH SOME fifty or sixty pages of 'Historical Sidelights', or documentation, the complete text of the controversial play by a young and previously unknown German writer which the Royal Shakespeare Company presented in London in autumn 1963. The acting version is drastically reduced, by more than half, but the whole play deserves to be read; the reader will then see what truth there is in the criticism that, by the shortening, certain 'guilty men' have been exonerated, and the guilty responsibility of the Pope unduly stressed.

The substance of this very long play, which has stage-directions that are often essays designed to be read rather than acted upon, may be given briefly. It is a dramatization of the extermination of the European Jews by the Nazis, their exploitation by German 'big business' and, above all, the failure of the Pope to denounce the appalling crime of murdering between five and six million Jews because of their race. Especially emphasized is the failure of the Pope to stop the deportation of Jews from Rome. It is rather confusing that the writer mingles real with imaginary characters, and ascribes to them actions which are entirely derived from what, in his notes, he calls his 'intuition'. This is, of course, the practice and the right of historical dramatists, but it lays itself open to serious objection in a play dealing with figures in modern history, and portraying personages such as the Pope, known to millions of people, but not, apparently, to the dramatist. Thus, in the first scene, at the Berlin house of the Papal Nuncio, a real life character, Gerstein, another real life character, a man who is said to have joined the S.S. in order to frustrate their diabolical work, tells a young Jesuit— a quite imaginary and hardly credible portrayal—of the terrible

---

ROLF HOCHHUTH: *Der Stellvertreter, The Representative*. 274 pp. Paperback. Hamburg: Rowohlt. DM. 8.80. Translated by Robert David Macdonald. 331 pp. Methuen. 16s.

slaughter of Jews that is going forward day by day. Riccardo Fontana, the young priest, is shocked by the news and forms the opinion that only severe action by the Pope against Hitler will halt the slaughter. At Gerstein's request Riccardo exchanges his cassock with a Jew whom Gerstein is protecting, for a suit to which is pinned the Star of David, made compulsory for Jews who came under Nazi control.

The Roman scenes present Riccardo's father, a papal count and financial adviser to the Vatican, and an old-maidish kind of Cardinal, his mind on his orchids but occasionally remarking on the heavy responsibility of 'the Chief', as they call the Pope, in the face of Hitler's defeat and the probable consequent dominance of Europe by Stalin. There is also an abbot of a monastery where many Jews have been given asylum. It is admitted that the organization for saving Jews in this way has been initiated with the Pope's approval, but to Riccardo it is a trifling effort, and must, he thinks and hopes, be followed up by some dramatic action by Pius XII, such as denouncing the Concordat or excommunicating Hitler. The German Bishops' successful protests against 'euthanasia' seem to show that strong action by the Pope will stop the massacres of Jews. Gerstein and Riccardo discuss even more dramatic steps, such as seizing the Vatican radio to denounce Hitler's crimes, or even murdering Hitler or the Pope, and spreading the report that the S.S. did the deed. Allowing for Riccardo's hysterical reaction to the monstrous facts he has heard, this is a fantastic and incredible piece of melodrama. It, with a scene showing the arrests of Jews under the Vatican windows, leads up to the act that the writer calls 'Il Gran Rifiuto' where Pius XII gives what the dramatist conceives to be the sole motives for his failure to denounce Hitler by name: concern for the Vatican's investments, ambition to play the mediator between the Germans and the Allies, fear of seeing the balance of power disturbed in Europe to the advantage of godless communism.

By a smart piece of theatre the note of contempt for the Pope is struck in his first words, in which he expresses his 'burning concern' (his 'brennende Sorge', the title of Pius XI's famous encyclical against the Nazis). For what? His stocks and shares! Riccardo confronts him and says he will wear the Star of David until the Pope has done his duty. Pius then dictates a statement like one he actually made in 1943, denouncing crimes against people because of their nationality or race, but not specifically attacking Hitler. As he signs

this he gets some ink on his fingers, and is shown washing his hands
like Pilate. After this act it is no surprise to find that, in his notes,
the author calls the Pope a hypocrite, a cold sceptic, cold, callous,
a careerist, a 'neutrum', in short a criminal. Such unrelieved denigration, apart from its truth, fairness or otherwise, is a dramatic weakness, for it is hardly a tragedy to show the central character not
struggling as Pius XII may with good reason be conceived as doing,
between the terrible duty of saying too much and saying too little,
but as entirely contemptible, like the stock figure of Stalinist propaganda. What could have been a true tragedy is turned into a mere
denigration. Far more effective are the ensuing scenes, in which
Riccardo, forced to go and work in the crematoria, is confronted
with the sinister Doctor, and eventually killed—his faith destroyed
by the scenes of horror he has had to witness. These concentration-
camp scenes, in fact, bring to dramatic life the awful horrors of the
whole extermination procedure.

The 'Historical Sidelights' already mentioned are a collection of
documents, often interesting and useful, but clearly selected to
exclude anything which might modify or disturb the writer's notion
of Pius's action—which is an historical fact, in the sense that he
never denounced Hitler, or indeed anyone else, by name—and his
motives, on which there is room for much argument. It is legitimate
to point to the paucity of material from the Vatican archives; some
has been produced since the play was first staged, and it might,
had it been known to Herr Hochhuth, have enabled him to lighten
his black portrayal. There are other partisan features in the play,
side-hits at Krupps, at Chancellor Adenauer, minimizing the Allies'
part in the defeat of Hitler. Much of this is ephemeral journalism.
But the writer must be given the credit for an illustration, of true
dramatic power, of the almost incomprehensible story of the Nazi
obsession against the Jews and the cold inhumanity of the scientific
exterminators. Whole chapters of the Nuremberg trial documents
have been used to distil this concentrated essence of a prodigious
crime which was in some danger of being forgotten or belittled. It is
unfortunate that the searchlight is so much diverted from the
chief villains to the figure of the Pope, a fault, not only of taste and
injustice, but, especially, so it would seem, in the stage-version, of
dramatic construction. Quite truly, at the end, Herr Hochhuth says
that 'without freedom of choice there can be no dramatic conflict'.
But his Pope's inaction is determined by an innate and unrelieved

villainy. What might have been a tragic drama is turned, in this respect at least, into nothing more than a propagandist indictment.

* * *

SIR.—With your reviewer's estimate of the literary value of my play, *The Representative*, I have, of course, no quarrel. It does, however, seem necessary to me to take him up on one or two points of historical accuracy.

(1) It is not true, as your reviewer states, that, since the play was first staged, material has been produced, either by the Vatican itself or by historians, which, had it been known to me, 'might have enabled [me] to lighten [my] black portrayal', or which confutes my argument. The fact remains: neither did the Pope protest publicly against the massacres, nor did he attempt, through diplomatic channels, to suggest to Hitler that the massacres be stopped—whereas he did, for example, address himself, repeatedly and in writing, to Roosevelt, when it was a question of protecting Rome from further bombing.

(2) On the first page of the 'Historical Sidelights' I state expressly that neither the Vatican nor the Kremlin open their archives to researchers. It may, however, be assumed that the Vatican does not possess any document which exonerates them in this matter, since, in the seven months since the play appeared, they have neither produced nor published any such document. I shall not presume to judge the objective value of Pope Paul's statement against my play; but it should be remembered, in this context, that the attitude of Under-Secretary of State Montini to the deportations of the Roman Jews was made clear only after discussion on the subject with Hitler's diplomatic representative to the Vatican at the time (cf. English edition, page 308).

(3) Your critic writes that, in Act IV, I make Pius dictate 'a statement *like* one he actually made in 1943' on the occasion of the deportation of the Roman Jews. I would like to point out that the text of the statement in my play is that of the *actual* statement which appeared in the *Osservatore Romano*, and that it is quoted uncut.

(4) Your critic also writes that I imply Pius's silence to be based on 'concern for the Vatican investments'. This is not true; I have put into the Pope's mouth serious and statesmanlike arguments and apprehensions—apprehensions that were translated in great part, during the period 1944–47, into an unfortunate reality, which was more clearly foreseen by Pius XII than, for example, by Roosevelt. This political argument should characterize him as a statesman of some standing, and it is in this context alone that Riccardo's demand that a Pope should not simply be a diplomat is fully justified. Each feels his attitude to be entirely right, and from this arises the unresolvable conflict. Anyone who reproaches me for mentioning stocks and shares in this scene should, in fairness, not conceal the fact that I also mention the half-hundredweight of gold which the Pope was prepared to pay the Nazis as ransom for the Jews of Rome.

(5) Your critic suggests that I have failed to make a tragic figure out of Pius XII. This has at no time been my intention, as no single document

from the fifteen years during which Pius continued in his pontificate after the deportation of the Roman Jews has ever persuaded me to regard him in this light.

There is no word in all the twenty-two volumes of speeches and writings which he left behind him which suggests that he suffered retrospectively about the questions of the deportations from his own diocese and of his own silence regarding them. The tragic figures in my play are the two Fontanas, and the Jews themselves, in other words, the victims; *not* the man whose silence indirectly helped the murderers, in that he did not even fulfil the Christian duty of warning the Jews. Countless families in Western Europe demonstrably allowed themselves to be registered for the death-journeys, completely unaware of the purpose of these journeys, because not even the Pope, the great neutral figure, the one man whose word could be trusted in those times, not even he informed these people that the terrible rumours from Poland were *not* Allied horror-propaganda.

To attribute tragic stature to Pius XII is a blasphemy; he did not even once make personal intervention for any one of the 3,000 nameless priests whom Hitler, his partner in the Concordat, caused to be murdered. It is these priests, however, who are the true martyrs, in Kierkegaard's sense, of the Church in our century. In Riccardo Fontana, abandoned by his superiors, like the rest of the 3,000, I have tried to portray one of them. . . .

To your critic's reproach that Pius is made 'the stock figure of Stalinist propaganda', I can make no further comment. Nor can I make much of his claim that Chancellor Adenauer is attacked in my play. Before reading *The Times Literary Supplement* I had no idea that Adenauer's name was ever mentioned either in the play or in its appendix. On which page had your reviewer discovered it?

ROLF HOCHHUTH

Basle.

** Our reviewer writes: My reply to Herr Hochhuth is that he and I are talking about two different things. He asserts—and I do not contradict him —that Pius XII made no specific protest or public denunciation of Hitler during the war. I may remark that he did protest about the Poles at the very beginning, and was asked not to, as it merely increased the Nazi terrorism. My concern was, however, with the motives attributed to the Pope. Putting reasonable political arguments in the Pope's mouth, or mentioning his offer of gold for the Roman Jews is heavily outweighed by the setting in which Herr Hochhuth introduces the Pope; the words 'mit brennender Sorge' (title, of course, of Pius XI's vigorous and, unhappily, ineffective encyclical of 1937) are followed by some three pages of discussion about investments. The gold episode is history; the chat about investments in this context is invention. Then when the dramatist makes the Pope dictate a short protest making no use of his two, long, moving statements about atrocities, with their clear allusion to racial persecution—he interrupts it with talk of Hungarian railway shares, and tops it with the hand-washing scene.

I am sorry Herr Hochhuth should feel it necessary to condemn in such extravagant terms my idea that, with more knowledge, he might have moderated his presentation. I was alluding chiefly to Pius XII's letter to Bishop Preysing, of Berlin, of 30 April 1943. To the impartial reader this, I think, reveals the Pope as deeply troubled about what worse things his more specific public action might provoke. When I wrote my review I did not know that Herr Hochhuth, writing to the *Frankfurter Allgemeine Zeitung* on 30 May 1963, said that he would, in future productions, put passages from this letter in the Pope's mouth. This leaves me even more puzzled.

Someone lately has pointed out that Brecht allowed some sort of humanity even to Galileo's inquisitors. Herr Hochhuth, in the book, gives the Pope no moral credit at all, calls him 'a criminal', 'a cold sceptic', 'a neutrum', 'an introverted mystic', and so on. He also says 'never perhaps in the whole of history have so many paid with their lives for the passive attitude of one man'. Taken literally, this seems to 'let out' Hitler, Himmler, and all the rest, which I am sure was not Herr Hochhuth's intention. The view he gives of the Pope's character has been decisively contradicted by people who knew him well. It is a pity Herr Hochhuth, in his researches in Rome, could not find material for a better balanced portrayal. As for Pius XII's writings, full of religious and moral guidance and laying down Christian principles on which the late Pope built his last encyclical—they are dismissed as 'trivialities'.

I named Dr. Adenauer because I took the sarcastic references to Bonn politicians and 'Germany's economic miracle' as pointing at his government. It is unimportant compared with the fact that, by exhibiting in such a contemptible light a recent Pope known to millions the play becomes a rather lopsided piece of propaganda.

I should, however, like to make clear that it was the book that I reviewed and not the acting version. On the London stage the crudity has been softened in some degree; one might gradually be brought even to think Mr. Alan Webb's Pope is deeply sincere; while in the final scene the play, to my mind, rises above contemporary history and takes on an impressive moral symbolism. In my review I said the last scene was of real dramatic power; this is even more so of the acting version, reduced to two main characters, the Jesuit and the Doctor. For this impressive scene the writer must be given credit, though some is, of course, due to the producer, the translator, and adaptor, and the actors concerned.

II

AWAY FROM THE ABSURD

IONESCO'S PROGRESS

IT WILL PROBABLY be agreed that with *Rhinocéros*, the play which opens the third volume of his collected works, Ionesco's writing took a rather different turn. Although vestiges of the absurd are still present in certain scenes, particularly in the arguments about logic and language, the central theme is traditional and non-absurd. Bérenger, the hero, may be a bit of a Bohemian anarchist and a drunk, but these are the weaknesses of the common, more or less rational man. In fact, the choice of the name Bérenger, which occurs in all three major plays of this new period—*Rhinocéros, Le Piéton de l'air* and *Le Roi se meurt*—is perhaps meant to imply that Ionesco-Bérenger sees himself as expressing the average emotions of the average man in an immediately comprehensible way, like the nineteenth-century songwriter whose name was identical in sound if not in spelling.

Rhinocéros is a straightforward symbolical play; the horny, phallic-nosed pachyderm can only signify mindless, gregarious animalism, that is, the undifferentiated natural drives in man, against which he has to struggle by means of 'reason' and 'decency', like any old-fashioned humanist. Bérenger's final cry: 'Je suis le dernier homme, je le resterai jusqu'au bout! Je ne capitule pas', is an unequivocal assertion of rational individualism, very different from the paroxysmic or cyclical endings of the really absurd plays. In the latter, the irrationality of the world is boiling up within the major characters themselves, and the spectator or reader is left with no rational handrail to cling to. In the more recent plays, we are clearly invited to identify ourselves with Bérenger, who sometimes, indeed, speaks openly in Ionesco's own name. In *Rhinocéros* he is protesting

---

EUGÈNE IONESCO: *Théâtre*. Volume III: *Rhinocéros. Le Piéton de l'air. Délire à deux. Le Tableau. Scène à quatre. Les Salutations. La Colère*. 305 pp. 12 fr. *Le Roi se meurt*. 157 pp. 7 fr. Paris: Gallimard. EUGÈNE IONESCO: *Plays*. Volume Five: *Exit the King, The Motor Show, Foursome*. Translated by Donald Watson. 113 pp. John Calder. 21s.

against totalitarianism of all kinds; in *Le Piéton de l'air* he seems to be thirsting for a peep behind the world of appearances and coming as close as he ever gets to a religious emotion; in *Le Roi se meurt* he is facing the anguish of his own inevitable death.

If Ionesco has now moved over, or back, to symbolist theatre, he has to be judged according to the intellectual and dramatic effectiveness of his symbols. That he has a genuinely dramatic imagination there can be no doubt: in fact, it is rather curious that he should have written some of these later plays originally as short stories (published as a collection under the title *La Photo du Colonel*), because he is clearly much more gifted as a dramatist than as a prose narrator. The boldness and simplicity of his basic images—the rhinoceros as a representation of animal nature, levitation as a sign of metaphysical yearnings in *Le Piéton de l'air* and death as a crumbling of the individual's kingdom of life in *Le Roi se meurt*—are eminently suited to the stage.

It may be wondered, however, whether they are handled in a completely satisfactory way. *Rhinocéros*, for instance, is very enjoyable theatre while it lasts, but the broadness of the symbol may, to some extent, defeat its own purpose. The play can be interpreted as a satire on Nazism or communism or any other collective movement, and the message is that a collective hysteria may break down the resistance of the most unlikely people. This point can be readily admitted; the weakness of the play lies in the absence of any detailed analysis of hysteria or of individual reactions to it. The characters are differentiated before they succumb, but the peculiarity of each psychological collapse is not shown. The big metamorphosis scene is superbly done as stagecraft, and at the same time empty, because it is purely physical. Nor are we made to understand how Bérenger resists the general temptation to conform; he survives, one suspects, merely because the central character has to remain untouched in order to utter the final cry. He is not even tempted, as most dramatic heroes are. In spite of his slight failings—his tendency to drink and his indecisiveness—he does not participate in the general human weakness. Therefore, the play as a whole seems to be an image of the isolation of the author, who sees the rest of the world going mad. It is valid on this level, because such a sense of isolation is universal. One cannot help feeling, however, that the level is not the highest possible one; to accept and illustrate solitariness as if it were a final truth is to fall back on solipsism, which is always in some degree self-righteous.

The impact of *Le Piéton de l'air* is less definite. The action is set in a kind of grammar-book England like that of *La Cantatrice Chauve*; indeed, in a moment of self-indulgent winking at the audience, Ionesco produces a hairless little girl and presents her as the bald prima donna. The group of English people includes several old ladies and a journalist who repeat unimaginative commonplaces while Bérenger becomes aware of the fourth dimension and finally walks off into it, to the dismay of his wife and daughter. He soon returns in a state of disillusionment, having found the Other World as horrible as this one.

The English reader may be tempted to think of this play as a kind of *Peter Pan* gone sour. The meaning presumably is that there is no metaphysical solution to the anguish of living. The platitude-chewing characters, ruminating in English meadows, are like harmless rhinoceroses, almost devoid of any higher impulse, and Bérenger has nothing in common with them. He feels that if he could make himself immortal his problems would be solved. He walks out of time into the sky but, instead of discovering paradise in Never-Never Land, he experiences a nightmare and comes sadly back to earth.

The play contains a great deal of complicated stage business, which must make it the delight of any energetic producer. The question is: what does all the movement add up to? Here again, the central point seems rather too simple. Ionesco is saying that the human imagination can create only heaven or hell, and he appears to be trying to prove that hell is more genuine than heaven. This may well be so, but it is unconvincing to make a character go behind the scenes (in the literal sense of the expression) and then come back to bear witness. We know that he was yanked up out of sight by means of a nylon cord and that, far from having the authority of a traveller from another bourne, he is no more than the principal boy in an *avant-garde* pantomime.

In *Le Roi se meurt* Ionesco deals directly with his own fear of death. King Bérenger is due to die '*à la fin du spectacle*', which is to say that the play itself is his death agony. His court has been reduced to his two queens (one a Martha, the other a Mary), his bodyguard, his doctor, and a maid. The royal palace is falling to pieces, whole tracts of the country have subsided into oblivion, and the vestigial population consists of old men and imbeciles. The interest of the action lies, in the first place, within the king himself; he has to be made to understand that he is going to die and, when this has been accomplished, he begins to appreciate the pure phenomenon of living, independently of any particular quality life may have. The conflict between the two queens provides a second theme; the older woman is all for making the king face reality and die with dignity; the younger one would like to keep him in ignorance and surround him with affection.

It is a very bold step to announce, in the opening scenes, that the main character will die precisely with the final curtain-fall. This may make the spectator feel that Bérenger is an unconscionable time a-dying and, certainly, in the production at the Théâtre de l'Alliance Française this impression was not entirely avoided. Yet Ionesco shows an almost classical ingeniousness in spinning out the play for the required time, and Bérenger's regretful farewell to the ordinary things of life can be counted as one of his most moving pieces of writing. Such final doubts as the spectator may have are connected rather with the inward-looking and limited nature of the symbol. It is true that ageing and death consist in a shrinking of the sensory domain, in a moving back of the frontiers of interest, so that the whole world, in fact, is destroyed each time a consciousness is extinguished. But for the symbol to be complete, it should also suggest that other lives are still going on. After all, *Le roi est mort, vive le roi!* could be the motto of all organic creation. It is at once a pain and a consolation to know that life is expendable because it is perpetually recreated. But Ionesco, being as self-absorbed here as in *Rhinocéros*, does not indicate this dimension, and so his play remains claustrophobic, instead of being fully and generally poetic.

Perhaps, then, the movement from the absurd to the symbolic has not been an unqualified success. Ionesco's handling of symbols, although powerful and admirably theatrical, is less subtle, less impersonally effective, than his exploitation of the principles of the Absurd.

The English version of *Le Roi se meurt*, which was performed at the 1963 Edinburgh Festival, is of the same high standard as Donald Watson's previous translations. The volume also contains two slight earlier pieces. Through some oversight, it gives neither the dates of composition nor the original titles of the three plays. One imagines that the English reader would have liked to know, at least, in what order the plays were written.

12

NOVELS OF 1963

(f) MURIEL SPARK

The Girls of Slender Means

FEW PEOPLE WOULD CHOOSE to remember the life lived in the cratered, blacked-out, austerity London of summer 1945 as an idyll of the Golden Age. Fewer still—perhaps, indeed, only Miss Spark—would see in a Kensington hostel for young ladies of respectable country background and poverty the subject of a novel about Hell and lust, about the savage joke of time which makes nonsense of the beauty and ideals of gregarious youth. There is no obligation for Miss Spark's readers to be perturbed by such sombre themes, or to speculate on the significance of her characters, however, because *The Girls of Slender Means* is a lot more straightforwardly enjoyable, and splendidly witty, than anything she has written since *Memento Mori*. Her provocative, anarchistc asides about sin and salvation melt so blithely and neatly into the narrative that even Mr. Waugh would approve their sophistication. She introduces Nicholas, later reported to have met a martyr's death in Haiti, as a sort of poet *flâneur*, who looked 'slightly dissipated, like the disappointing son of a good English family that he was'. His brothers are dentists and accountants; 'he could never make up his mind between suicide and an equally drastic course of action known as Father D'Arcy'. Another character, Joanna, a parson's daughter much admired by the other girls for her recitations of 'The Wreck of the Deutschland', falls to her death chanting the evening psalter of Day 27 because, even naked and smeared with cold cream, her hips, measuring more than thirty-six and a half inches, are too wide to squeeze through the lavatory window.

(f) *The Girls of Slender Means*. 183 pp. Macmillan. 17s. 6d.
(g) *Radcliffe*. 376 pp. Longmans. 21s.
(h) *The Centaur*. 303 pp. André Deutsch. 21s.
(i) *The Group*. 360 pp. Weidenfeld & Nicolson. 18s.
(j) *One Fat Englishman*. 192 pp. Gollancz. 18s.

But the gaps round such ambivalent images are, as one expects from Miss Spark, filled in with the usual appealing attention to trivia. With brilliant, eccentric glimpses she evokes the strange city of staircases leading up and up, 'like a new art-form', out of the bomb-ripped buildings, and the people all carrying shopping-bags in hope of finding something off the rations. The May of Teck Club has survived the bombs, although one of the older residents is always talking about an unexploded one in the garden. On its top floors live Joanna and Jane and Selina, and a mad girl called Pauline Fox, who is always off to dine with Jack Buchanan—a drive in a taxi round Hyde Park, as it happens. Clothing coupons are short, and somebody's red taffeta Schiaparelli dress changes wearers nightly, though Selina, the slim beauty and Nicholas's great love, wears it most. Selina slips easily through the lavatory window, to spend nights on the roof with Nicholas, making love under rugs. Jane, who is fat and keen on her 'brain-work', is employed by a crooked publisher; to earn a little more she writes pathetic letters to famous authors in hopes of selling their autographs. It is Jane, the bystander, who introduces Nicholas to the May of Teck—dinner for boy-friends is allowed, cost two-and-sixpence; she hopes that her literary interests are what intrigue him. She does not see her shilling-meter life as beautiful heedless poverty nor her bartering little community as Eden. She might, if given the chance, have grasped his vision of perfection better than Selina.

But only years later, trying to tell the girls in their various destined successes and smugness about Nicholas's death, does Jane uncover how soon the bonds of shared love and shared privations are forgotten. Time destroys, and Miss Spark deliberately juxtaposes its destruction with 'the way things were' to suggest that only in retrospect does the violence of a passing incident become apparent. The unexploded bomb does, of course, go off one night, and Nicholas from the roof watches Selina escape the burning building not with her trapped fellow-occupants of Eden, but with the Schiaparelli. 'A vision of evil may be as effective to conversion as a vision of good', Jane notes from his manuscript, Nicholas makes the sign of the cross, and reminds Joanna's father, up for the funeral, that his daughter had been afraid of Hell. When during the rather frightening exuberance of the celebrations on VJ night, Miss Spark says simply 'It was a glorious victory', she is not being crudely satirical. Gestures must be made, and the girls who are so delightful, so movingly lovely, are also savage—perhaps because their hold on perfection is so precarious and so brief. With the jerky, ironic precision of which she is a master, Miss Spark has caught a kind of perfection from what has now become part of history, and her evocation, like that of an old newsreel, is no less moving because it is also slightly ridiculous.

(g) DAVID STOREY

Radcliffe

A mountain stream which comes early on in the scene in Mr. Storey's new novel is described as having a 'quiet ferocity', and this would serve as a description of his writing for a good part of the way. It does not stay quiet, however; it builds up into something more like a subdued roar, and all—characters, readers, and carefully assembled setting alike—is overwhelmed in the final torrent. Anyone who feared the contemporary novel to be a danger of death from emotional anaemia has Mr. Storey to reckon with. Garlanded with golden opinions his earlier books have won for him he works in heroic dimensions, and with something of a pagan impulse to affirm the reality of man in a menacing universe by constructing huge statues, massive emblems and outrageous myths.

Only the smallest claim is made on normal plausibility from the start. The scene is set and the mood established with brooding, confident, highly visual strokes. On the crest of a hill near some unspecified northern town is a once-proud house, the seat of the eccentrically decaying Radcliffe family. A building estate is rapidly invading it, and a smouldering relationship develops between young Leonard, the last of the Radcliffe line, and a dangerous boy named Tolson from the local school. No gleam of irony disturbs the doom-charged picture: no reader has the least excuse for expecting any development along Rotary or rugger-club lines, or any other familiar pattern of regional fiction. 'Red fangs of cloud' show on the horizon; a 'murderous line of rocks' also meets the eye; the rooks have 'fierce shapes like torn segments of cloud' and the encroaching houses are 'hard red knots, clenched like fists'. Domestic detail is equally ominous—from a broken suitcase the clothes spill out like entrails, and when the hero gets dressed 'a slim red tie runs down from his throat'.

These hints are not wasted on us, and all the subsidiary characters have an air of creatures locked in a legend or a nightmare. Soon, indeed, we begin to suspect that it is a region of hell we have to contend with, as the violent, proletarian Tolson and the blue-blooded Leonard, with the rot of the old house in his bloodstream, clinch their way to mutual destruction through several rounds of intensifying horror while the landscape glowers and bleeds in sympathy. When we come to the ravings at the end, after Leonard has murdered Tolson with a claw hammer as a final act of demented love, it is a little as though Dostoevsky had set his hand to rewriting *The Fall of the House of Usher*.

(*h*) JOHN UPDIKE

The Centaur

Prometheus stole fire from Zeus, fire enough to make the pith of a stalk of a giant fennel smoulder. And he gave it to men. For this Zeus chained him to a rock in the Caucasus. He was finally released through the intercession of Hercules, but Zeus insisted on the life of another immortal in exchange and accepted Chiron the Centaur. Chiron gave his life readily. John Updike's new novel is forged with the fire of this myth and from it he has created a novel which is outstandingly good. The weekly reviewer (or indeed the regular reader) can sift to his own satisfaction the new novels that spring up week by week into categories—good, bad or indifferent, but once or twice a year his pulse quickens as he recognizes what the horse breeder calls 'real class'. His judgement becomes a little distrait and he struggles to make a decision which time and reflection alone can make.

Hedging oneself about with these cautionary thoughts, *The Centaur* makes it clear that Mr. Updike is now one of the best, if not the best, of the American prose writers at work today. His first novel, *The Poorhouse Fair*, was a clear and simple account of an old people's home and a surprising first novel as there was a slight atmosphere of 'Finir' about it. His second, *Rabbit Run*, was extraordinarily good, but it was essentially and deliberately a small town novel and the whole kept rigidly within the bounds of the town. But in *The Centaur*, while maintaining his concentration on particular people in particular situations so that there is nothing airy-fairy about the novel, he has produced an intellectual and emotional creation with a universal application which lifts the book from the national to the international level.

There are many reasons why the book is outstanding, but the following three attract the reader's attention immediately. First, the successful introduction of the myth into the book. It must be made clear that the author does not merely use the Chiron legend as a basis for his novel, but actually introduces the Centaur into the book. In the opening section the hero, George Caldwell, is teaching his class when one of his pupils fires an arrow into his ankle and George leaves his class to have it removed. He goes down the hall listening vaguely to voices from other class rooms and then, the text goes on,

Each time the feathers brushed the floor, the shaft worked in his wound. He tried to keep that leg from touching the floor, but the jagged clatter of the three remaining hooves sounded so loud he was afraid one of the doors would snap open and another teacher emerge. . . . His great gray-dappled flanks twitched with distaste, but like a figurehead on the prow of a foundering ship his head and torso pressed forward.

It makes a startling opening. Obviously this device could easily become strained or merely whimsy. But it doesn't and the mythical characters blend with their mortal characters easily. Mr. Updike avoids overworking the trick (which must have been a temptation) so that in the second half of the book the mythological part of the character is seldom overt. But it is the undertones of this story—of Chiron the wise teacher of the world—that makes the humdrum of Caldwell's everyday difficulties at Olinger school into a story for every man.

The character of George Caldwell himself is a second factor in the book's impact. He is one of those rare people in modern fiction, a really convincing good character. Caldwell is not in any way a rebel, he is anxious to be thought well of by his headmaster. He is frightened of the head (one Zimmerman, or Zeus for short) and cannot see through him, though even his 15-year-old son can see that Zimmerman is only a 'befuddled old lech'. But it is in fact precisely his determination to make everything mean something which makes George Caldwell into the man he is. He is not in any way humourless, but he makes everything he does *mean something* and this feeling of the significance of life is the wisdom he tries, not wholly unsuccessfully, to pass on to others.

Finally, there is the creation of Prometheus who is Caldwell's son Peter. This is a logical extension of the myth. When Chiron forgoes his immortality he hands it to his son. Peter has a third dimension; he is allowed to reflect on his father through the distance of years and from the bed of his coloured mistress with whom he is not quite at ease. As many an unchained hero has found, somehow the freedom his father won him has not been fulfilled and he looks back nostalgically, trying to see why he has failed where his irritating father succeeded. The very act is in some way a failure because his father would never have indulged in this kind of nostalgia, daily events crowding in and absorbing him too much.

It is interesting that we never learn either in the mythological or the Olinger side of this story who shot the arrow into Caldwell's leg. It was, of course, Hercules, who, while fighting off the other centaurs, accidentally put an arrow into Chiron. The same Hercules who later unbound Prometheus from his rock. It is also curious how little Hercules appears in the story and it is tempting at times to equate Mr. Updike himself with Hercules as the manipulator behind the tale. Either way, this Labour has not been in vain.

(i) MARY McCARTHY
The Group

'The Group' are eight girls who have graduated together from Vassar in the first year of the New Deal and meet from time to time in New York to share gossip, wedding parties and crises: all except Lakey, that is; she was always aloof, beautiful and intelligent, and she goes off to Europe. But for the others, bliss was it in that dawn to be alive, though somehow things don't turn out quite as they might have done. Miss McCarthy has hit on the brilliant device of telling most of her story in the style of a woman's magazine romance. This underlines the all-girls-together motif, the lesbian element of which is not fully revealed until the end of the book. Parody is itself parodied (for there is no end to Miss McCarthy's technical cleverness) by Helena, who as Class Correspondent, must take notes on the girl's doings and render as chummy gossip the failures and disenchantments of her class-mates:

Yestreen I saw Kay Strong Petersen's new husband in Norine Schmittlapp Blake's arms. Both were looking well . . . Kay and Harald have an elegant

H

apartment in the East Fifties convenient to the river, where Harald will be able to throw himself when his marriage goes 'on the rocks'. Re this, an-thropology major Dottie Renfrew opines that the little things, like lying, become so important in marriage. . . . How about this, '33? Write me your ideas and let's have a really stimulating discussion.

Much of the novel is devastatingly funny and the only question is, are we dealing with anything more than an extended and classier version of the Nausicaa episode in *Ulysses*? Most of Miss McCarthy's eight heroines (each an aspect of *das ewig Weibliche*, New York social register variety) fail to establish a satisfactory personal life. Only Libby, bright, eager, irritating, unrebuffable Libby, becomes a career girl, rejecting sex and competing with men on their own terms. But Norine, Dottie, Priss, and Kay (whose death ends the book) all sacrifice them-selves to men, all exhibit a basic insecurity and anxiety to please which merely emphasizes the corresponding insecurities of the men. At the end of the book Lakey's lesbianism is offered as a dramatic comment on the failures of the rest of the group. Harald, himself a repressed homosexual, turns on her bitterly: 'You have no part of America', he says—the America of canned food, daily sessions on the analyst's couch and canned sex. Lakey seems to have escaped into a kind of freedom (though one based on concealment) but even her lesbianism raises doubts: who wears the trousers, she or her baroness? 'And yet these could be disguises, masquerade costumes.' Society has become a vast transvestite parody, morally indefensible, intellectu-ally unsatisfying, spiritually destructive.

The Group has something in common with the work of Mrs. Lessing and Mme. de Beauvoir. Its heroines are women of courage, intelligence and charm, but with a fatal streak of masochism which elicits a corresponding sadism from men trying to assert their virility in a society where conformity and bohemianism are both aspects of a single complex malaise. A significant episode is Priss's attempt to please her husband by breastfeeding their child in the age of the bottle: in an artificial society the natural act is endlessly justified and intellectualized until, or so it seems, even the baby rebels.

The weakness of *The Group* is that, with so much material to hand, Miss McCarthy takes refuge in documentary rather than analysis. She has taken some striking and revealing photographs, and has written some amusing captions. But too much is left out. We get pages on the fitting of a contraceptive, but at the end we know much more about Dottie's vagina than ever we do about Dottie. Lakey is a *dea ex machina*, the lesbian hints are too pat. For the first time in her distinguished career Miss McCarthy has over-exploited the fact that she is a woman. She has given us a collection of case histories on the sex war. But she has told us nothing new. The novel tails off with a Fitzgeraldian dying fall as the cars full of returning mourners glide back to New York; back to the neurotic society which has methodically undermined the girls' all too vulnerable zest for life. But it is too late for the reader to be moved; the photographs, as we flick back in search of clues we might have missed, remain 'stills' and, for all their glossy finish, obstinately refuse to come to life.

(*j*) KINGSLEY AMIS

One Fat Englishman

With *One Fat Englishman* Mr. Kingsley Amis completely emerges from the doldrums he was lying in with his last two novels. It is a small book, no bigger than a man's fist—but it plants that fist with precision and force square in the belly of the fat English publisher who is its main character. This is satire of a wit and intelligence that class it with the best.

A few days during the visit of Roger Micheldene to the States are enough for Mr. Amis to do all that he wants with him. It is a fine bit of strategy. We settle down in the opening pages to what promises to be an orgy of comedy at America's expense. Everything is portrayed through the eyes of Micheldene, who can pick out at a glance the ridiculous features of anything he looks at—and conveys his conviction of his own superiority in an unbroken stream of discomforting nuances. In America, food for his conceit and polished rudeness falls around him like manna: the American publisher he is staying with, who is continuously at war with the world of objects, and cannot move a chair without having a stand-up fight with it; the man from one of the valleys in West Virginia in which pure eighteenth-century English is allegedly spoken ('I'm a horrible Anglophile, you know. And believe me there aren't too many of them around these days, brother'); the unmemorable wives and, still worse, unforgettable children; the whole setting, where he is, of large wooden houses well apart from each other in the trees, with 'the look of a semi-temporary encampment for a battalion of parvenus'.

But slowly and firmly the reader is forced to acknowledge how thoroughly gross and stupid Micheldene's snobbery is. The demonstration is the more effective for the fact that we have been lured cunningly into sympathy with Micheldene's point of view at the start. As the general decency and good will of the majority of the Americans he meets becomes plainer—as his own discomfiture by them, rather than their discomfiture by him, proves more and more to be the outcome of his bland and beastly sallies—the fist swings round, past the Americans, straight for its real target.

Of the seven deadly sins Roger considers himself most distinguished in anger; but qualified too in gluttony, sloth and lust. His fate when possessed by the last of these follows a parallel course to his fate when trying to lord it socially. Insatiable in his desire for women, unbudgeably sure that he knows how to get them, he ends up with one ageing sex-starved wife, who has a car and a blanket and a spot outside town waiting for anybody who turns up; and another wife— a Danish girl, his greatest desire—who he is forced to acknowledge at the end has never felt anything for him but horrified pity. The whole pattern of his past conquests and his two failed marriages seems clear in the light of these days in America.

In fact there is a note deeper than that of satire being struck grimly at certain moments in the novel. Part of Mr. Amis's epigraph to his last novel, *Take a Girl Like You*, ran 'Go, gentle maid, go lead the apes in hell'. It was perhaps a bit premature for that rather sentimental book. But Roger Micheldene might well be considered an ape in hell—in a hell conforming pretty closely to modern theologians' notion of it.

'Look, Roger, I know you're stoned, but if you go on this way, you're going to say something you'll be sorry for.'

'You're probably quite right, my dear. Trouble is those are the only things I really enjoy saying.'

The point is lightly made; but the ugly paradox of Roger's life is there. He is a tragi-comic Iago; the only things he really enjoys doing are those that end in harm, discord and torment. Is it very significant that Mr. Amis for the first time makes his hero a Catholic? Roger prays regularly to God but always abuses Him, and his wildest outburst of rage is against a priest, Father Colgate, who complacently preaches that God is love—Roger knocks him up at night, and dipping him in one of his fish-tanks three times curses him in Latin for 'making a good living out of telling the rest of us we put all the bad things there ourselves'. This picture of God the tormentor—failing, in this case, to do any good by all His tormenting—equals anything in Mr. Graham Greene's books. Seen in its reflection, even the comic agonies that Roger suffers from his great stomach have the air of an analogy to the pains within the soul.

One Fat Englishman is very funny, then—splendidly slapstick, in some of its American vignettes—and serious, too, on a couple of planes. Its satire—for its 'one' fat Englishman is very evidently one of many—has a lot to say about a very English type of absurd, as well as nasty snobbery: that of the vulgar aesthete, the petulant intellectual, the kind of ambassador who thinks he is keeping up standards by being rude to his guests when they are late. And plunging below satire, it marks the first clear effort Mr. Amis has yet made at locating the roots of human misery.

13

BATTLE OF THE SENSES

THE TECHNOLOGY OF LETTERS

THIS IS A MOST difficult book to judge. Much of it consists of quotations from other men's work (H. J. Chaytor, Giedion, W. Ivins, Father Ong). It uses typography—variations in type face, ornamental asterisks, broad leads, oddities of pagination—to articulate and enforce its argument. Each chapter, or rather, surge of statement, is heralded by a gloss. The tone and cadence of these glosses is patterned on Blake's *Descriptive Catalogue* and Brecht's placards: 'Marlowe anticipated Whitman's barbaric yawp by setting up a national PA system of blank verse—a rising iambic system of sound to suit the new success story'; 'Heidegger surf-boards along on the electronic wave as triumphantly as Descartes rode the mechanical wave'.

The Gutenberg Galaxy bristles with oracular assertions: 'China and India are still audile-tactile in the main'; Russia, 'where spying is done by ear and not by eye', is still 'profoundly oral'. The Chinese ideograph 'is a complex *Gestalt* involving all the senses at once'. The Germans and Japanese, 'while far-advanced in literate and analytic technology, retained the core of auditory tribal unity and total togetherness'. Numerous pronouncements have a majestic simple-mindedness:

The miseries of conflict between the Eastern and Roman churches, for example, are a merely obvious instance of the type of opposition between the oral and the visual cultures, having nothing to do with the Faith.

Some statements are slipshod; 'the Koreans are reputed to have a phonetic alphabet'; others are false: 'the Viennese musician Carl Orff'. The bibliography is eccentric. An accurate notion of the Babylonian and Greek treatment of volumes and spatial relations is vital to Mr. McLuhan's theory; yet he discloses no awareness of Neugebauer.

MARSHALL McLUHAN: *The Gutenberg Galaxy*. The Making of a Typographic Man. 294 pp. Routledge & Kegan Paul. 40s.

110

More disturbing is the nervous cheapness of Mr. McLuhan's style—language being the very matter of his concern. He tells us of woman's 'haptic bias, her intuition, her wholeness':

What a fate, to be integral and whole in a fragmented and visual flatland! But the homogenization of women was finally effected in the twentieth century after the perfection of photo-engraving permitted them to pursue the same course of visual uniformity and repeatability that print had brought to men. I have devoted an entire volume, *The Mechanical Bride*, to this theme.

Referring to Professor Mircea Eliade's *The Sacred and the Profane*, Mr. McLuhan questions 'the quality of insight that causes a human voice to quaver and resonate with hebdomadal vehemence'. Used in this (non)-sense, *hebdomadal* is a real comic find.

It would be easy to anatomize *The Gutenberg Galaxy* in this way: easy and stupid. This is a maddening, uneven, but brilliant work. Many of the irritants in Mr. McLuhan's method, many of the crudities of presentment which exasperate or bewilder, are strategic. *The Gutenberg Galaxy* is an anti-book. It seeks to enforce, physically, the core of its own meaning. Its bearing on traditional modes of philosophic-historical argument is deliberately subversive. It is precisely part of Mr. McLuhan's achievement that we should be irked and affronted by the strangeness or inadequacy of his resources. He is saying to us, in a verbal mime which often descends to jugglery but also exhibits an intellectual leap of great power and wit, that books—a linear progression of phonetic units reproduced by movable type—are no longer to be trusted. He is making, triumphantly, what Mr. George Steiner has called 'the retreat from the word'. And because the classic verbal medium is inimical or irrelevant to Mr. McLuhan's purpose his argument is difficult to follow. But the effort yields reward.

Mr. McLuhan posits that western civilization has entered, or is about to enter, an era of electro-magnetic technology. This technology will radically alter the milieu of human perception, the reality-co-ordinates within which we apprehend and order sense data. Experience will not present itself serially, in atomized or linear patterns of causal sequence, but in 'fields' of simultaneous inter-action. To offer a very crude analogy (and the process of analogy may itself be a vestige of an earlier logic), our categories of immediate perception will shift from those at work in an Ingres drawing to those we experience in a Jackson Pollock.

But we are unready to master the new spontaneity, randomness, and 'totalization' of the electronic experience-field, because print, and all the habits of feeling and thought print has grafted on the western mind, have broken the creative, primal unity of the senses. By translating *all* aspects of the world into the code-language of *one* sense only—the reading eye—the printing press has hypnotized and fragmented western consciousness. We lie rigid in what Blake called 'Newton's sleep'.

Yet obscure promptings bid us wake. Hence the present malaise, that feeling as sharp-edged in Klee and in Kafka as it is in the ferocities or pointlessness of our politics, that western man is no longer at home in the world:

We are today as far into the electric age as the Elizabethans had advanced into the typographical and mechanical age. And we are experiencing the same confusions and indecisions which they had felt when living simultaneously in two contrasted forms of society and experience. Whereas the Elizabethans were poised between medieval corporate experience and modern individualism, we reverse their pattern by confronting an electronic technology which would seem to render individualism obsolete and the corporate interdependence mandatory.

Mr. McLuhan's reading of ancient and medieval history is related to Nietzsche's indictment of Socrates and Henry Adams's vision of a golden age of unified sensibility. He argues that the phonetic alphabet began the fatal dissociation between the senses, that it splintered individual consciousness from the creative immediacy of collective response:

Only the phonetic alphabet makes a break between eye and ear, between semantic meaning and visual code; and thus only phonetic writing has the power to translate man from the tribal to the civilized sphere. . . . Nor is this to give any new meaning or value to 'civilization' but rather to specify its character. It is quite obvious that most civilized people are crude and numb in their perceptions, compared with the hyperesthesia of oral and auditory cultures. For the eye has none of the delicacy of the ear.

The printing press and the associated development of the conventions of perspective (precisely what *is* the correlation between these two great steps?) have made our apprehension and use of sense data explicitly linear, sequential, discrete. We are imprisoned in the unexamined assumption or unconscious illusion of a homogeneous, forward-flowing space-time continuum. Our notion of the categories of past and future is mechanistic, as if the universe were itself a printed book and we were turning the pages. The vast majority of literate men are unable to cope, sensorily or imaginatively, with the new 'vitalistic' space-time concepts of Einsteinian physics and electro-magnetic field theory. Hence the widening gap between the picture of physical reality on which we base our lives, and the mathematical-statistical image proposed by the natural sciences: 'The new physics is an auditory domain and long-literate society is not at home in the new physics, nor will it ever be.' The fascinating concomitant is the possibility that 'primitive' cultures will find it much easier to work with concepts of indeterminacy or with the idea that space is altered by the quality of neighbouring events.

Print helped to initiate and formalize the economic ambitions of Renaissance Europe. It gave spur to the new forces of nationalism and cultural arrogance. Mr. McLuhan conjectures that movable type 'enabled men to *see* their vernacular for the first time, and to visualize national unity and power in terms of the vernacular bounds: "We must be free or die who speak the tongue that Shakespeare spoke." ' The world-image codified by typography made of western man a unit at once impersonal and private, unique and repeatable. In that light the modern city, the warren of crowded solitudes, is a product and expression of the Gutenberg galaxy. We move through it scarcely calling on the manifold, subtle functions of ear, nose or touch; when we die, our name survives for a spell in the typographical pantheon of the telephone directory.

By its exclusive stress on visual order, on Cartesian logic and abstract nomenclature, the Gutenberg mode of perception has divided and sub-divided the categories of action and knowledge. The Baconian dream of a total, rational classification, of a universal taxonomy, in which every art, science and technology would have its distinct place, is emblematic of a typographic sensibility (Miss Elizabeth Sewell's brilliant, neglected study of Bacon in *The Orphic Voice* is relevant here). The dissociation of sensibility which Mr. Eliot discerns in post-metaphysical poetry was merely one tactical aspect of that larger intellectual attempt to conquer all knowledge through division.

But already, as Mr. McLuhan suggests, we are moving into a phase of creative disorder; everywhere the lines are blurred. Physics and biology have reached outside their classic bounds; the important work is being done within the shifting, undogmatic contours of 'middlefields' such as biochemistry, molecular biology or physical chemistry. A Calder mobile asks of us, as it might of Aristotle or

Lessing, why statues should not move. Novels are presented as loose pages, randomly gathered in a folder; we may, if we choose, arrange the narrative in varying sequence. Elements of improvisation and calculated hazard are being introduced into modern music; an orchestral statement has been described as a 'cluster of possible simultaneous tonal occurrences'. In the book of modern life (a Gutenberg simile) the hinges are loosening. But where Yeats saw the coming of 'mere anarchy', Mr. McLuhan speaks of 'the greatest of all human ages' resulting from 'this dramatic struggle of unlike modes of human insight and outlook'. Beyond the present chaos lies the possibility of 'new configuration' of perception; man's dormant senses, his powers of integration, the chthonic, magic fibre of his being, will be liberated from the closed, passive system of Gutenberg literacy. Else a great prince in prison lies.

These are the main lines of Mr. McLuhan's case. The obvious objection is a matter of cart before horse. What evidence is there that printing and the typographical world-order were the cause rather than the technically inevitable consequence of the specialization and diminution of sensibility? Can we assert, except by romantic, utopian convention, that the era of oral and manuscript communication possessed the gift of integrated perception? The Henry Adams-T. S. Eliot myth of a twelfth or a seventeenth-century organic unity is no more than a useful *canard*. It sharpens our alertness to some of our own difficulties and limitations; but there is no responsible evidence for it. In signal respects the medieval community was as fragmented, as riven by doubt and economic antagonisms as any we have knowledge of. If Dante or Donne could extend their poetic reach to a more comprehensive range of experience, it was because the sum of available matter was smaller and because words could give a more inclusive, adequate map of reality. Today we confront a topography of experience in which the word occupies only a central precarious domain; on each side lie the realms of number.

Historically it is likely that the phonetic alphabet and the development of movable type (a technical, not a metaphysical innovation) were themselves the end-process of a long evolution. The syntax and structure of the Indo-Germanic languages are strongly disjunctive; the bias toward logical stylization, toward linear progression and analytic delimitation, is rooted in the morphology of our speech-patterns. It obviously antedates not only Gutenberg but also the adoption, by pre-classical Greece, of the Phoenician alphabet. Moreover, it may well be that those forms of aural mass-communication which Mr. McLuhan regards as heralding the new age have, in fact, persisted beneath the surface of visual literacy. Where Mr. McLuhan assumes a Spenglerian sequence of historical epochs, there is most probably an overlapping simultaneity of mental habits and techniques.

But even if one balks at the general argument, the local insights of *The Gutenberg Galaxy* are rewarding. This book has a Coleridgean breadth. Mr. McLuhan points out that the notion of private ownership of ideas and words—the notion of plagiarism and the correlative of acknowledged citation—only evolve with the printed text. His own use of a cluster or mosaic of long quotations is meant to illustrate an earlier attitude, a 'collectivity' of truth. He points acutely to the source of the characteristic problems and symbolic proceedings of contemporary philosophy:

As our age translates itself back into the oral and auditory modes because of the electronic pressure of simultaneity, we become sharply aware of the uncritical acceptance of visual models and metaphors by many past centuries.

An apt quotation from Hopkins's letters leads to a discussion of how much major literature—poetry in particular—was never intended for silent perusal by the private eye, but demands recital and the live friction of voice and ear. Though Mr. McLuhan's reading of *King Lear* is absurdly unconvincing, he has fascinating marginalia on Rabelais, Cervantes, Pope and Joyce. He describes *Gargantua, Don Quixote*, the *Dunciad* and *Finnegans Wake* as the 'four massive myths of the Gutenberg transformation of society'. Looked at closely, the idea seems beautifully right. Might one add Swift's *Tale of a Tub* and, as myth of the combat between ideogram and letter, Canetti's *Auto-da-fé*? It is with awed impatience that one hears Mr. McLuhan has a new book ready.

14

NEW WAYS WITH TYPE

FACES TO LAUNCH A THOUSAND BOOKS

TYPEWRITERS HAVE LATELY become a growing threat to the printer's traditional methods of text composition through the introduction of computers into typesetting techniques. The literary reader of these columns may well shy away from the intricacies of computers, but he is probably as familiar with a typewriter as he is with a pen, and he is certainly familiar with typescript of many different kinds from business letters to weird numerals on cheques. It is therefore likely that he is already equipped to understand some important aspects of the new threats to traditional methods of text composition, and it will be assumed that he will want to know how recent developments are likely to affect his own activities both as a reader and as a writer.

Although readers will notice several changes in the appearance of printed texts, a more profound change will probably occur in writers' opportunities for making proof corrections. For many years publishers have provided writers with a great temptation to make unnecessary corrections to printers' proofs by an assurance in their contract that no charge will be made to authors for proof corrections, provided that these do not exceed twelve and a half per cent of the costs of composition. Only in recent years has a publisher had the courage to change his contract to read 'The publisher shall provide the author with a finally edited copy of his manuscript. If the author makes any corrections subsequently to a proof the cost of it shall be borne by the author'. Even this brave statement glosses over a vital fact by referring to a manuscript, although the publisher has in mind a typescript.

The fact is vital because a typewriter can now enable a publisher to eliminate the need for a printer's compositor. This can be simply achieved by transferring a typewritten image directly on to a lithographic plate, an operation which is little more complicated than making a stencil for a duplicating machine. Another more elaborate method is to adapt the typewriter so that it produces punched tape, which can subsequently be used to control the operation of un-manned typesetting or filmsetting machines. Not only can such things be done: they are already a daily occurrence in the production of an American daily newspaper.

On 5 March 1963 the *Oklahoma City Times* brought into use two IBM 1620 computers for the faster production of news copy. Although one press report in this country made unfounded claims that these computers were able to find and correct mistakes, some startling results were nevertheless achieved. The typists who produce punched tape for the computers do not have to concern themselves, as compositors must, with spacing out lines or with hyphenating at the end of lines. Instead the typists merely give coded instructions for the computer to determine choice of type, length of line, paragraphing and indenting. Punched tape from the typists is processed by the computers, which take the edited but unjustified tape, add spacing to fill the lines out evenly, hyphenate where necessary to break off a word at the end of the line, and produce a fully justified tape which operates a typecasting machine.

The hyphenation process illustrates both the versatility of the computer and the tremendously complex planning involved in preparing the computer programme. Word division is accomplished by an editing routine and by a table of hyphenation built into the computer's memory after analysis of nearly three million words. The production manager of the *Oklahoma City Times* predicts that ultimately the initial tape will originate at the reporter's keyboard, and, after editing, will move through the computer justification process direct on to a press plate, using offset reproduction.

When book printers start to make similar use of computers and punched tape in book production, authors will no doubt be deprived of any opportunity to make proof corrections after they have given their approval to a finally edited manuscript. Authors can never-theless expect some substantial advantages in return for this sacrifice. Their works should be printed faster and cheaper, and with greater flexibility. Before elaborating on what is meant by 'greater flexibility', it needs to be said that printing by any existing methods could immediately be made cheaper and faster if author's corrections were confined to the removal of printers' errors, instead of being regarded as an opportunity to make stylistic improvements, or to add new material. But if books are produced faster authors may no longer be so strongly tempted to make purely stylistic changes, since their ideas on style will have had only a short time in which to change; certainly there will be less need for authors to add new material in order to bring their work up to date with recent developments in their field, because there will be a shorter delay after a typescript is sent to the printer.

The use of computers and punched tape will not only speed up book production; it will also enable printers to use punched tape for different settings for the same text—for a cloth-bound edition in a large format, and subsequently for a paperback edition reset in a smaller format, or in conformity with an existing series. As such new methods become more widespread, it may be possible for the same tape to be used by newspapers, journals and book printers. These possibilities show how great is the potential flexibility of the new methods.

Although these methods are still in very restricted use for newspaper production to control the operation of typesetting, the actual technique of typesetting is itself rapidly losing ground to filmsetting, or to other systems which combine the use of special typewriters and cameras. Some of these systems are suitable only for certain kinds of work such as directories and lists, but the range of alternative methods to composition with the printer's type is now so extensive that work of any description, from Bibles to telephone directories, from the Beeching Report to a requisition form, can now be produced without specially cast 'hot metal' type. (The term 'cold type' is sometimes used as a generic term to describe all forms of typewritten composition.)

What effect will the use of alternative methods of cold type composition have upon the appearance of printed matter? A booklet containing 'some suggestions on filmsetting with reflections on the declining use of hot metal . . .' has recently been produced by the Westerham Press in Kent, which already enjoys a high reputation for the quality of its letterpress composition. Its suggestions are more substantial than its reflections, but this booklet includes a report that many firms like the Westerham Press are heavily involved in research into ways of making a complete type family from one upper and one lower roman alphabet. The Westerham Press is experimenting at the moment with a roman upper and lower case letter form which will distort to italic, expanded and condensed versions. Control over the distortion will be available at the keyboard. This may well result in a typeface 'midway between the typewriter and printing, but will result in a very much easier and cheaper form of filmsetting which may prove suitable for certain classes of work'.

Any new type which appears to be midway between the typewriter and printing is unlikely to disturb a reading public already accustomed to reading so much printed matter containing typewritten text. To some lay or lazy eyes, it is already difficult to distinguish between printer's type and the best results produced by typewriters of various kinds—manually operated, electric or Vari-Typer. Most electric typewriters have the advantage of letters made with proportional spacing (so that narrow letters such as i or l are not distorted to fill the wider spaces needed by m or w); furthermore these letters are struck with uniform weight through a strip of new carbon paper, which produces a clear and crisp impression on every letter, without any of that blurring or fading which often mars the appearance of ordinary typescript. In comparison with the best results achieved by hot metal composition, typewritten texts can be easily faulted; but the common practice of reducing typescript in size before reproduction automatically diminishes its imperfections.

Much more could be done to improve the appearance of typescript. Some manufacturers such as IBM and Olivetti have already gone to great trouble to commission handsome new letter designs which attain excellent results, despite the limitation imposed upon the designer by mechanical restrictions on the number of standard letter widths—no electric typewriter admits as many variations in letter width as normal printer's type. Unfortunately other firms such as Vari-Typer have concentrated their efforts on the production of designs which carry the names of famous printing types, such a Bodoni, Caslon, Garamond and even Times New Roman, but which bear little resemblance to the originals. The Vari-Typer machine is remarkable for its versatility, but the manufacturer's boast that it is 'the machine with a thousand faces' deserves respect only as a feat of production and not as an achievement in design.

If the Vari-Typer lacks a face which could launch even a single ship, it has the immense advantage of a tower, not the topless kind of Ilium, but a practical little rotating turret, on to which can be fixed semi-circular plates embossed with a wide variety of type designs. The machine can therefore carry out composition in an extensive range of foreign alphabets, and it can also be equipped with the symbols required for mathematics and other technical work. Quick changes can be made from one style of type to another by changing plates on the turret. The IBM 72 typewriter, introduced in 1961, is fitted with a typing head similar to a golf ball, which can also be changed in a matter of seconds to provide a change in type style, but so far only a limited range of types is available for this machine.

The Vari-Typer Corporation and Messrs. Kodak both manufacture high-speed mechanized cameras to transfer information from typed cards on to continuous rolls of film. This method has been employed since 1961 by the *British National Bibliography*, and it is widely used in many countries for telephone directories, catalogues and other compilations which have to be kept up to date and frequently reissued. A special model of the Vari-Typer has been constructed to type information in precisely the same position at the top of each card, the lower portion being left free for coding by normal punched card methods, if required.

Great economies can be made by storing information on cards, instead of keeping it in the form of standing type. Type metal is expensive in comparison with pasteboard; it is heavy and awkward to handle; and it cannot be sorted or rearranged mechanically. Methods have also been devised for combining the card system with film-setting. The typographical results of filmsetting give better definition, greater compactness and a more pleasing appearance than the product of any variety of cold type composition. At present filmset material has to be stuck down on cards, but it is only a matter of time before a satisfactory method is found for filmsetting direct on to cards. It will then be possible to achieve the appearance of printed type without the uneconomic features of hot metal composition.

The reader who wishes to study the latest advances in filmsetting techniques will have an opportunity to do so later in 1963 at the vast International Printing Exhibition (IPEX) which will occupy Earls Court and Olympia from July 16 to 27. In addition to demonstrations by improved models of several existing filmsetting machines, it is expected that a new British electronic system for photocomposition will be shown. Unwin Brothers, printers at the Gresham Press, will give a field test to this system, which meets their own specifications. It is designed to reproduce at speeds far in excess of present filmsetters, and it will be equipped with a much simplified keyboard. Pioneer work with electric keyboard composition has been carried out since 1959 by Unwin Brothers, who already have a large department of specially trained typists. The future of much text composition is likely to pass into the hands of typists with special training.

15

THE STATISTICS OF STYLE

JUNIUS AND THE COMPUTER

RARELY HAS LITERARY HISTORY produced a problem so worthy of a detective-novel treatment as that of the identification of 'Junius'. Letters on political subjects appeared above this signature in George Woodfall's newspaper *The Public Advertiser* from 1769 to 1772. What caused them to make their mark on the political and literary scene of the day was not so much their outspokenness (for compared with contemporary political writings they were quite mild in their abuse) but the elegance, succinctness and wit of their style. They were, however, outspoken enough for the writer to wish to conceal his identity; this he did so well that it may be only now that the riddle is finally solved.

The solution, if such it be, is the achievement of Mr. Alvar Ellegård, who has spared no pains in ferreting out the author. In his more general book *Who was Junius?* Mr. Ellegård sums up the extensive controversy on the subject in a manner that manages to convey the excitement of the hunt, while losing nothing of the elegance of style that he has doubtless caught from Junius himself. Much of the evidence that has been used to support candidates for the Junian crown of laurels has been of an historical or biographical nature, and, like so much evidence of this sort, alas, open to at least two interpretations.

At the time of the Junius correspondence many names were canvassed round literate society; a favourite was Edmund Burke, who was, by all accounts, not unflattered to be thought the author. It was only in 1816 that one John Taylor put forward, as a likely candidate, Sir Philip Francis, at one time a War Office official, and from 1773 a member of the supreme council of Bengal (when he was

---

ALVAR ELLEGÅRD: *Who was Junius?* 159 pp. Sw. kr. 25. *A Statistical Method for Determining Authorship*. The *Junius* Letters, 1769–1772. 115 pp. Paper bound: Sw. kr. 23. Cloth bound: Sw. kr. 30. Stockholm: Almqvist & Wiksell.

the implacable foe of Warren Hastings). Taylor's earlier theory (in a book published in 1813) was that young Philip had collaborated with his father, the Rev. Dr. Philip Francis, in the writing of the letters. Later, however, after Taylor had discovered that he had underestimated Philip's age, Philip himself was claimed to be sole author. The claim was substantiated mainly by biographical material but some (very unconvincing) linguistic evidence was introduced. Certain words and phrases, held to be characteristic of Junian style, were also to be found in Francis's voluminous writings: for instance, *uniform* was said to occur particularly often, and *force to* was preferred to *oblige to*.

Even though the linguistic evidence was so lame, because based on insufficient comparative material, the other evidence used by Taylor was convincing enough to make Philip Francis by far the strongest favourite in the Junian stakes. Francis himself was obviously not averse to being considered a runner: his sole denial was couched in ambiguous terms and he did all he could indirectly to convince his wife that he was indeed Junius. Viscount Samuel has told us (letter to *The Times*, 18 September 1962) that Jowett believed Francis 'was much too vain a man to have kept it to himself, if he had really been the author'. George Tierney, the Whig politician, puts another interpretation on Francis's self-conceit: 'I know no better reason for believing the fellow to be Junius than that he was always confoundedly proud of something, and no one could guess what it could be.'

A later commentator, Dilke (in articles in the *Athenaeum* 1848–50), poured cold water on Francis's claims: the linguistic evidence was useless; the biographical evidence complex and unreliable; and the calligraphical evidence extremely important. Indeed, Junius's handwriting has provided the stumbling-block for all candidates: his manuscript letters to Woodfall are written in a beautiful distinctive hand that does not in the least resemble that of Francis. Could it be a disguised hand? The calligraphic expert Chabot (in 1871) admitted that Francis could, at a pinch, have used it. The plot thickens with the discovery of a single sample of the Junian hand, other than the Woodfall letters: it is a covering note to an anonymous poem addressed to Miss Gibb, a Bath belle. Miss Gibb apparently always believed that the poem was composed by Francis; indeed, it has long been thought that it was written in Francis's hand. Alas, Chabot tells us that it was not Francis who copied the poem, though it may well have been his cousin, Tilghman. The mystery of who wrote the covering note remains.

Mr. Ellegård, dissatisfied with the widespread identification of Junius with Francis, first of all attempted to elucidate the handwriting mystery. He scrupulously examined Oxford and Cambridge matriculation lists, and similar documents, to see if he could find a signature that resembled the Junian hand. Our hearts must go out to him for performing this thankless and, in the event, fruitless task. Given the complexity and uncertainty of the historical and biographical evidence, he was left only with stylistic criteria. For his examination of style Mr. Ellegård has used a series of highly original statistical tests described in detail in his more technical book.

The author was driven to devise his own system of stylistic tests after finding that those suggested by the great Cambridge statistician G. U. Yule—measuring 'concentration' of vocabulary, and sentence-length—were insufficiently sensitive for his purpose. The characteristic of style that he investigates is the use of 'typical' words and expressions—Valéry's *mots-clefs*, an idea that has been developed in rather a different direction by Professor Guiraud, of Groningen. By careful combing of the undoubted Junian texts (numbering 157,100 words) and a sample of other contemporary texts (numbering more than a million words) he picked out words and expressions that were used particularly frequently (plus-words) or particularly rarely (minus-words), and calculated for each of them a 'distinctiveness ratio'—a ratio of frequency of occurrence in Junius to that in general usage. For instance, the word 'uniform', already noticed by Taylor to be a favourite of Junius, was found to have a relative frequency in his works of 280 per million words, whereas in the million-word general sample there were 65 occurrences of this word: the distinctiveness ratio of 'uniform' is thus 4·3 (280/65). Words with a distinctiveness ratio of between 1·5 and 0·7 were found to be of little use in the tests, for Junius did not distinguish himself clearly enough from his contemporaries in either his predilection for them, or his neglect of them.

Within the Junian texts themselves there were, of course, considerable fluctuations of frequency of occurrence, only very partially attributable to sample size. The fluctuation that could reasonably be expected to occur by chance was estimated simply by calculation of the standard deviation and coefficient of variation in a 'basic' Junian sample of 80,000 words: an author whose usage fell within the Junian range might well be Junius himself. The testing list's systematic bias, owing to its inclusion of rare items that were picked up 'by chance' in the sample material examined, was estimated in a similar way. Mr. Ellegård carefully avoided another pitfall: many of the characteristics of Junian style might be common to political pamphleteers, or to correspondents in the *Public Advertiser*. After eliminating words that were decidedly plus or minus in these types of writing, Mr. Ellegård was left with 272 items in his testing list, representing only 1·8 per cent of occurrences in the million-word general sample and 2·5 per cent of the Junius material.

The fact that the items occurred so rarely (as they are bound to, given that the vastly greater part of any text is made up of a small number of the commonest words) raised yet another problem: in the short texts to be examined calculation of probability of a rare item occurring is subject to disproportionate error. In practice the effects of this factor were reduced by a simple and rather neat, device— 'grouping'. Words with similar distinctiveness ratios were grouped into eighteen categories: nine for plus-words, nine for minus-words. This led to a certain amount of 'blurring' of information: if the summed frequency of two words, w_1+w_2, is the same in authors A and B, it may be that A uses w_1 a great deal and w_2 hardly at all, while B uses them both equally often. This drawback is less important if the tests concentrate more on the extremes of the distinctiveness range; the paramount advantage of grouping is that there is much more probability of a small sample picking up one of a *series* of rarities than any one rarity.

When it comes to presenting the results obtained by comparing the relative frequency of the eighteen-plus and minus groups in the Junius texts, the million-word sample and a corpus of Francis texts (of 231,300) Mr. Ellegård's clarity of exposition fails him. He claims (page 50, *Statistical Method*) that 'a glance' at his tables will show the reader that the Junius values and Francis values are close, and 'indeed, . . . overlap'. These tables are apparently reproduced directly from his electronic computer material, with tiny figures and almost no explanatory notes (for instance, we are not told that text size is quoted in hundreds of words). If we do examine the figures carefully (bottom row of Table 5F, two bottom rows of Table 5E, and the whole of Tables 5G, H and I) it can be seen that, on the whole, the Francis values are nearer Junius than the general values, but the raw data is by no means striking. To make things a little easier Mr. Ellegård extracts some figures from the tables and presents them in the text (page 51): he calls them 'averages'—of what he does not say! It is only by dint of painful searching that it can be discovered that these figures are summarized from Tables 5E and 5F, columns R1, R2, R3, D^+ D^-, rows for texts 68–76+77–106, and texts 265–131. Even then the reader will be puzzled by the errors of simple arithmetic that appear in the summations: $(10\cdot00+9\cdot00)\div2=$ $9\cdot9$ for instance!

This vital table (page 51, *Statistical Method*) compares certain scores by Francis and Junius: on the whole they are similar, but it surely cannot be claimed that the figures in fourth series quoted (Francis seventy-two, Junius twenty-nine) are very close. These figures represent the difference between the relative frequency of plus-words in the texts under examination, and that of the Junius control material (texts 1–67, numbering 127,100 words). Mr. Ellegård seems to say (page 51) that only two texts (158 and 159) approach as nearly to Junius as Francis, in this respect; but 'a glance' at Table 5G (political pamphlets and speeches) reveals that three others (148, 259, 262) do so.

These irritating errors of exposition and fact do not, however, prevent Mr. Ellegård's material from being striking; it is most obviously so in the graphic representation of Diagrams 1–8 (also found in *Who was Junius?*, but there insufficiently explained). According to calculations devised by Per Sigurd Agrell F.K. (who provides an elegant and subtle statistical appendix), less than one writer in a hundred could have scored so many near hits on the Junian target as does Francis himself.

This means, of course, that, if there were 100,000 literate Englishmen at the time, Junius could be, by this test, any one of upwards of a thousand people. True, none of the usual candidates seem to be included in this thousand, but who is to say that there is no outsider who could claim to be Junius? Mr. Ellegård had to reduce the field by introducing more variables: this he did by an 'alternatives test'. This test is based on the observation that Junius prefers some synonyms to others: for instance, he, unlike his contemporaries, uses *in effect* more than *in fact*. Fifty-one sets of synonyms were divided into four groups: the relative frequency of use of these groups in the various samples was compared. Francis again attained the highest score.

Having incorporated this new test, it can now be calculated that only one in 30,000 of the 'population' could be as nearly Junian in his style as was Francis; but, as Mr. Ellegård explains very clearly, this calculation is not the one we need. The aim is rather to attach 'confidence limits' to the identification of Francis—to estimate the chances that identification is correct. To do this, Mr. Ellegård has to ask, in the conventional statistician's manner, 'how large could the population of potential "Junii" be, while still leaving Francis's candidature a hundred to one odds-on bet?' If, from evidence completely outside the linguistic material, the population of potential Junii can be confined to something less than 300 in number, the bet is sound.

At this critical point Mr. Ellegård, like a tired mathematics lecturer, appeals, perhaps rightly, to intuition. As a specimen of the sort of evidence available, he asks how there could possibly be more than a few hundred people who heard Lord Chatham's speeches in 1770, as both Junius and Francis did. But he himself admirably summarizes Dilke's case (pages 59–62, *Who was Junius?*), denying Junius's presence at the debates: Junius could have read about them in the newspapers (typically, copies of the 'great reporting journals' that appeared at the time seem no longer to be extant). That Francis himself may have been the reporter who took down the speeches does nothing to strengthen his claim to be Junius.

If only Mr. Ellegård had more use of his electronic computer and had examined more stylistic features! The introduction of more variables might have reduced the 300 figure, and convinced us completely that Francis was indeed Junius.

Having set up the machinery, it was a comparatively simple matter to proceed to the attribution of doubtful Junian texts. The main difficulty was that of the smallness of the samples, so that the tests were not sensitive enough to be wholly reliable: Mr. Ellegård discusses clearly the ways in which this disadvantage can be minimized.

There is no doubt that Mr. Ellegård's is a remarkable achievement. Thus it is all the more a pity that his work is marred by a number of minor slips and obscurities (for instance, he tells us that he scrutinized a text-mass of 1,604,800 words—if we examine his scattered, and not wholly clear, references to the composition of this text-mass, we arrive at a total of 1,605,200 words). It is a shame, too, that having laboured so hard he could not have done just a little more, by extending his investigation beyond the examination of mainly vocabulary items. If he had had the use of an electronic computer earlier, he might have been able to include more syntactical and morphological data in his investigation. In the event, however, he has managed almost to solve a long-standing mystery, and, more important, he has opened the way to further work on the statistics of style.

*   *   *

SIR.—In a very generous review of my books on Junius (your issue of 25 January) your reviewer finds my presentation of the statistical material lacking in clarity. I will not dispute this point, nor will I deny 'minor slips and obscurities'.

I should like to point out, however, that what I say on page 51 on the difference between Francis and other writers with respect to their Junian characteristics is quite expressly limited to texts of 4,000 words or more. The three texts adduced by your reviewer are smaller, and hence, of course, more subject to chance variations. They are all discussed separately in my book.

Secondly, the 'errors of simple arithmetic' are not the ones your reviewer instances. The table on page 51 (which is meant to be purely illustrative) is based on the absolute numbers of occurrences in the texts, not on the relative frequencies given in Table 5E. Hence the slight differences.

ALVAR ELLEGÅRD
Gothenburg University, Sweden.

*** Our reviewer writes: Mr. Ellegård's first point is well taken. It should be pointed out, however, that it is an extremely minor detail, and that my mention of the three texts was, as I stated in the review, based on a superficial glance at tables printed in excessively small type, without explanatory notes.

The second point Mr. Ellegård makes is illuminating. My identification of his table on p. 51 with items from Table 5E was the result of laborious searching: certain discrepancies seemed only explicable if we assumed arithmetical errors. Now we are informed that the table is 'purely illustrative'! I feel Mr. Ellegård should have allowed us more opportunity to check his conclusions, by reference to the actual data he used.

These petty quibbles, it should be stressed, concern only a few pages of two otherwise excellent books—and then only the exposition, and not the content. They do not affect my overall view that Mr. Ellegård's is a remarkable achievement.

16

POETS TODAY

(a) LOUIS MacNEICE

The Burning Perch

A LITTLE BEFORE HIS DEATH, Louis MacNeice had written and produced the last of his Radio-Features, *Persons from Porlock*. Many
listeners will have winced at the sad irony of the circumstance, for
the theme of this broadcast was the constant interruption to which a
creative artist may be exposed; and some interruptions are final.
There are further ironies in that MacNeice's last and barely posthu-
mous collection of poems should contain some of his best work and
a pathetic promise at the end of the dedicatory poem to

> keep my appointment
> In green improbable fields with you.

Only hindsight, perhaps, would have noticed how many of these
poems are concerned with the sinister, with 'what is past, or passing'
and with death itself. For it is strange how often, throughout his
writing career, MacNeice's amazingly sharp and unexpected vision
undressed the familiar and found something eerie. As the poet himself wrote ('Experiences with Images', first published in *Orpheus*,
Vol. 2, 1949), 'the mental climate of our time, and our own peculiar
background' are even more important in forming a writer's imagery
than are the perennial themes:

Now about this peculiar background . . . The guinea pig I am using . . .
myself, was born in 1907 in Belfast and brought up on the northern shore of

---

(a) *The Burning Perch*. 58 pp. Faber & Faber. 12s. 6d.
(b) *A Group Anthology*. 127 pp. Oxford University Press. 21s.
   The Owl in the Tree. 59 pp. Oxford University Press. 18s.
(c) *Advice to a Prophet*. 64 pp. Faber & Faber. 12s. 6d.
   Selected Poems. 61 pp. Eyre & Spottiswoode. 12s. 6d.
(d) *Another September*. 47 pp. Dolmen Press. London: Oxford University Press.
   10s. 6d.
   Downstream. 63 pp. Dolmen Press. London: Oxford University Press. 10s. 6d.
(e) *Addictions* 80 pp. Chatto & Windus. 12s. 6d.

Belfast Lough, i.e., in a wet, rather sombre countryside where linen mills
jostled with primitive rustic cottages and farmyard noises and hooters
more or less balanced each other. Thus the factory entered my childhood's
mythology long before I could place it in any social picture. As for the sea, it
was something I hardly ever went on but there it was always, not visible
from our house but registering its presence through fog-horns. It was
something alien, foreboding, dangerous, and only very rarely blue. . . . My
father being a clergyman, his church was a sort of annex to the home—but
rather a haunted annex (it was an old church and there were several things
in it which frightened me as a child). Which is one reason, I think, though I
would also maintain that the sound is melancholy anyhow, why church
bells have for me a sinister association. . . . On top of this I had more
than my share of old wives' tales from our Roman Catholic cook and others,
of calvinist alarums from our Presbyterian housekeeper, and of nightmares
from various causes, I also had certain early contacts with both mental
illness and mental deficiency (these latter may explain the *petrifaction*
images which appear pretty often in my poems, e.g., in 'Perseus'). I should
add that our house was lit by oil lamps (not enough of them) and so was
full of shadows. And in general the daily routine was monotonous, there
were few other children to play with and I hardly ever went away to stay.
These circumstances between them must have supplied me with many
images of fear, anxiety, loneliness or monotony (to be used very often
quite out of a personal context).

Add that during the past thirty years 'the mental climate of our time'
cannot often have been soporific for an alert and sensitive mind.
MacNeice has been accused of developing too little, since his early
works. In so far as this is true, which is not so far as some critics
pretend, the reasons are here.

Even the happiest and most singing of Louis MacNeice's lyrics—
and none in the present volume is quite of that kind—are at least
lightly tinged by the sombre, the wistful, or the uneasy. It is as if, in
his most personal poems, his inward world became appreciable to us
only through faintly-coloured and slightly rippled glass, or as if it
were lit by a sun different from ours. The result is often beautiful,
always vivid, always arresting both intellectually and emotionally;
but always disturbing, too. In more objective poems (some of the
Burnt Offerings, for example, or 'Memoranda to Horace' in the
present collection) there is always urbanity and wit, rapid and allusive intelligence; there is always the superb assurance of craftsman-
ship, and rightness both of technique and of organization that we
find also in the intimate poems. But whether the prevailing tone
be an apparently classical reasonableness, or a restrained lyricism, or
—occasionally—an almost outrageous humour, still there will be

undertones of the sub-sardonic, or even of something fiercer. Is the famous 'Bagpipe Music', for instance, really a comic poem? In another bagpipe-poem, the first section of 'Cock o' the North', we are not expected to feel straightforward high-spirits. Two poems from *The Burning Perch* itself, 'Children's Games' and 'The Taxis', are 'light verse' only at first sight: the former, full of distorted echoes, is a savage satire; the latter, off-hand and unemphatic, has an aftertaste of nastiness.

The work of minor poets, such as Walter de la Mare, often gives one the impression that they were happy people. That of major poets, of whom Louis MacNeice was one, will do this very seldom. Those who knew him personally will agree that what occasionally seemed in him remoteness, watchfulness, wryness, by no means indicated a melancholy or unsociable temperament.

(*b*) EDWARD LUCIE-SMITH and PHILIP HOBSBAUM (Eds)
A Group Anthology

ANTHONY THWAITE
The Owl in the Tree

Over the past ten years, since about 1953, the year of the death of Dylan Thomas, the year also of the appearance of some of the most interesting of Mr. Oscar Mellors's Fantasy Press pamphlets of young Oxford or Cambridge poets, reviewers have found themselves, in England, looking less for remarkable new individual talents among younger English poets than for the development of a tradition. The tradition, on the whole, that has been most consistently developed is one of plain style, down-to-earth, near-prose English poetry; poetry very much as a 'criticism of life', in the sense of the application of ideas, hesitantly defined and empirically controlled ideas, to areas of the texture of contemporary life.

Lyrical intensity, concentration of phrase, sustained nobility of mood, loyalty to a vision, even strong and simple emotional drive, have not been main marks even of recent poetry that has been rightly admired: the memorable quality of good recent contemporary poetry has been like the quality of fingernails scratching silk stockings, of a cat's fur stroked the wrong way, of the noise a shovel makes among small coals, of a smoothing plane cutting against, rather than with, the grain of wood. There has been what might be called a 'sick mood', a certain preoccupation with the ugly, the cruel, the nasty, the poetically grotesque and pathetic, in recent poets, notably, perhaps, Mr. George MacBeth and Mr. Peter Redgrove and Mr. Philip Hobsbaum; but this mood has not been combined with a tone of hysterical protest or overt social rage, and not divorced, for instance in Mr. Hobsbaum's work, from a mood of realistic social compassion.

Clogged with detail, recent poems of this sort have been often oddly emotionally low-pressured, the low pressure expressing itself in a certain ordinariness and unconcentration of diction, a disparity between the disagreeableness of the images or events presented and the poet's, if not flat or perfunctory, at least implicit, at least un-insisted-on, emotional response. It is hard to think of a youngish modern poet whose response is mainly to beauty; on the other hand, of Mr. Eliot's famous triad for the attention of the poet, the horror, the boredom, and the glory of life, the boredom and, in a rather glum way, the horror are more in evidence than the glory. What one finds oneself looking for in good contemporary verse is, perhaps, a rational compassion working through a controlled and not frantic distaste or disgust. The distaste or disgust may be livened, and mitigated, by half-sympathetic humour. Much recent poetry could be covered by Professor Northrop Frye's definition of the mode of much modern literature as being 'low mimetic', shading into 'irony'. Poets no longer imitate the actions of gods or heroes, or allegorical repre-sentatives of ideal virtues, or states of *bourgeois* well-being, or intense and exciting states of subjective feeling; they imitate the untidy, shabby, incoherent pattern of everyday life as it is, and this imitation arouses in them no strong and simple negative or positive feelings, but rather a peculiar and rather low-toned feeling, like the feeling of somebody swallowing with a grimace a tepid and flocculent half-pint of bitter beer, towards the dimness, and yet the necessity, of things as they are.

A Group Anthology illustrates admirably these generalizations. It owes its existence to a 'poetry workshop', started by Mr. Philip Hobsbaum in Cambridge in 1955, carried on by him for some time in London, and more recently carried on, in weekly sessions, by Mr. Edward Lucie-Smith. At each session one poet presents a set of several poems on cyclostyled sheets and these are criticized in detail by other poets present at the gathering; only coffee is served, so the criticism is sober. The group is what Professor Karl Popper would call an 'open society'; nobody is excluded in principle and the only principle generally accepted is, in Mr. Lucie-Smith's words in his preface (probably Rimbaud, Hart Crane, Dylan Thomas would not have accepted it), that 'poetry is discussable, or, to put it another way, that the process by which words work in poetry is open to rational examination'. In a fascinating epilogue, Mr. Philip Hobsbaum prints fragments of transcript from a tape-recorded discussion of a poem; the discussion, vivid as it is, seems to spring rather from first attempts at apprehension or comprehension of the spoken word than from really close 'rational examination' of the printed page.

The volume as a whole is full of poems interesting, as Mr. Lucie-Smith says in his introduction, as 'very frank autobiographical poems', 'poetry of direct experience', and as 'dramatic monologues', rather unfull of poems which immediately grip the attention through the power or attraction of the voice, the personality, the technical skill of the poet. There is perhaps no line, phrase, or rhythmical cadence which imprints itself at once, and for ever, on the remembering ear and mind. Yet this is probably the most soberly intelligent, and in a sense the most representative, anthology of English poetry that has been published for several years. What is unattractive in it is the unattractiveness of the age we live in, not of these poets. It is perhaps the unattractiveness of the low-mimetical and ironical concept of what a poem should be.

Mr. Anthony Thwaite (so far as one knows, he has not been an attender at the sessions of the group) is also a low-mimetical and ironical poet, but he allows himself often a piercing directness of personal feeling, a naïve self-exposedness, which is rather aside from the general group tone (though one finds something like it, for instance, in the work of Mr. Martin Bell, Mr. Peter Porter, Mr. Edward Lucie-Smith, and Mr. Philip Hobsbaum).

The fact is that low mimesis and irony are, for him, a kind of polite social mask; and high mimesis, compassion, and admiration are never very far under the surface of his verse. A splendid poem, 'Mr. Cooper', about finding in the outside lavatory of a Manchester public house an enigmatic card with the words written on it, 'Mr. Cooper—dead', *could* be a conventional, low-mimetic short story poem (it is full of convincing small details) but manages to be a rather fine and large poem about the loneliness, transitoriness, noncommunicableness of human life. Mr. Thwaite has a number of poems about being a father, about the odd relationship of fathers to small children, who seem to have their own separate and calm civilization. He manages to handle this without being either twee and whimsical, or sentimentally, or consciously unsentimentally, portentous:

> The woolly animal with rabbit ears
> And pom-pom tail sits at the table. There
> Biscuits are wooden and the tea is air.
> A random guest appears—
> Myself—and blundering in I take a seat.
> No one says grace. There is, in fact, no meat.

Taken together, *A Group Anthology* and Mr. Thwaite's volume are, on the whole, very encouraging symptoms, or perhaps emblems, of the present state of English poetry. They contradict the notion of the poet as somebody fantastical, arrogant, aggressive, withdrawn from, or hostile to, current life, living in a kind of make-up world of his own; on the other hand, there are poets, Yeats, for instance, and perhaps Mr. Robert Graves, who fit that notion, and are also more memorable poets than Mr. Thwaite, or any of the poets in *A Group Anthology*.

(c) RICHARD WILBUR
Advice to a Prophet

GREGORY CORSO
Selected Poems

Ever since Mr. Edmund Wilson first divided American authors into Palefaces and Redskins we have all been happily engaged in playing Cowboys and Indians with American literature. American writers themselves seem to have taken very kindly to the game and readily type their work as belonging to one or the other camp. While Mr. James Purdy and Mr. Bernard Malamud patrol the plains, tending their herds of words, Mr. Norman Mailer has taken to the hills and is busy sending up smoke signals to Mr. Jack Kerouac and anybody else who can interpret his hip lingo. But the truly classic confrontation of Cowboy and Indian has happened in this country, recently and quite fortuitously, through the publication within a week of one another of books of poems by Mr. Richard Wilbur and Mr. Gregory Corso.

Not that the encounter is classic in scope; Mr. Wilbur is no James any more than Mr. Corso is a Melville. But it will do to define the class to which these clashes belong. Never did a United States Marshal appear more immaculate among the roughnecks of the West, not to mention the even scruffier Indians, than Mr Wilbur does among the generation of the 'beats'. An imposing, elegant figure, he indubitably stands for Law and Order. He has an air of absolute, though tolerant, rectitude, and would obviously be prepared to eat his boots on a desert trek rather than trifle with a participle or insult an adverb. Even more, he stands for 'the due processes of the Law', with all the paraphernalia of precedents the phrase implies. We are, therefore, hardly surprised when a seemingly simple description of a fire engine turns out to contain allusions to Henry Adams's *Letter to American Teachers of History* and that his present volume includes translations from writers as different as Molière and Quasimodo. One feels almost disappointed, in fact, that he has not yet turned his attentions to Horace. If any living writer could give us an adequate version of that propagandist for civilized good living, it is surely Mr. Wilbur.

Mr. Corso, on the other hand, is an Indian. Were he to be invited to stay the night at the Sabine farm, he would probably regard Horace as one of the 'old poetmen' he hates. Since he has committed himself to

> rip out their apology tongues,
> and steal their poems

he could hardly be regarded as an ideal guest. But what would he do with the poems once he had stolen them? He could hardly pass them off as his own. Or could he? For, in spite of his slipshod techniques, his occasional havering, his over-anxious anger, Mr. Corso possesses a directness, a simplicity and a sense of humour which would not have been foreign to the author of the *Satires*. He is able, that is, to describe accurately something he has seen—a puma in a Mexican zoo or a building in Harlem—and to convey his feelings about it with total and amusing lucidity. He is able, too, to laugh at himself—an exercise very uncommon among the poets with whom he is usually grouped, completely unknown among the Indian tribes who inhabit the cinema screens, though, probably, by no means unusual among the original inhabitants of the American plains. In this, indeed, he is much more like Horace than Mr. Wilbur, who seems incapable of laughing about anything, unless he has the written permission of Molière.

That Mr. Wilbur has succeeded so brilliantly in translating Molière shows that he is far from being a humourless man. But without these translations the reader would be hard put to it to recognize the fact in his original pieces. He has one or two witty epigrams in his present collection but, for the most part, all hint of levity is drowned in the kind of dreary uplift one associates with the heavenly choirs of films. Were he alone in this, it would merit mention but little more. But he is far from being alone. Almost all serious poets today seem to feel compelled to be very serious indeed, to enlighten us or preach at us from whatever rostrum they find handy, even if it be no more than, in one of Mr. Wilbur's poems, a hole in the floor.

This determination to be serious often leads them into over-valuing an experience or an object and devoting too many words to evoking it. And verbosity is a close relative of poetic diction. The fault of poetic diction has always been that it tends to smother simple observation under a smog of words, that the smog gives pneumonia to whatever meaning was intended and the poem dies. One realizes this immediately if one turns to the eighteenth century and finds out that 'all who crop the verdant food' means cattle and 'celestial Muse' refers to Melpomene. But the tricks of our own time are harder to detect, partly because they are usually more original and, conversely, partly because they are more in the spirit of the times—one of the strongest contemporary spirits, and one on which most of us have been drunk at one time or another, being originality. Covert as they are, however, they are by no means less ridiculous than those of earlier eras and when so intelligent and sensitive a writer as Mr. Wilbur is able to label darkness as:

> . . . a shuttered kiosk, standing
> Where the only news is night

it is high time that somebody cracked down and tried to restore us to sanity; and this is what Mr. Corso, quite effectually at times, attempts.

He can, of course, be absurd, nonsensical, outrageous, inconsequential. His technique, unlike Mr. Wilbur's, is very much a matter of hit and run or, equally often, hit and miss. In this, as in most other matters, he is a typical Indian. But his hits have a habit of being very clean and his running is remarkably fast. Many poems in this selection are reminiscent of the later Lawrence, except that his humour is wiser and gentler than was Lawrence's. He does not—and who does?—possess anything like the power of Lawrence at his best but, strangely enough, his social attitudes are in some ways more mature than those of the master. He does not, for example, take sex as a simple or complex revelation of the meaning of life or whatever, but regards it, in his excellent poem called 'Marriage', as something which ties us into all manner of experiences.

Nor is Mr. Corso incapable of a certain tenderness and a degree of rhythmic subtlety. To give the reader a chance to judge these for himself, it is best to quote an entire poem called 'Mortal Infliction':

> I think of Polyphemus bellowing his lowly woe
> seated on a high cliff
> sun-tight legs dangling into the sea
> his fumbling hands grappling his burnt eye
> And I think he will remain like that
> because it's impossible for him to die—
> Ulysses is dead
> by now he's dead
> And how wise was he
> who blinded a thing of immortality.

There is something to be said for judging poets by the way they use the word 'immortality'. If they mean by it 'a very long time' they are usually bad poets—and it is difficult to create contexts in which it cannot be interpreted as such. Yet here Mr. Corso has created such a context and, in so doing, has added an element of pathos unfelt even by Homer. There could hardly be a higher achievement.

(d) THOMAS KINSELLA

Another September,   Downstream

A poet today born or living in or near London is not expected usually to have Mr. Eliot's or Mr. Betjeman's specific feeling for the London scene and atmosphere or to see himself as a spokesman for the culture, if there is such a thing, of the great south-eastern conurbation. He can speak for the times and himself. On an Irish, Scottish or Welsh poet circumstances force a more conscious locally representative role; he is not asked necessarily to be a nationalist or a writer of historical-patriotic poems, but he is expected to have a strong sense of history and place, and to be in some sense a spokesman for his less articulate countrymen, a voice for some of the deeper instincts of the tribe. This expectation can strengthen him, give him a confidence that somebody, at least, is interested; but it can also sometimes freeze him into poses of rhetorical stiffness.

Rhetoric, the rhetoric of a nation of wits and orators, is at once the great strength and weakness of Irish poets; even of the greatest of them, Yeats, who flattered himself vainly in his youth that he was going to wring rhetoric's neck. To transform rhetoric into style is the great technical problem for all Irish poets; where the problem for many young English poets is how to squeeze style out of a habit of articulate hesitation. Mr. Kinsella can rank, with Mr. Richard Murphy and Mr. John Montague, as one of the finest conscious stylists among recent Irish poets. He enjoys, it might be said, the feel of words in his mouth, their sweetness or sourness, and their weight:

> Road and river parted. Now my path
> Lay gleaming through the greasy dusk, uphill
> Into the final turn. A concrete cross
> Low in the ditch grew to the memory
> Of one who answered latest the phantom hag.
> Tireless Rebellion, when with mouth awry
> She hammered at the door, disrupting harvest.

The artistry of that passage can be even better appreciated if a reader remembers that the Irish 'r', even in forward positions, is fully sounded as a consonant and that in initial positions it is softly aspirated. There is fine art also in the play of the contrasting sense and similar sound of 'gleaming' and 'greasy'. The whole passage also suggests a tendency in Mr. Kinsella to modulate, to play down, a manner of high rant which would be natural to him if he let himself go. The burring 'r's embrace every image with a kind of affectionate rust:

> as a froth
> Locked in a swirl of turbulence, a shape
> That forms and fructifies and dies . . .

and the inner chime of the ending of 'fructifies' and the word 'dies' is like the subtle chime of 'greasy' and 'gleaming' and the thick, half-stammering alliteration of 'concrete cross', where the short 'o's also echo. It may be, as Mr. Skelton suggests in his introduction to his anthology *Six Irish Poets* (O.U.P. 25s.), that a knowledge of Gaelic

K

poetry often helps Irish poets to give their English verses a peculiar richness of texture.

It must be confessed, however, that this conscious richness of texture, so delightful in itself, does often tend to rob Mr. Kinsella's poetry of immediate emotional directness; or the emotion seems more in the poet's feeling about the words than in the meaning of the words: there is a poem about a dead young woman, whose family have come to bring her home from Dublin to bury her:

> They dither softly at her bedroom door
> In soaking overcoats, and words forsake
> Even their comforters. The bass of prayer
> Haunts the chilly landing while they take
> Their places in a murmur of heartbreak.

There, the artful choice of words like 'dither' and 'bass', the three long 'o's and 'soaking overcoats', even the final 'heartbreak'—In Irish English, this is not a trochee, *'heart*-break' but a kind of rocking spondee, *'heart-break'*—all give us more of a sense of Mr. Kinsella's skill in manipulating our emotions than of the urgency and pressure of his. Yet this remains a most distinguished volume.

(e) D. J. ENRIGHT

Addictions

We are now in the tenth year of D. J. Enright, poet, teacher, and moralist. Just over ten years ago an article in these pages stated that he 'shows signs of exciting achievement'. With Mr. Enright's fourth collection, *Addictions*, we now have some two hundred of his poems; enough, one would think, for someone to do a hard vacation's work and tell us just how exciting that achievement has been. One or two approaches are offered here for a critical discussion of Mr. Enright.

His most exciting book still remains his first, *The Laughing Hyena*. Mr. Enright has never quite regained the power over language which he shows, for example, in 'Black Country Women', whose opening image,

> Did they burn in their men's furnaces

creates a pointed correspondence between people and the landscape in which they live; the women, described as 'small deities of coal', come burning into life. Mr. Enright showed, in his first volume, an earnest, questioning mind, divided between his idea of humanity and his observations of the misery of people; the latter evoked in him a pity which sometimes assumed an antique dignity, fusing individual humans into humanity:

> Rest,
> Rest your eyes here, wash them in these beneficial waters,
> they are very old, but very good.

Here, probably, for the first time in Mr. Enright's work, something of an intellectual resolution by way of an empathy with nature is achieved and the conclusion is presented in an undisguised moral stricture. It is also one of the rare occasions when he uses a symbolist technique.

Right through *Bread Rather Than Blossoms* and *Some Men are Brothers,* his second and third volumes, to *Addictions,* his language becomes increasingly direct, stripped of ornament or the conspicuously sharp image, until what we have in *Addictions* is an unforced, but still vigorously tense, language which will hold commerce only with meaning, providing few incidental pleasures. The occasional pun—'sloe-eyed (though far from slow-witted)'—intrudes jarringly from the past; otherwise, there can be few poets writing today who depend so heavily and almost exclusively on the vitality they confer on their language; sometimes figurative, Mr. Enright is always plain and commonsensical.

Common sense may indeed be said to be an ethical principle with Mr. Enright. While his poetic development has mainly meant a refinement of his language, his theme has hardly varied from what preoccupied him ten years ago. He is a wanderer: his poems take us from Alexandria to Berlin, from the Black Country to the Hiroshima country; but, whatever the setting, humanity is almost always his subject.

Addictions offers us mostly the Far East and Mr. Enright's further variations on the technique of irony. 'An Unfortunate Poem', for example, describes the shooting of a man against a library wall:

> To wound a Library wall with bullet nicks!
> Really hardly cultured. No respect for books.

The poet controls his comment by mimicking a superior attitude and refrains from assuming an obviously satirical pose; the effect is a sort of shrugging of shoulders which takes on the power of vituperative speech without needing explosive words with which to express itself.

In 'Freshman Poetry', one of the best poems in the book, the irony comes from a contrasting of subjects, The poet, lecturing a class in literature, is made uneasy by his environment; the meanings of life which literature seeks are contrasted with the usefulness attributed to science:

> ... the bench I lean on also holds a sink, a Bunsen burner
> And electric points. I'm here by courtesy of Science.

Often the irony comes from a particular word, as in the title poem:

> Uneasy embers of our race,
> Glowing and fading in their licensed place.

The word 'licensed' places the poem right in the middle of the twentieth century.

Sometimes a poem fails because the statement is banal and the mode of expression poetically uninteresting, as in 'Names':

> Meanwhile the rest of the alphabet smile to themselves,
> Who never write anything, who only work five days a
> Week, eight hours a day, who are assured of a pension,
> Whose names are on monthly cheques, who have succeeded.

This stanza contains in it, potentially, all the vices peculiar to Mr. Enright's poetry. The language just does not sustain itself to make a significant enough statement; and this is the level to which any poetry must lapse which tries to keep itself alive with the force of language without the artificial, but sometimes essential, respiration of formal devices.

On the matter of form, one would, indeed, be inclined to reprehend much of Mr. Enright's work, though successive readings reveal details of technical precision which one did not suspect on first reading. He uses the long, five-stressed line oftener than any other, but sometimes the stresses are so far apart that the lines seem to become entangled with themselves. This is because Mr. Enright uses speech rhythms for his cadences; the danger of depending too much on the ear is to suggest that anything which sounds right to the 'auditory imagination' is also metrically right, and that is a fallacy. Rhythm, as Hopkins showed, follows metre.

On this subject, and not without relevance to Mr. Enright's poems, one can quote a remark by Cowley: 'And though the *Liberty* of them may incline a man to believe them easie to be composed, yet the undertaker will finde it otherwise.' Cowley was commending his own poems; this reviewer commends those of Mr. Enright.

ROBERT CONQUEST (Ed)
(*f*) *New Lines*

No one has ever done more than hum a few guesses about why particular poets write as they do—or, to tell the truth, about why poets write at all. This is what makes it so absurd for critics to get irritated when people write bad poetry, or, grim-browed, to hunt down the sources of the corruption in other poets' (or critics') villainous influence. Poets will write as they will and can. What a reader can do, though that is often a tricky enough problem for him, is to say whether he wants what the poets write—then read it again, or graciously decline to.

Let it be said without useless recriminations, then, that the great mass of serious English poetry of the last eight or nine years has had a quite distinctive flavour; that many people who care about literature like it very much; and that many people would resolutely never read it again. Mr. Robert Conquest's newly published anthology, *New Lines 2* (Macmillan, 21s.) raises all the issues afresh.

New Lines 2 contains work by eight poets from his first *New Lines* anthology in 1956, and sixteen others. It is an extremely interesting, and genuine, successor to the first book, inasmuch as it reflects, again, Mr. Conquest's own taste—and Mr. Conquest's taste is precisely for those qualities that most recent English poets have sought to put into their work.

Of course a few individuals stand out: Miss Elizabeth Jennings, the only woman poet in the book, has a gift in no way equalled by the others here for letting the music of her lines convey her mood before the sense of the words does. Mr. Thom Gunn, still, it seems, the most striking poet of his generation, has some poems that seem physically to force one into states of delight in nature or of metaphysical terror. Mr. Thomas Kinsella knows how to stare at very real scenes, and feel about them with a peculiar dreamy intensity.

But the majority of the contributors write in a style that makes one think of them as members of a kind of poetic common market. All, as represented here, write well—testing their words, putting them down in the most telling place, letting their rhythm and rhymes tap their points home. But this very adroitness, this very aptitude for getting their ideas across at the conference table, so to speak, is the first feature that unites and at the same time limits them. With all their unmistakable sensibility, they are still very much of the same

company as the lawyers and businessmen. At the conference table
there is moreover very little disagreement. The themes recur: the
world's work must go on as best it can; it's no use having illusions
about either other people's possibilities or one's own; let's make
ourselves responsible for the jobs we find we've got, but not expect
very much of use to come of them: women are bound to be disappointed by men, and men to be haunted by guilt; the best times are
the wonderful prelude of childhood, that no child must miss, and
after that the occasional moments when mind and conscience go
through a lull. To such themes the concentration and intensity we
find in great English lyric poetry are not appropriate. The most
common type among all these poems are what might be called last-
moment lyrics. They deftly and dryly outline all the mundane
details of some domestic dullness or amorous failure, and save till
the final verse or the final line one pang of feeling at 'what might
have been'.

Mr. Conquest himself, in a loyal but haywire introduction, presents his contributors as returning to 'the cardinal traditions of
English verse'. This, in the face of the deliberate refusal of almost all
of the recent poets to write outside the limits of a very small range of
feeling, will strike anyone who reads on as a simply ridiculous assertion. (He accommodates the more strong and original talents found
in the book by claiming later that it shows 'the persistence and
variety of the central current of English verse', which seems a mere
piece of paradoxical play on words.) His carefully chosen selection
helps the new poets considerably; his large claims, and pages of wild
insults at those who, he thinks, would distort English poetry by
imposing critical fashions, seem pointless and even harmful to his
contributors. It would be better rather to say that we have a new
body of poets in England now, writing well—and writing how they
want to—about familiar moods and situations of the post-war years;
that we are lucky to have them; but that they, in their evident
despondency, must be wishing quite as strongly as anyone else that
some great poets would come and write them on to the sidelines.

*   *   *

This article was followed on 20 and 27 September by correspondence between Mr. Conquest and the reviewer.

17

A WRITER'S CONSCIENCE

THE COLLECTED HERMANN BROCH

HERMANN BROCH is not an easy writer to place, for he was 'a creative writer *malgré lui*'. He is known here, as in Germany, primarily for that massive trilogy, *Die Schlafwandler* (*The Sleepwalkers*, translated by Edwin and Willa Muir), which was first published in the early 1930s, and secondarily, to a more limited circle of readers, for *Der Tod des Vergil* (*The Death of Virgil*, translated by Jean Untermeyer), published just after the end of the war. The first of these two books is an outstanding narrative work; it earned Broch his reputation as an important writer; and it is the work by which he will be remembered. Yet it is not purely as a novelist that he must be assessed at the moment, now that his Collected Works have appeared. For despite the achievement of *Die Schlafwandler* and despite the assertion of his close friend, Hannah Arendt, that he was 'after all primarily a creative writer', he has left a record testifying both implicitly and explicitly to the contrary.

*   *   *

Broch made many very emphatic statements about his reluctance to commit himself to literature and about the ancillary function he allotted to it. Both such remarks as: 'What I don't get into my epistemology, mathematics, &c., turns into the novel-structures' (*Romangebilde*) and the Collected Works themselves demonstrate that although he was in later life forced, by a combination of circumstances and his undeniable literary gifts, into the position of a

HERMANN BROCH: *Gesammelte Werke*. Volume I: 263 pp. Swiss fr. 19.80. Volume II: 687 pp. Swiss fr. 26. Volume III: 541 pp. Swiss fr. 26. Volume IV: 599 pp. Swiss fr. 19.80. Volume V: 367 pp. Swiss fr. 19.80. Volume VI: 361 pp. Swiss fr. 19.80. Volume VII: 298 pp. Swiss fr. 19.80. Volume VIII: 459 pp. Swiss fr. 19.80. Volume IX: 443 pp. Swiss fr. 24.80. Volume X: 420 pp. Swiss fr. 24.80. Zurich: Rhein Verlag. ERICH KAHLER: *Die Philosophie von Hermann Broch*. 84 pp. Tübingen: J. C. B. Mohr (Paul Siebeck). DM. 8.60.

man of letters, he always thought of himself essentially as a mathematician and a philosopher. Also, although his friends and executors are not entirely astray in speaking of his mysticism, this term has to be understood in a sense so wide as to make it, again, almost meaningless; for what above all impelled and directed his work was a feeling not so much of religious as of moral urgency and—again in a very wide, one might say almost metaphysical, sense—political responsibility. He did not wish his work to be 'mere "literature"'.

There are radical differences between the German and the English approach to literature and learning, differences that we overlook only at the risk of some confusion. The German literary tradition is broken by appalling political upheavals and is therefore much shorter than ours. It begins, to all intents and purposes, only in the eighteenth century. This fact might seem irrelevant to the problem of the novel, which is, broadly, of eighteenth-century origin. But the point is that since that time the Germans have regarded both learning and literature with awe and tend to expect that literature should partake of the nature of learning; a situation the reverse of our own, for we expect learning to be informed with the graces of literature. For us, with a tradition as rich as it is long, there are not the same sharp distinctions between being beguiled, being elevated, and being instructed. It would be idle to discuss Broch's narrative writing without the premise that its aim is not to entertain or transport the reader but to instruct him.

*   *   *

Hermann Broch was born in Vienna in 1886. He read mathematics and philosophy at the university there, but was for a long time prevented from pursuing these studies further, as was his inclination, through having to take charge of the family textile-manufacturing business. He was in his forties and, as he once sardonically said, a captain of industry when he began to write his first novel, *Die Schlafwandler*. The next decade, that in which almost all his literary work originated, was one of financial crises and political terror. It was in the United States that he died in 1951, an exile honoured and supported by a number of foundations for the encouragement of art and scholarship, an honorary faculty-member of Yale University and having been recently proposed by the Pen Club for the Nobel Prize. (Unlike Thomas Mann, who had much earlier been awarded the Nobel Prize, Broch did not receive any honorary degrees, an honour that he wistfully thought would have been useful.)

It is doubtful whether he could have attained his somewhat esoteric reputation as a sage anywhere but in the United States, where his earnest striving for a central unifying value met with eager response, perhaps because many American intellectuals assume that these are things that can be constructed or at least uncovered by research. Broch himself does not seem to have believed that philosophical inquiry could be a direct means of approach to the fundamentals of which he was in search, yet he made it plain that if the direct approach had to be made through art, this was not because of art's primacy as a mode of experience but because art might serve as a substitute for religion when religion was not available. And for him art, specifically literary art, *Dichtung*, was as much didactic as heuristic.

*   *   *

His problems were representative, the problems of our age. Thus his novels are the works of a man who, if not a professional philosopher, wished to devote himself to mathematics and logic and yet found himself compelled by conscience to state the immediate problems—social, historical, mass-psychological, psychopolitical—as philosophically as possible. His narrative writing, which is varied and sometimes unusual, is not that of the story-teller, the impassioned portrayer of human destinies in terms of heart and action. To be fair to his novels other than *Die Schlafwandler* one should perhaps come to them only after making some acquaintance with his strictly theoretical writings. But it is not likely that many people will do so.

As early as 1906, when he was a student, Broch had been confronted by

The problem of the loss of the Absolute, the problem of that relativism for which there is no absolute truth, no absolute value and hence no absolute ethic, in short, the problem and the phenomenon of that gigantic Machiavellianism which has been intellectually developing for some fifty years and whose apocalyptic consequences we are experiencing today in reality.

During the 1920s he worked on a theory of values that enabled him, as he said, 'to break through crudely empirical relativism and re-establish the type of the objectivity valid value'. But 'the metaphysical need' remained, and the religious sphere, most truly the sphere of this need, was 'closed'. The fact that Broch, by birth a Jew, became a Roman Catholic on his marriage does not affect this (his extra-dogmatic position can be seen from, for instance, the description of the Easter Mass in *Der Versucher*, where the author's attitude is one of respectful detachment and the rite is made the occasion for a piece of prose-poetry in the manner of *Der Tod des Vergil*). That towards the end of his life he was apparently drawing closer to Judaism is relevant only in so far as it also testifies to what his friend Erich Kahler has emphasized: a profound striving towards oneness that is 'particularly intense in all great Jews, in Spinoza, in Marx, in Einstein, and even indeed in the renegade Paul'.

* * *

As Kahler's heterogeneous examples in *Die Philosophie von Hermann Broch* indicate, this striving, however intense, is not necessarily associated with a sense of the numinous. And this is indeed a sense in which Broch—in this as in much else a curious counterpart to his fellow-Austrian and contemporary, Robert Musil—was deficient. Thus, although he could say that 'the metaphysical need' is 'inextinguishably and eternally rooted' in the human soul and that the way into the soul 'has always been through art (*Dichtung*), art in its God-seeking mission', and gave this as 'doubtless' the first reason why, about 1930, he turned to a non-scientific, literary mode of expression, it is plain that he attached at least as much weight, if not more, to his 'second and actually more rational reason for doing so', namely that the literary medium has a 'directly ethical effect'. Such a duty-ridden attitude speaks for the moral seriousness of him who holds it; but as a principle on which to set out as a creative artist (one who, as Keats said, has a commission from Heaven), it is discouraging.

Nevertheless, the first product of this resolve to use literature as a means of exerting a moral influence is a very distinguished work. *Die Schlafwandler* (reviewed in *the T.L.S.* on 20 October 1932) traces the disintegration of values in Germany from 1888 to the revolution of 1918, and the three self-contained but inter-linking novels of the trilogy are written in three different styles, each intended to correspond to the spirit of the age.

The first, *Pasenow oder Die Romantik*, which portrays the insidious spiritual ruin of the Prussian *Junker*-class, is the most satisfying— possibly the nostalgic quality of the subject-matter opened up in Broch that vein of mournful simplicity, that awareness that the glories of our blood and state are shadows, not substantial things, which is characteristically Austrian. The general effect is at once urbane and unnerving, and nowhere more memorably so than in the final pages, which show Lieutenant von Pasenow and his bride on their wedding-night pensively avoiding consummation of their marriage.

*   *   *

The second novel, *Esch oder Die Anarchie*, which has all too often been called Joycean, already shows the faults arising from Broch's theory of the function of literature. The third, *Hugenau oder Die Sachlichkeit*, in spite of such *tours de force* as, for instance, the wounded officers' ball, with its fragments of bitter and pathetic dialogue, suffers further from theory, indeed from theorizing; for not only are the interpolated chapters entitled 'The story of the Salvation Army lass in Berlin' sometimes, in conformity with his theories, in verse, but also ten sections consist of an excursus, 'The Disintegration of Values', a philosophical intrusion that manifests itself also in the last pages. Broch once referred to this excursus as an important and original step towards creating the polymath novel. Posterity will draw its conclusions from the fact that these sections of the novel also appear in the second volume of his Essays.

If *Pasenow* is so remarkable as to suggest that Broch might have become a major novelist, the same cannot be said for *Die Unbekannte Grösse* (*The Unknown Quantity*, translated by the Muirs). It is a professionally but also perfunctorily written short book (completed in a few weeks) that has dated badly, and it is a relief to know that Broch was against letting it be reissued (it nevertheless appears in the Collected Works and has just been translated into Italian). Once again the reason for the weakness in Broch's treatment of his theme—here the mystery of the mathematical, indeed the ontological unknown quantity—lies in his theory of literature, which leads him to use his plot as an intellectual scheme, the characters being clichés. The curse of this theory becomes glaringly evident in *Die Schuldlosen*, a so-called novel that he put together after the war by manipulating several stories that his publisher wished to reissue in one volume and with which 'something had to be done'; they too are linked by some of those home-made verses that German writers for the past century have been so ready to run up on their sewing-machines. Although Broch at first had qualms about republishing his old stories, he was not only not embarrassed by the result, but even considered the process justified and provided the book with a note giving an account of it.

The hand of the theoretician, the constructor, is apparent in a different way in *The Death of Virgil*, the German text of which was published in 1945, simultaneously with Jean Untermeyer's English version made with Broch's collaboration. (It appears that Willa and Edwin Muir, Broch's devoted translators and friends, were so critical of the book that they preferred not to undertake the translation.) It presents the last day of Virgil's life, beginning with his arrival at Brindisi after the voyage from Athens with Augustus. Broch's own claim that few works in world literature have stalked the phenomenon of death so closely may be accepted with reserve, as may his assertion, put into the mouth of his American translator, that the book is 'almost untranslatable'. There are no adequate grounds for his declaring it to be an internal monologue—when in fact it contains much description, comment and explanation, interventions by the author—and that 'accordingly' it is a lyrical work, 'nothing but a poem'.

*   *   *

The disaster here originates in the assumption that a sufficient mass of 'fine writing' lifts a work from the solid ground of prose into the lyrical ether. These page-long sentences with their cottonwoolly thump of pointless repetition (both deplored by Aldous Huxley, who in one of his interesting letters to Broch called the book 'valuable socially') can, alas, often be read to the rhythm of Old Man Kangaroo. Two random but representative examples of the distension of style into verbiage are: 'Wann, ihr Götter! wann, o wann? o wann war sie . . . ' (page 418) and (in outline only), 'sie vermag. . . . , hingegen vermag sie nicht . . . , sie vermag es nicht, weil . . . weil . . . , weil . . . , weil all dies . . . zwiefach . . . , zwiefach . . . , zwiefach aber auch . . . ', &c., ending: 'oh . . . , unerreichbar der Dichtung, und doch, oh doch ihr erreichbar . . . ', &c., (page 208 f.). To suggest, as has wildly been done, that this style is comparable to that of Sir Thomas Browne can only indicate deafness to language.

What is so disappointing is that after his magnificent start with *Die Schlafwandler* Broch ceased to apply his appreciation of the values of language in narrative. How finely intelligent an appreciation it was can be seen from his long and detailed letter (*Briefe*, 397 ff.) to his French translator, on the necessity of extended translation, and from his essay on the art (significantly he does not call it the art, but 'the philosophy and technique') of translation, which contains a brilliant analysis, in the light of an attempted English version, of Claudius's poem, 'Der Mond ist aufgegangen'. Both letter and essay are urgently to be recommended to all English translators of German verse.

* * *

The blight of portentousness that eats at the very root of *Virgil* also creeps upon the posthumously edited *Der Versucher* (*The Tempter*), which is about the spell that a Hitler-like newcomer casts upon a mountain village in Tirol. This novel, which was intended to be the first in a religious trilogy, had through the years grown out of a short story. It is excessively long and may well raise the question to what extent a novel developed from a short story can be artistically successful. Much of the psychological detail is striking, and the descriptions of landscape and weather, which recall Stifter, show Broch at his simple best, as in the passage about the frosty air in the woods, at once crystalline, ethereal, and cosmic. It is the introduction of allegory in the early nineteenth-century romantic manner that overloads and before long sinks what might have been a good book, and the most damaging of the allegorical elements is Mother Gisson, a tediously folky old herb-gatherer who not only represents Mother Nature but also continually speaks in that role, uttering such wisdom as: 'The fear of a man is darkness, he shuns the snake that lies upon the ground, and longing is always for the far off light, the invisible light', and so on. Yet the theme is sufficiently important to keep the reader leafing through the book for scenes between the old doctor, who tells the story, and the villagers: little essays, in dialogue form, on such matters as tolerance, social justice, and the psychology of power.

Broch's novels, after *Die Schlafwandler*, are not likely to be read for long, except by the student of literature. While it is true, as Mr. Rayner Heppenstall has recently reminded us, that the novel as a form is infinitely elastic and that even the concept of the anti-novel (a term coined by the Seigneur de Souvigny in 1633) is inherently part of the tradition, a distinction must be made between the 'novel of ideas' that is written primarily out of a creative urge and one that is written primarily for the sake of the ideas. The first kind turns out to include all the great novels, from the rag-bag into which the writer stuffs anything he has to say—*Wilhelm Meister, Lavengro, Moby Dick*—to such elaborations of the precious particle as *The Wings of the Dove, The Possessed*, or *Emma*. But none of this was what Broch meant when, a few months after the publication of *Pasenow*, he wrote to his publisher: 'The age of the polymath novel has dawned' (*Briefe*, page 60). Had it in fact dawned any more then than at any other moment?

Broch went on to point out that what he meant was not what had already been done in novels by Gide, Thomas Mann, Musil, and Aldous Huxley, in all of which one finds 'the frightful device of "educated" talk as a means of getting the polymathy in', the information (*Bildung*) being apart from the novelist's 'real business', as it were a crystal block from which bits are constantly being chipped off to decorate the story. With this he contrasted the polymathy of Joyce, which was inimitable because his sovereign virtuosity was unique. Apparently unaware that Joyce was great not because of his learning, that his art emerged from what Joyce himself once called the mind of a grocer's assistant, and unaware that the 'frightful device' in two of the four cited cases was often stimulating and amusing. Broch used a device still more 'frightful', the excursus in *Hugenau*, which is a whole series of blocks and thus an impediment far larger than his contemporaries' chips.

While finishing *Die Schlafwandler* Broch wrote to a friend that what he was aiming at, although he had only hinted at it in the novel in progress, was

the '*epistemological novel*' instead of the psychological one, i.e., the novel in which there is exploration beyond psychological motivation, back to basic epistemological attitudes and to the real logic and plausibility of values, just as it has been philosophy's task to free itself of psychologism

(*Briefe*, page 23). What he was proposing was a novel about what he called the philosophical *Angst* that always obtrudes through the chink between 'I think' and 'thinking is going on'. (From the absence of editorial comment here it must be presumed that whatever manuscript of this novel existed was among those lost as a result of the Nazi search of Broch's house in Vienna when he was arrested and imprisoned in 1938.) What is disconcerting is that he could seriously have such intention while recognizing that behind what he called epistemological plausibility there were 'still further layers, layer upon layer full of myth', significantly adding: 'and *there* Joyce has already arrived'.

His respect for Joyce (whom he mentions very often and on whom he published a long and perceptive essay in 1936) led him to draw some infelicitous conclusions. On the one hand his admonition to a critic preparing an essay on his (Broch's) work that Joyce should not be mentioned casually in one breath with himself and Musil,

Joyce being infinitely superior to both, bears witness to his critical intelligence as much as to his integrity. On the other hand, since he was of a preponderantly theoretical constitution, the influence that Joyce's work, in particular *Ulysses*, had on him was of a theoretical and not of a seminal kind; it accounts for, among other things, the inordinate length of *Virgil* and for its uncertain, as opposed to subtly shifting, focus. Yet the sense of multidimensionality that enabled him to appreciate Joyce's musical and associative method is one of Broch's most remarkable gifts. It is also the gift that makes him worthy of investigation as a seeker after a new synthesis. For Broch did believe that there was a centre, even if it seemed to be lost; and, with all his reiterated respect for Joyce, the writer whom he most admired was Kafka, of whom he said that in his work the primal experience, i.e., the sense of the centre, remained intact (*Briefe*, page 282).

What had been done in modern painting, most particularly by Picasso, has been done in part, Broch said, by Joyce and Kafka in that they gave expression to 'a second reality' (*Briefe*, page 266). But this, as he said, represented only one aspect of a task that could perhaps never be fulfilled; the other was moral and political, and consequently a matter both of education and of action. Undoubtedly it was an increasingly urgent sense of the need for education that made him say, shortly before his untimely death, that he wished to devote whatever might be left of his life to finishing his theoretical works, 'simply because I regard them as more important than literature' (*Briefe*, page 416).

*   *   *

Action, which is always likely to be a problem for a writer, with Broch in his last years, as an exile, was of the invaluable but obscure kind which is acknowledged chiefly in obituaries. It is typical at once of his practical common sense and of his delicacy of conscience that at the end of the war he proposed that every 'C.A.R.E.-package' sent from the United States to Germany should be balanced by another sent to the countries recently enslaved by Hitler. In stressing that this was also politically right, as a measure to educate American public opinion, he also demonstrated once again that his political sense was moral, a sense of the humane.

The nucleus of 'the whole problem', he had written in 1938, lay in the realm of ethics and religion. Democracy, with its approximately adequate measure of humaneness in relations between the individual and society, he saw as doomed unless people could recognize and put an end to their indifference to one another's welfare. Modern man, he saw, moves about the technical world in a state of concussion that reduces him physically to a primitive level and thus exposes him to assaults of the irrational against which he is helpless. (One must regret that Broch wrote nothing expressly dealing with Jung's work.) In his awareness of the menace in this state of things—which he had experienced in person after the invasion of Austria by Nazi Germany—Broch in 1946 began 'A Study of Mass Hysteria', a project that was sponsored by Princeton's Office of Public-Opinion Research and financially supported by the Rockefeller Foundation. This undertaking was still in progress at his death.

It was an ambitious and specialized work, the ultimate purpose of which may be summed up in a passage from a letter of March 1946, a letter mainly on political matters of the day, as sad as it is penetrating, and which reveals the essential humanity of Broch's psychological and therefore of his political insight. Speaking of the swastikas on the walls of Yorkville, the German district of New York, he denied that the inhabitants' emotions were necessarily Nazi; but even if much of it was *Vaterland*-sentimentality, the result might be the same. He pointed out that the hysterical crowd-behaviour he had witnessed in Yorkville at the fall of Paris in 1940 was not specifically German, and added, 'What Yorkville is today, this whole country can be tomorrow' (*Briefe*, page 253). In short, his aim in the *Massenpsychologie*-project was 'the search for such possibilities of conversion as exist (do still exist) today'; and the word 'conversion' is a reminder that with Broch we are never very far from 'the realm of ethics and religion'.

A new spiritual synthesis must be achieved, he was convinced, if civilization is not to perish and human beings are not to become 'brutalized half-beasts'. Time was running short, not only his own but also the world's time. In his last years, immediately after the end of the war, the urgency of his self-imposed task drove him, an ailing man in his sixties, with seven books on hand and an enormous correspondence that he felt it was his duty to deal with often at great length, to reduce his sleeping hours to five. Yet his dread of 'not being able to finish in time' does not in the least seem to have been obsessive. His many references to it, though sometimes accompanied by realistic remarks about the necessity of attaining an academic position and hence financial security, are singularly devoid of hysteria, and this is obviously because he recognized his need to say what he still had to say as an expression of 'a metaphysical, irrational compulsion that is connected with some sort of notion of spiritual salvation'.

* * *

Together with the Essays, the Letters will be for many readers the most interesting part of the Collected Works. They are also the most attractive, above all those to Edwin and Willa Muir (hers to him, which he said were the most charming he had ever received, have not been traced). These latter are to be found not in the *Briefe* volume, but in Volume X. This is merely one example of the exasperating way in which these Works have been arranged. While it is much to the credit of publishers and executors that the ten handsome and compact volumes contain scarcely a misprint, even in the many pages of text extant only in Broch's laborious English, acquired after the age of fifty, it is not helpful to supply only a general index at the end of Volume X, with references to the other volumes, by numbers, when only Volume X has received a number; the clue to the missing numbers is tucked away on page 419 f. (not on page 421 as stated at the head of the index). If there is another edition, these faults should be mended. Further, the deplorable word *Jargon* in the notes to the Letters, which precede the translations of Yiddish words, or of Hebrew words current in Yiddish, should be replaced by a true description; the fact that when educated Central-European Jews, who are rarely Yiddish speakers, use such words it is usually with mildly humorous overtones does not excuse the silliness, much less diminish the offensiveness, of equating Yiddish with pidgin or thieves' slang. Broch would surely have objected.

Hermann Broch embodied what a friend of his called *politesse du cœur*. He had a peculiarly unselfish awareness of the dignity of others and the attention that should be accorded to their efforts, and wore himself out with, as much as anything, his efforts on behalf of others, not only other victims of the Nazis and of the war, but also, most admirably, other writers. Whatever view may be taken of his own last intention, to contribute to evolving a political philosophy that, as he believed, could be the most effective means of combating Marxism in that it would be a similarly close-knit and consistent system, this project too was in the last resort an attempt to answer his fundamental question, the profoundly moral question that is at once politically and mystically of desperate urgency: 'What are we to do?'

L

SIR.—The failures of sympathy and critical insight in your front-page article of Hermann Broch should not pass unchallenged.

Though he was, indeed, revered and loved by a circle of friends, and had received occasional support from scholarly foundations, Broch died under circumstances of solitude and financial stringency. He was not 'an honorary faculty-member of Yale University', but simply an honorary fellow of one Yale college. Contrary to hopes and expectations expressed on Broch's behalf, this association carried no stipend. He died alone in a coldwater flat in New Haven.

To assert that *Die Schlafwandler* is Broch's greatest work is to deny those achievements which are most original and most distinctive of his genius. *Der Versucher* is one of two major German novels to grapple with the spiritual and psychological roots of the coming of the night. It is, perhaps, an even greater achievement than *Doktor Faustus*, because Broch goes deeper than Mann and seeks to apprehend the mystery of Hitler's own daemonic force. Though incomplete, *Der Versucher* ranks among the finest novels of the twentieth century, both through its treatment of nature and of the diverse modes of human love. The famous episode of the narrator's love affair with Dr. Barbara would, alone, justify the belief in Broch's classic stature.

Your reviewer's account of *The Death of Virgil*, by way of a few snippets, is irresponsible. To many of the few who have actually read the whole work, let alone wrestled with its intense stylistic originality, it seems the only advance beyond Joyce in the matter of technical form. Though Broch himself regarded Joyce as the master, *The Death of Virgil* may, in fact, have achieved that realization of the quick of inner consciousness and of the life of sleep, of which *Finnegans Wake* gives only a fragmentary, stylized version.

The book is built in the manner of a quartet, and the language renders with uncanny precision alternances of key, mood, and cadence, such as are inherent in musical notation. The last movement—Virgil's entrance into death—carried speech to its exact limit: silence. Like Wittgenstein's *Tractatus* and the works of Kafka (with both of which *The Death of Virgil* has notable affinities), Virgil's meditation on the inadequacies of the word poses the central dilemma for the modern artist; what can we *say* in the face of present inhumanity? Can we speak, without making language corrupt or blind, of what is unspeakable?

Because it asks that question (in a form which is, paradoxically, of immense eloquence). *The Death of Virgil* is crucial to Broch's achievement. In Virgil's plea that the *Aeneid* be destroyed Broch prefigured his own turn toward sociology and toward mathematics—that other language of silence. But his life had in it a marvellous unity of design. The genius of the artist and the haunted nobility of the man are inseparable. To say that 'Broch might have become a major novelist' is an absurd epitaph: the work lives to deny it.

GEORGE STEINER

Churchill College, Cambridge.

SIR.—Mr. George Steiner finds 'failures of sympathy and critical insight' in my article on Hermann Broch (29 March).

I am surprised and sorry that anyone should overlook the respect I was at pains to express for Broch as a significant figure of our time. As for 'critical insight', this is what we often feel to be lacking in those who do not share our partisan passions. I see no profit in arguing with Mr. Steiner, who, while admitting that 'few' have 'actually read' the whole of *The Death of Virgil* during the twenty years of its existence, 'let alone wrestled with' the virtues that he sees in it, nevertheless contends that Broch's work 'lives to deny' my view that the later novels are not likely ever to be much read. Surely a literary work 'lives' only in the sense that it is constantly read over a long period?

I regret having taken on trust a slightly inaccurate description of Broch's honorary status at Yale, though it is presumably clear that any honorary position 'carried no stipend'. The financial stringency of Broch's last years has no bearing, however, on the nature of his literary achievements.

Mr. Steiner is scarcely doing Broch a service by seeking to inflate his literary importance at the cost of what was indisputably important in this remarkable man.

YOUR REVIEWER

SIR.—Recently, from three different sources, I received copies of your 29 March issue, with its leading article, 'A Writer's Conscience'. I was too ill at the time to answer it, and meanwhile, in your issue of 19 April, George Steiner has called attention to its major inadequacies. Since your policy is to print your articles unsigned, I must rely on your fairness to print the following, in order to correct some errors of fact, not covered in George Steiner's letter.

On page 210 (29 March) your reviewer wrote: ('It appears that Willa and Edwin Muir, Broch's devoted translators and friends, were so critical of the book [*The Death of Virgil*] that they preferred not to undertake the translation'.) The facts are as follows: Broch wrote to Willa Muir in October 1940—letter in Volume 10 of the *Gesamtausgabe*—in what he, with self irony, called 'a kind of English' that he hoped the Muirs would translate the *Virgil*, which was then being read at the Viking Press. But he warned that there was little likelihood that enough money would be forthcoming to compensate for the immense labour of translating a prose-poem of nearly 500 pages. Subsequently, Broch told me that he had ceased to hear from the Muirs. It is understandable that the Muirs would not wish to undertake such a long and exacting work without guarantee of a commensurate recompense; it is unthinkable that they, with their sensitivity and wide culture, would not recognize the stature of *The Death of Virgil*. More than that, it is highly questionable that, even though they themselves were not its translators, they would cast misprision upon it. That, it seems, was the unjustified inference of your reviewer who, of course, has the right to be wrong.

Early in the summer of 1940, Broch wrote to me at the MacDowell

Colony, where I was correcting proof on *Love and Need*, my own book of poems that appeared in November 1940. He said he had showed the manuscript of the *Virgil* to Stefan Zweig, who said: 'This is the greatest thing to come out of Europe in the last hundred years. Too bad, it is untranslatable.' (That stricture came from Zweig and was not 'put in the mouth of his translator' by Broch.) Since I had already translated the five Elegies on Fate, Broch showed these to Zweig, who (so Broch wrote me) exclaimed: 'Unbelievable! This is your only chance.'

When the Muirs failed to respond to several letters of Broch, he—an almost penniless refugee, deeply perturbed by the war—was in a panic. He begged me: 'Since you were so successful with the Elegies, please try to do the first ten pages so that Huebsch [then the vice-president of Viking Press] will see it *can* be translated. Otherwise, he will take Zweig's word for it.' I was dismayed and reluctant. But his plight awoke my compassion and with great difficulty I completed the ten pages. Whereupon Broch wheedled: 'Ten pages are so little. Finish the first twenty-five pages. That is the end of the section, and would make sense.' Before the twenty-five pages were completed Viking Press rescinded their option. I kept on, at Broch's pleading, believing and hoping that the Muirs would again get in touch with their friend and author. This did not happen. The story of the translation that was literally forced upon me is a long one that I have written into a literary memoir that I hope soon to finish. It is enough to say here that as I persevered, with no contract or hope of remuneration, I became so fascinated by the book and so dedicated to it, that it was my constant task of from ten to fifteen hours daily for nearly five consecutive years. My only 'vacations' came in the form of nervous breakdowns. Rebuffed and ridiculed by practical friends and family with 'Why are you not in Washington, using your writing gifts for the government and making some money besides?' I had only this extenuation. 'When the Napoleonic wars were despoiling Europe, two geniuses laboured steadily at their appointed tasks. Today, we have ceased to prize Napoleon but know the work of Goethe and Beethoven as precious heritages. I believe the same will come to pass with Broch.'

While it may be that few people read Broch in England the same is not true in America. The English version of *The Death of Virgil* has long been sold out, and second-hand copies, hard to come by, are at a premium. I have received a number of letters from readers who treat this book as a kind of modern scripture, reading and rereading it for its revelations and its relevance to their own lives. They thank me for having made it available to them in their own language.

JEAN STARR UNTERMEYER

235 East 73rd Street, New York City 21, N.Y., U.S.A.

Sɪʀ.—With reference to Hermann Broch's *The Death of Virgil*, may I say that it was entirely because I did not like it that I jibbed at translating it? Possible remuneration did not enter into the question. Had I liked it, with the enthusiastic appreciation I felt any work of literature must have from a translator if it is to be well translated, I should have taken it on. *The Death of Virgil* was, and remains, a blind spot of mine.

Well before October 1940 I made this clear to Broch. This I am certain of, because in the summer of 1940 I was very ill and nearly died in a St. Andrews hospital. When I came out, I was in no shape to undertake anything, not even to write or answer letters. But well before then I had told Broch, impertinently, that *The Death of Virgil* was a tombstone on Virgil, with other even more impertinent remarks which I think Hermann rather enjoyed; at least, I hope so.

Edwin did not like the book any more than I did. Your reviewer was justified in saying that the Muirs were critical of it.

WILLA MUIR

Priory Cottage, Swaffham Prior, Cambridge.

18
ANTE OR ANTI GATTOPARDO?
WRITING AND SICILY

THE SUCCESS ALL ROUND the globe of Giuseppe Tomasi di Lampedusa's *Il Gattopardo* (*The Leopard*) has had a stimulating effect on
Sicilians which is oddly at variance with the fatalism of the book
itself. This is particularly noticeable in Palermo. For the first time
for nearly two centuries, since the days of the dialect poet Giovanni
Meli, the inhabitants of the island capital are becoming conscious of a
literary life of their own, distinct from that of Catania or even
Agrigento. Flaccovio, the Palermo publisher who is the most enter-
prising on the island, has for years been producing, in collaboration
with the Regional Government, a magazine, *Sicilia*, which is quite
outstanding typographically and artistically. His pioneering volumes
on living Sicilian folk-lore are splendidly illustrated, yet scarcely known
abroad. Recently, with *Il Gattopardo*, book and now film, focusing
attention on Palermo and its environs, a new Italian and foreign
interest is beginning to produce results that seem likely to spread.

What, till now, has been considered to attract the more-or-less
civilized visitor to Sicily can be seen by a glance into a bookseller's
window in Taormina at the height of the summer season. On display
would be one or two of those large picture books on Greek-Sicilian
temples, usually seen against orange-blossom; nothing remotely
satisfactory on more modern architecture, apart from an unexpected
book on Sicilian castles, no volumes on, say, 'Exasperated' Sicilian
baroque or on the villas of the Conca d'Oro. History, until Mr. Denis
Mack Smith produces his long-awaited book, is even barer; the old
'Garden of the Mediterranean' type of travelogue, in which the
author mingled what the *carrozziere* told him with, often, a considerable knowledge of the island's classical history, is now out of date.

GIUSEPPE MAGGIORE: *Sette e Mezzo*. 430 pp. Palermo: Flaccovio. L. 2,400.
ANDREA VITELLO: *I Gattopardi di Donnafugata*. 300 pp. Palermo: Flaccovio.
L. 3,500. LEONARDO SCIASCIA: *Il Consiglio d'Egitto*. 185 pp. Turin: Einaudi.
L. 1,200.

No British Arabist has ever taken more than a superficial interest in the centuries of Arab occupation. To cover the gaps there is only Mr. Vincent Cronin's admirable *The Golden Honeycomb* (the bookseller's window will show copies in two or three languages) with its splendid pages, rather *à thèse*, on the Norman kingdom.

To Sicilians, a concentration on their classic or Arab Norman past by visitors to their island could also be a bitter-sweet reminder of days when it was at the centre of civilization, functioned as one of the great crucibles or catalysts. To offset this, and rub their noses in an unwelcome present, that bookseller's window might show, tucked away discreetly to one side, a more recent foreign interest; translations of Danilo Dolci's factual if one-sided accounts of horrors in western Sicily, Gavin Maxwell's nordic exploitations of the same subject. The Mafia is becoming a growing and justifiable obsession, in which even mainland Italians see a reflection of the worst in themselves. But Sicilians are a self-critical people, and few visiting writers or journalists today avoid being asked their opinion of the Mafia, or, such is the fascination of the subject in northern climes, on returning home telling many a spicy tale about that most grisly of living European folk-lores.

Il Gattopardo, though the Mafia is mentioned in it so glancingly as to be discernible only by initiates, has opened up Sicily again in historical perspective. With it some of the old catalyst quality has come back; 1860, the year of Garibaldi's Thousand, has begun to take on to the outside world something of the sense of crystallized change, of epoch-making myth, accorded so far in the west to the American Civil War. To Sicilian writers the Year of Unification and those immediately before and after have been a source of inspiration for three-quarters of a century; long before Lampedusa nearly every major island novelist, from De Roberto and Verga to Pirandello, wrote at least one book in which the crisis of 1860 was a main theme. But never until now has this crisis begun to be seen as of almost universal interest. Once again poetry, in this case Lampedusa's, looks like being an unacknowledged legislator.

One effect in Sicily has been retrospective. This spring another novel on the same period, written in Palermo just over a decade ago, and originally published at the author's expense in 1952, when it passed quite unnoticed, has suddenly been discovered and is now arousing interest all over Italy. Flaccovio, who first recommended *Il Gattopardo* to Mondadori and Einaudi, now republishes *Sette e Mezzo* himself. This is a long, discursive novel about Palermo in the

years immediately after the Unification, and the troubles that cul-
minated in the abortive, and little known, popular revolt against the
Piedmontese that lasted seven and a half days in 1866—hence the
title. What has helped to focus attention on it are a few, if undoubted,
resemblances to *Il Gattopardo*.

The chief character, or what appears to be until the author almost
loses sight of him in his ramblings, is a massive Marchese called Don
Fabrizio; we find him brooding in his palace about family and politics
while awaiting Mass; he has a nephew who represents the new times,
with a name, like Tancredi's in *Il Gattopardo*, taken from Ariosto,
Goffredo. But, unlike the Prince of Salina's nephew, Goffredo is an
idealist rather than an opportunist, and through him we follow Garibaldi's second descent on Sicily that ended disastrously at Aspro-
monte in 1862. The resemblances between the two books do not go
much further, though to a non-Sicilian eye backgrounds and references are apt to link. Maggiore's inspiration ranges from D'Annunzio
to Manzoni, his style is sometimes crisp, at times witty, then diffuse
and descriptive, then didactic. Donna Teodora, Don Fabrizio's wife,
is a self-destroyer reminiscent of one of those heroines of Roman
high-life at the turn of the century, and there are some splendid, if
rather exterior, set pieces of her at a ball (for the British fleet, at
what looks like the old Palazzo Butera), at a theatre, at a 'fox-hunt-
ing'. Suddenly we leave these cloying splendours for a long glimpse of
the Sicilian countryside, and a description of an attempt at distributing a feudal estate to peasants which ends in the owner panicking
and putting the restoration of order into the hands of the local Mafia.
Finally, in the last fifty pages, comes the revolution itself, the disillusionment of Goffredo (who eventually searches for a saintly Capu-
chin amid a cholera epidemic like Renzo in Manzoni's *I Promessi
Sposi*), and the funeral of Donna Teodora. In these last pages there is
genuine compassion though not, alas, the artistry that Lampedusa
put into the expression of his bitterness.

That Lampedusa must have read this book, which came out just two
years before he began his own, there seems no doubt; and controversy
is still going on in Palermo about how well he and its author knew each
other. Professor Maggiore, one of the most distinguished experts on
penal law in Italy and at one time rector of Palermo University, with-
drew to private life after being relieved of his appointments in 1944
as an active Fascist. He died in 1956. Lampedusa was never a Fascist,
or a Separatist as the other seems to have been, too. But just as the

Prince wrote from a poetic conviction of decay due to being a member of the dying class he was describing, so the Professor, though seeing the same class from the outside, wrote from an inner pressure to express his own experience in historical form. No artist of the same calibre, Maggiore obviously loved his native island, and his novel is full of details, comments, information, about its customs, ambience, and history, all apparently authentic. It would be a pity if what the Italians calls a *caso* were made out of its few resemblances to *Il Gattopardo*. Like the theme of the times, the pattern of reactionary uncle, modern nephew, and family chaplain (Don Azzardi in *Sette e Mezzo* is far more of an intriguer that Don Pirrone in *Il Gattopardo*) was after all quite usual in such Sicilian families of the period. And one of the mysteries of inspiration about Lampedusa's novel is that nearly every character, Don Pirrone included, was taken down to the details of names from his own family history and then transposed into the land of poetry.

This world of Lampedusa's background has now been explored to almost every available detail by Dr. Andrea Vitello in his imposing tome, *I Gattopardi di Donnafugata*. Signor Vitello is a doctor practising in the town, Palma di Montechiaro, which was once the centre of the Tomasi di Lampedusa family estates; he does not mention it is now such a horror-spot that visitors are often dissuaded from going there, or explain that its condition now is largely due to grants made to the Church by past Tomasis, and so to the effects of the expropriation of Church property in 1862. Here, amid the open drains and the decaying balustrades. Dr. Vitello traces every prancing and legless leopard on the coat-of-arms, follows every detail of the family history, tracks down names, stories, buildings, mentioned in the novel. There is an admirable opening preamble on the word 'gattopardo', the animals concerned, the North African and American hunting-leopards (he does not mention the Indian hunting-leopard or cheetah, an exact translation whose Sanscrit origins precluded its use as the English title of the novel). He plunges fearlessly into heraldry, adds detailed genealogical tables. Every adventure of the manuscript is given, with the help of information supplied by the author's widow, friends (names given), publishers. Dr. Vitello also supplies a rather sketchy biography, and some comments on Lampedusa's character based on his own experience as a doctor and psychiatrist. There is a bibliography (not, however, of articles, many of which are mentioned in the text), and elaborate indexes.

It is a scattered, diffuse work, a labour of enthusiasm and love. But it is not the book of a writer, nor does it say the last word on the subject. Though Dr. Vitello attempts a review of the novel's political implications seen against the background of Sicily, he does not approach any literary assessment, or try to place *Il Gattopardo* in modern writing, either Italian or European. Nor has he ventured among the shoals of literary controversy about the book still rife in Italy, a subject which would make a wry study in itself. Such mistakes as there are do not seem of any particular importance, though it should perhaps be put on record that the Princess of Lampedusa, the author's widow, objects to some of Dr. Vitello's conclusions about her husband's religion and finances. Some of his facts also need cross-checking. There is no mention of Monsignor Potino, chaplain for twenty years to the Lampedusa sisters, now secretary of the Sicilian Società di Storia Patria and a fount of accurate family information. And Dr. Vitello must have been warned off investigation into the origins of the Angelica of the novel; by failing to brave this jungle he has not quoted two important extant letters by Lampedusa on the subject. A defect general to all Italian biography is that the central figure has no background, no setting in place and period; one would like to know more, for instance, of the effect on Lampedusa of the Allied landings of 1943. But the book is a gold-mine for the writers of theses.

As an amateur and an enthusiast, Dr. Vitello shows the defects of his qualities. He has followed the labels given by a photographic agency in Palermo which has been distributing old photographs (one has even appeared in the *New York Times*) of various Palermo houses as those of the destroyed Palazzo Lampedusa, and gives a double page of interiors which were in fact those of Palazzo Butera. In the controversy which has been raging for the past three years about the setting of Donnafugata between Palma di Montechiaro and Santa Margherita Belice he lets himself go in *campanilismo* for his native town. One can only hope that this internecine struggle will soon reach a peaceful conclusion without (for tourist money as well as prestige now begins to be involved) the intervention of the Mafia, which already last year prevented the director Luchino Visconti from using Palma for his outdoor shots of Donnafugata in the film.

We always come back to the Mafia, in Sicily now. One of the leading young Sicilian writers, Leonardo Sciascia, whose novel on it, *Il Giorno della Civetta*, was one of last year's best-sellers and has now inspired an excellent play, enters the new lists with an historical novel about Palermo, *Il Consiglio d'Egitto*. His political supporters have not hesitated to call this 'l'anti-Gattopardo'. Certainly of any of the books linked to Lampedusa's this is the most diametrically opposed in spirit. As if to emphasize his detachment, Signor Sciascia has set his novel a hundred years earlier, in the Palermo of the 1780s and 1790s. Perhaps more than a novel he has tried to write a modern parable in terms of history. 'Il Consiglio d'Egitto' was the name given to a document, purporting to have been drawn up by the Norman kings of Sicily, which disproved, on the eve of the French Revolution, the hitherto sacrosanct feudal rights of the nobles over their lands. It was in fact a complete fabrication by a certain Abate Vella, who had been encouraged in this enterprise by his successful forgery of an Arab document called 'Il Consiglio di Sicilia'. The subject, which is an authentic story, gives Signor Sciascia a chance to paint a convincing picture of the mentality of Sicilian nobles at the time (and, it is to be feared, often now), and give some brilliant 'genre' sketches of Palermo social and literary life. But behind it he has a serious rationalist purpose, never quite worked out. A moment during the faking Abate's trial gives a young Palermo lawyer, Di Blasi, an intuition about honesty which eventually leads him (with a summary break in narrative) into a Jacobin conspiracy which is also historical fact. He is tortured and executed and the Abate, now alas with no basis in history, has a change of heart. This is an impressive sketch by a writer of whom more will be heard; but Signor Sciascia seems to be trying to dig deeper than he can with the tools he allows himself, and we are left with what looks like a teasing essay in Marxist dialectics.

Il Gattopardo, gattupardù, the ghepard, the pard, *panthera pardus nanopardus* (Dr. Vitello lists them all) could not range much farther.

*   *   *

Correspondence on 16 August 1963 included a letter from Mr. Gavin Maxwell, querying the term 'exploitations'. The reviewer replied that he was speaking of artistic exploitation only.

19

THE SADDEST STORY

MR. MOOREHEAD LOOKS HOMEWARD

FOR BATHOS FEW OTHER nations' stories can hold a spluttering candle to the history of Australia. Of the aeons that preceded the arrival of the *Duyfken* in 1606 we know virtually nothing, because the aboriginal inhabitants of the land never learnt how to write: of the centuries since we remember almost as little, because nothing in particular has happened. There have been no frontier wars, no blazing revolutions, no great movements of religion, no catastrophes, no soaring triumphs, no hilarities and few great men. Independence came to Australia in slow easy stages. The world wars summoned her splendid soldiers to Gallipoli and Tobruk, but scarcely reached her own shores. To contemporary events her principal contributions have been made on the track, at the wicket, in the swimming pool, or by her myriad gifted expatriates. She is a prodigy indeed, but prodigious chiefly, for all her images of beer and beaches, in an albino kind—pale, blue-eyed, and rather eerie.

Thus in all the range of literature few forms of composition are duller than an Australian history-book, and there are perhaps only three purely Australian episodes that can instantly capture the artistic imagination. One is the complete disappearance of Ludwig Leichhardt's expedition in 1847, the inspiration of Mr. Patrick White's *Voss*. Another is the saga of the bush-ranger Ned Kelly, the subject of Mr. Sydney Nolan's famous series of paintings. The third is the first crossing of the continent from south to north, achieved by the Burke and Wills expedition in 1860; and it is this tragic story which Mr. Alan Moorehead, returning at last to his native land, has now enshrined in *Cooper's Creek*.

Australia is still an emptiness; a vast brown slab of nothing, inhabited only on its fringes. The Australian, said D. H. Lawrence, is 'always aware of the vast empty spaces of his own consciousness: like his country, a vast empty desert in the centre of him'. Even now there

ALAN MOOREHEAD: *Cooper's Creek*. 222 pp. Hamish Hamilton. 30s.

is something flat, pallid and monotonous to most things in Australia, despite the grandeur of her size and the pungency of her isolation. Whether the visionaries are right in prophesying a glittering future for her, or the cynics in supposing that she is never going to come to much, she will always feel incomplete, unfulfilled. She will always be mostly desert. There will always be something dry and drained to her, a feeling that, as her spindly aborigines dream away the days and her kangaroos leap and lollop through the twilight, something stood still, long ago in Australia, and has never budged since.

It is this sense of hush that Mr. Moorehead now evokes, for of those three events the story of Burke and Wills is much the most hauntingly suggestive. Leichhardt disappeared, and that was that. Kelly was a thug, and was riddled with bullets in the hotel at Glenrowan. But the expedition led by Robert O'Hara Burke and William John Wills had as its climax a moment of ironic tragedy. The two leaders—one a showy Irishman, the other a Devonian of scientific bent—had established a depot at Cooper's Creek, in the very heart of Australia, and had set off with two others to complete the journey to the Gulf of Carpentaria. They hoped to return to the Creek, rejoin the depot party, and go home all together, refreshed with supplies and mounted on fresh horses. Burke's instructions were, however, unwritten and often vague. They were four months on the journey to the coast, and on 21 April 1861 William Brahe, the depot commander, decided that they had either perished or were returning to the south by another route. He therefore packed up his camp and set off for Adelaide. Just nine hours later the explorers, reduced to three by the death of Charley Gray, stumbled into Cooper's Creek. They were almost starving and terribly exhausted, but all they found was a message carved on a coolibah tree, and a small cache of food buried beneath it.

To every Australian, this is a supremely familiar moment of the national epic, heavily immortalized in a picture by Sir John Longstaff and a gigantic statue by Charles Summers (which was itself portrayed, for many years, in every school-reader in the State of Victoria). Burke and Wills both died as they struggled on from the Creek, only their loyal assistant John King surviving, by the kindness of the aborigines, to tell the tale and point out the graves. There was a Royal Commission of Inquiry, and a long bandying of recriminations. The route to the north so painfully pioneered presently opened up great new grazing grounds and orefields. It is that one day at Cooper's Creek, though, that has branded itself upon the public mind—were it not

for the accident of tragedy, Burke and Wills would now be almost
forgotten. Any Australian who stood before the Longstaff painting
as a child, says Mr. Moorehead, will recall the emotions it aroused.
'Death on the field of glory, one felt, must be a very fine thing, and
death in bed very bearable. But this was just death, stark, despairing,
and meaningless, the monster in the dark'.

Stark, despairing, meaningless; yet this is the episode that Mr
Moorehead has chosen to depict as, in the full powers of maturity,
he turns his great gifts to bear upon his own country. He has described
for us, in the past, the glories and miseries of Gallipoli. He has
roistered through the marvellous adventures of the Nile, consorting
with many a bewhiskered greatheart and surviving many a bloody
skirmish. He has written about Lord Montgomery and other wild
life, about the desert wars, about the Russian Revolution, about
Italy. For such a writer, at the peak of such abilities, the whole world
stands waiting, like a royal family before a Velazquez; yet Mr.
Moorehead has chosen that one moment at Cooper's Creek, that one
knell of Australian tragedy, and has built around it a chronicle of
events that are mostly tedious, men who are mostly ordinary, and
landscapes which contain, now as then, nothing whatsoever. Perhaps
he did not wish to epitomize the history of Australia; but in his
calm and elegant way that is precisely what he has done—with six
pages of drama embedded in monotony.

He belongs, of course, to the nation of artists, who can seldom be
pinned down to race or creed, and stand far above any footling
restraints of origin. Now that he is writing about Australia, all the
same, it is curious how Australian he turns out to be. His clarity
and straightforwardness are perhaps specifically Australian, and
perhaps specifically Australian, and so is his lack of humour; but
most of all it is a certain stillness of style, poised somewhere between
dream-time and disillusion, that marks him, now one comes to think
of it, as a man touched by the wide melancholy of Australia. Mr.
Moorehead can often, almost in spite of himself, move the susceptible
reader to tears: and so can Australia, too, so strange and lonely is
her quality, and so tinged with disappointment.

'Often for months at a time nothing of consequence happens,
lizards scuttle about the tombstones in the sunshine and time goes
by in an endless dream.' Mr. Moorehead was writing about the ceme-
teries of Gallipoli, forty years after the evacuation, but is there not a
hint, in the sad cadence of that sentence, of the Outback over his

shoulder—so still, so timeless, so empty? In all Mr. Moorehead's books one comes across such sudden pools of contemplative and passive quiet—a sort of cool stagnancy, into which the narrative, whether it is dealing with war, politics or adventure, sinuously slides for a moment or two of repose. It is as though every now and then Mr. Moorehead, so vigorously professional a writer, succumbs to some old instinct of soil or heredity—that 'vast empty desert at the centre of him'—and looks behind him to the distant south.

Beautifully accomplished though these passages are, in his previous books they have often struck an anomalous note, as though the author's own personality, normally so unobtrusive, has momentarily pushed its way into the theme, and held up the flow with a block of emotion. In *Cooper's Creek* they feel altogether at home; indeed so threadbare is the story itself, so desolate its setting, that their effect is reversed, and they seem to bring new life to the chronicle. In his books about the Nile Mr. Moorehead matched himself, willy-nilly, against some of the most strikingly colourful characters ever to stride across the human chronicles—and some of the best story-tellers, too. Burton had the wit that Mr. Moorehead lacks; Baker could tell a tale almost as well; Stanley was a reporter of the first class; Livingstone, Slatin Pasha, Gordon, Napier, Mohammed Ali, the Emperor Theodore of Ethiopia and Napoleon Bonaparte himself—these were characters such as few novelists would have the temerity to invent, and no historian, taking them on in a body, could hope to dominate.

Much the most interesting man in *Cooper's Creek*, however, is Alan Moorehead. The cast of the drama itself is mostly humdrum and often sordid. Burke was an Irishman of conventional mould, dashing, attractive, and careless. Wills was an Englishman of the worthy kind—always brave, always diligent, never inspiring. The lesser characters are embroiled in petty ambition, inefficiency, rivalry, and misunderstanding. Most of them, far from dying in the odour of glory, petered out into obscurity, and the only member of the expedition who seems to have been graced with any creative talent was the German naturalist, Dr. Ludwig Becker, who perished on the march—'too gentle a man', says Mr. Moorehead, 'to engage in all this violence'—and whose sketches *en route* oddly prefigure, in their sense of lonely immobility, the painting by Mr. Nolan that also illustrates this book. Faced with all the bickering mediocrity of the tale, from the pompous nonentities of the organizing committee to the dubious evidence presented to the royal commission, one can only settle in one's chair with pleasurable relief, when for a paragraph or two we are left alone with the author, to see that wilderness through his kind and honest eyes, and watch the lilac kingfishers come winging down the creek.

For out of *Cooper's Creek*, as from the legend of Ned Kelly, there emerges some of the meanness that has pinched the history of Australia, and has sprung, no doubt, partly from the ghastly inhospitality of the interior. It is sap that is missing from the Australian past: the fructifying sap of religious conviction, such as took the Pilgrims to America, or the stimulating sap of political aspiration, that nourished the Jeffersons and the Bolivars on the other side of the world. There is a disgruntlement to the Australian spirit, and it is doubly reflected in this book; first, by the awful disappointment of the Outback, which offered those desperate explorers such arid prizes; secondly, by the feeling that one party had failed the other, that somebody else was to blame, that the orders had been wrong, or the plan misconceived, or the organizers negligent. The story, says Mr. Moorehead,

perfectly expresses the early settlers' deeply-felt idea that life was not so much a struggle against other men as against the wilderness—that wilderness that made all men equal anyway. The quarrel, basically, was with nature, and to be 'let down' by a companion when one was out in the hard, implacable bush and absolutely exposed—this was the final treachery.

Australia's first struggle is still against nature, against the inescapable presence of the wastelands, and it is the lack of national fulfilment that this book, dealing as it does with the events of a century ago, still most poignantly embodies. It is much more than the story of an ill-conducted adventure: it is the emptiness and loneliness of Australia, packed between stout boards, and skilfully indexed. Mr. Moorehead rightly describes it as 'a story of predestined anticlimax', and it is all too proper that Burke and Wills, though they succeeded in crossing the continent, never did set eyes on the northern sea; the mangrove swamps were in the way, it was raining miserably, and they contented themselves with tasting the saltness of a creek, and watching the tides raise its level.

> O True Romance, whose splendour gleams
> Across the shadowy realm of dreams
> Whose starry wings can touch with light
> The dull grey path, the common themes;
> Hast not thou thrilled with sovereign might
> Our story, until Duty's flame
> Is one with Fame?

Thus the poet George Essex Evans once honoured the State of Queensland, upon whose northern shore Burke and Wills achieved this bathetic moment of success; but the splendour has not often gleamed, and those starry wings are sometimes drably furled. Mr. Moorehead, like Mr. Nolan, has sought to master the gauntness of Australia by transmuting it into art; and so he has, cobber, so he has.

20

IN HOMER'S WAKE

'HEUREUX QUI, comme Ulisse, a fait un beau voyage.' The quotation is inescapable, for what Mr. Bradford has made is a profitable voyage, or rather a series of them. To voyage hopefully at the helm of one's own sailing boat in the Mediterranean is without doubt a better thing to do, from the point of view of the doer, that to write another book about the *Odyssey*, but he has managed both feats. His particular achievement in *Ulysses Found* is to have brought down Odyssean studies to a new level. This may seem ambiguous praise, but not so when the level referred to is eye-level in a small boat. From this privileged point of view Mr. Bradford can see with an Homeric eye. His descriptions of landfalls and harbours, of winds and currents, are authentic. He is indeed justified in his claim that the sailor can contribute more than the scholar to the solution of Iron Age geographical problems even though his identifications of Odyssean place names can almost all show some scholarly support.

Snatched from the Classical Sixth at Uppingham by the outbreak of war Mr. Bradford served under Admiral Cunningham in the Mediterranean fleet as rating and officer. In a position which must have seemed, in 1941, as desperate as any in which his hero found himself he carried with him in his kit-bag two small green volumes of the Loeb edition of the *Odyssey*. After the war he returned and, in his own words:

spent most of the years between 1950 and 1960 sailing the Mediterranean, the largest vessel I owned being an old 20-ton cutter and the smallest a 7-ton sloop. For one period of two and a half years while sailing the central and eastern Mediterranean I only slept ashore on five nights. I grew to know this sea, and in doing so I also grew to know the Odyssey, almost as thoroughly as the charts that led me through the Messina Strait, or across the Ionian to the islands and to Ithaca. In the course of my wanderings I

ERNLE BRADFORD: *Ulysses Found*, xvii, 238 pp. Hodder & Stoughton. 25s.

came to a number of conclusions about Homeric geography and the navigations of Ulysses.

He has also drawn on Robert Graves's *The Greek Myths* (though Mr. Graves has led him astray about the pseudonym Ulysses gave to Polyphemus) and on Professor Taylor's *The Haven-Finding Art*, that wonderful compendium of information on ancient methods of navigation.

It is never quite clear, but it matters very little to the book, whether we are supposed to read it as a reconstruction of a real voyage made by a real Ulysses ('short-legged and red-haired') or as an attempt to show that the places visited and courses made good could correspond to real facts. (On either hypothesis Mr. Bradford admits that parts of the poem are drawn from a different background, perhaps from the saga of the *Argo*, and parts from fairy tale.) Mr. Bradford clearly would like to take the former line. He tells the history of Ulysses's life before and after the voyage in a way which is meant to present a real person, though he is sometimes unaware that the material he draws on is not very reliable. And, as Professor Burn points out in his foreword, even Homer did not say *in propria persona* that his hero had these adventures but only that this is what Ulysses told the Phaeacians, when dining out on the strength of them.

The Lotus-eaters are firmly located, in accordance with all tradition, on the island of Jerba, off the southern coast of Tunisia. Mr. Bradford's ship was torpedoed there, and he had a week of lotus-eating before returning to his life of 'clanging fights and flaming towns and sinking ships and praying hands.' But his identification is not based either on personal reminiscence or on tradition; he calculates that, running free before a Levanter, and this is the only wind likely to blow steady for the nine days Homer specifies, Ulysses's squadron would cover just 648 nautical miles at three knots, and this is the precise distance from Cape Malea, their point of departure. From Jerba he assumes that Ulysses, knowing how far south he had come, would steer on the Pole Star to get back to more familiar waters. Now in the first millennium, as Professor Taylor's diagrams show, the nearest star to the Pole was not our Polaris but Kochab, one of the 'Guards' of the Little Bear, and that was well East of North. On these reasonable grounds the next landfall, the island of wild goats off the land of the Cyclopes, is taken to be Favignana off the west coast of Sicily between Marsala and Trapani. Here again Mr. Bradford is on ground trodden before by Butler, though he rightly refuses to follow him into 'La Grotta di Polifemo'. There are plenty of caves to be found anywhere in the Mediterranean and the local inhabitants are only too happy to oblige the inquiring visitor with names and stories.

The Island of Aeolus he takes to be Ustica, fifty miles north of Palermo. Here also he can claim the support of Butler. The ancients looked for it in the Lipari group, eighty miles farther east, but a group of seven islands close together does not fit Homer's description. Ustica is mysteriously remote, an isolation which was put to use in more recent history. When the Italians in early September 1943 were seeking to negotiate their transfer from the German to the Allied side it was necessary to set up a group of Italian staff officers alongside the Allied invasion headquarters at Bizerta; they travelled to Ustica in an Italian ship and transferred there to a British MTB. The American General Taylor, sent to plan an air-drop on Rome, travelled in the reverse direction on 7 September; he too transferred to an Italian light naval craft in the waters of Ustica.

Apart from its isolation, its 'floating' appearance in the usual heat haze and its steep and inaccessible coasts there is a further conclusive argument in favour of Ustica and against the group now called the Aeolian islands. Aeolus presented Ulysses with a fine west wind which brought him back to within sight of his homeland. A west wind from Lipari would only have blown him on to the Italian coast, but Mr. Bradford demonstrates that, if we can stretch the name Zephyrus to mean any wind from a westerly quarter, a steady North-wester would serve all the way. On the starboard tack Ulysses could reach round the western end of Sicily, and then, bringing it first dead astern down the south coast of Sicily and then on his port quarter across the Ionian, he could run back triumphantly to Ithaca. The reconstruction holds water. 'West' was fixed by reference to the sunset, and in summer the sun sets farther to the north, by as much as 30° in these latitudes. A west wind in summer is therefore nearly north-west; and here the *Mediterranean Pilot*, perhaps the author's favourite authority, reinforces the argument by stating that 'North-westerly winds are in nearly all months the most frequent in these regions.'

It is by arguments of this sort that Mr. Bradford carries his readers along with him. He wins even more assent when he refuses to be dogmatic; on the land of the Laestrygonians, for example. There is something non-Mediterranean about this episode; more, something strongly Nordic. The short summer nights must derive from a tale told by amber traders from the Baltic, and surely the harbour with its narrow entrance and precipitous sides is reminiscent of a Norwegian fiord. There is a northern air, too, about the woman whom the Greeks met there 'big as a mountain, and they hated her'; such giants and cannibals are more at home in Scandinavian mythology. Mr. Bradford recognizes these northern elements but he thinks he has found the harbour which inspired the setting of the tale in Bonifacio on the south coast of Corsica. It may be so. There is, as it happens, one which fits pretty well, though it is small, on the south-east coast of Chios, Homer's own island. But it is a fair assumption that Homer could have heard a description of Bonifacio and introduced it at a point where he wanted to bring in a tale from another, northern, record of travel.

We get back on the traditional course when we reach Circe, firmly located on Monte Circeo. Though joined now to the flat mainland of the Pontine marshes it still looks like an island as many who gazed at it from Anzio can testify. Circe is a Mother Goddess, the Minoan 'Lady of Wild Things'. She shows a sound knowledge of the sea, and her sailing directions for the Straits of Messina, as elucidated by Mr. Bradford, are almost as explicit as the *Mediterranean Pilot* itself. The islands of the Sirens are the Galli, in the Gulf of Salerno, the Planctae are Stromboli and Strombolicchio, and Scylla and Charybdis are where they are today. Charybdis is splendidly described as from a small boat:

The heart of it was just abeam of us, about a hundred yards away. There was froth on the surface all round the boat, but the moving centre had a treacly consistency, like boiled sugar when it is cooling off.

Another result of the configuration of the straits may give a hint of the origin of Scylla. An American biologist, Dr. Paul Zahn, quoted by Mr. Bradford, explains that by reason of the topography of the sea bed,

waters farther down also feel the solar-lunar tug, and they too begin to move. When these deep-water currents strike the barrier shallows at Messina, they are violently deflected upwards, forcibly dragging with them a host of organisms from below. Hence, for these few hours twice a month [during spring tides] the surface waters in the Straits of Messina abound with living or half-living creatures, whose habitat is normally down where all is black and still.

And so, was Scylla a giant squid, as the Kraken of northern folk-lore almost certainly was? The largest known specimen of *Architeuthis* had an overall length of fifty-five feet and a weight of thirty tons; a specimen reconstructed on the basis of two of its arms was calculated to have weighed about forty-two and a half tons. Mr. Bradford may have been tempted to say so but he does not. He merely hints that the legend of Scylla could have been based on much exaggerated sailors' yarns of giant squids, perhaps from Phoenician voyagers in the Indian ocean.

He shows a similar restraint in his dealings with Ulysses's voyage to the land of the dead. He recognizes that this is an episode from another story, and contents himself with pointing out that at least the poet knew which was the right wind for a voyage from Monte Circeo to Gibraltar, and had heard of the strong east-going current through the straits which bore Ulysses swiftly back.

As convincing as any of his reconstructions is his location of the oxen of Hyperion at Taormina. He first shows that the Rada di Taormina is the only anchorage suiting Homer's description between Messina and Catania; then he works out that on the basis of tides and time under way this is 'just about where one would expect to find [Ulysses] towards dusk on an autumn day'. Less orthodox is his identification of Calypso's island with Malta, though not unprecedented. Mr. Bradford makes it seem all so reasonable with his calculations of southerly drift and his deductions from wartime experience of how long a man can survive on a raft. And if he is right in supposing that Malta was given its name by Phoenicians, and that it means 'shelter, haven or hiding place', then what could be more appropriate, etymologically, for Calypso? As for Scheria that, with all antiquity concurring, is Corfu where Mr. Bradford can lead us to the sweet river Ermones by whose gentle beach Nausicaa went to wash the clothes and Ulysses came at last safe to land. And Ithaca is Ithaca, not Leucas, and Ulysses is finally found, safe home after his wanderings.

Mr. Bradford is so reasonable and convincing, and so much at home both with tiller and pen, that it is hard to fault him. It must be said that he knows his *Odyssey*, and his Robert Graves, better than his *Iliad*, since he appears to think that the theft of the Palladium and Ulysses's revenge on Palamede occur in the *Iliad*. It calls for more hardihood to differ from him on a point of seamanship, but perhaps a query may be raised about his interpretation of the raid on Ismarus, the first exploit after the fall of Troy.

'The same wind that drove me from Troy brought me to Ismarus', says Ulysses, and on the face of it it looks as though the only reason for going there was that a southerly wind was blowing. Mr. Bradford thinks it was a deliberately planned raid 'for there was nothing to prevent the ships waiting safely at anchor to the north of Tenedos until the wind changed'. To do so, however, would be to offend against one of the laws of Aegean sailing. As the *Mediterranean Pilot*, Volume IV, explains in its stately prose:

A vessel may always anchor under the lee of an island with northerly winds, for though at times they blow with much violence, they never shift suddenly to the southward. It is not the same, however, with southerly winds; with these winds a sailing vessel should never anchor on the north side of an island, or any land, if it can possibly be avoided, as the winds from this quarter generally shift suddenly in a squall to the north or north-east, and blow with such violence that a vessel could not get under way.

Moreover the north coast of Tenedos has many off-lying dangers and no good anchorage.

That it is possible to argue with Mr. Bradford on such a point shows where his main strength lies; in the vivid actuality of his approach. The small boat sailor will enjoy his description of Ulysses's boat, half-decked and with an unhandy square sail of coarse flax or papyrus; the traveller will appreciate the skill in topographical description already shown in his *The Greek Islands*. The scholar, for all that he comes in for an occasional pasting, must relish a commentator by whom the seas and shores of the Mediterranean can be summoned as contemporary witnesses to the poem. And is, then, Ulysses found? Perhaps: and perhaps not so very far from where Bérard and his predecessors left him. At any rate there is no doubt that in what he has set out to do, to give the feeling of what the first voyages in these seas must have been like, and the smells and the sounds as well. Mr. Bradford has been completely successful. In this style there is no book to compare with his. Another quotation imposes itself: 'the surge and thunder of the Odyssey'. Here it is, from a passage describing a squall off Ithaca:

The island was not far away now, but we lost sight of it. We steered a compass course through the low-flying spindrift, and the lightning was all about us. No sooner had the flash dazzled our eyes than the thunder spoke, hard on its heels. . . . There was a broken, discoloured look about the water off our bows and the noise of the sea seemed to have changed. I had just got out the lead and line and was going forward to take a cast when a shift of wind disclosed the opening to the Gulf. The shore was less than a quarter of a mile away and the sea was slashing against the gap-toothed rocks.

21

NOVELS OF 1963

(k) IRIS MURDOCH

The Unicorn

JUDGED BY THE ORDINARY standards that we apply to narrative fiction, principally probability and truth to experience, Miss Murdoch's seventh novel, *The Unicorn*, is preposterous, a tale as remote and unlikely as the beast which gives it its title. This would not matter, of course, if it had properties, either alluring or allegorically illuminating, suggestive of some truth about experience on other levels, which gave sufficient inducement for the suspension of disbelief and the acceptance of the fable. After all the unicorn is a sort of truth. But these properties, if they exist, are difficult to discern.

To a remote house in a romantic and barren landscape—presumably the west of Ireland—comes Marian, an apparently progressive, fairly level-headed teacher. She has taken a job as governess there because she wants to get away from an unhappy affair. She finds she has been employed not as a governess, for there are no children, but as a sort of companion-cum-teacher of the mistress of the house, a mysterious, beautiful and eccentric lady who has been imprisoned there by a cruel, absent husband because she once betrayed him and perhaps attempted to murder him. There is a belief among the locals that if she goes outside the garden she will die; and there is a prophecy or a premonition that at the end of seven years something will happen, which seven years are now up. The imprisonment appears to be partly self-immolation, the voluntary aspect of it having some basis in the quite undefined religious side of the lady's nature.

(k) *The Unicorn*. 319 pp. Chatto & Windus. 21s.
(l) *A God and his Gifts*. 224 pp. Gollancz. 18s.
(m) *Les Fruits d'Or*. 227 pp. Paris: Gallimard. 9 fr.
(n) *L'Immortelle*. 210 pp. Paris: Les Éditions de Minuit. 12 fr.
(o) *Beautiful Feathers*. 160 pp. Hutchinson. 16s.
(p) *The Ginger Man*. 347 pp. Transworld Publishers. 5s.

Be that as it may, she is surrounded by an odd assortment of *quasi* servants and poor relations who to all appearances are gaolers; two male homosexuals and a lesbian spinster. There is also a secretive, fey sort of Celtic retainer who is secretly devoted to her, as Marian also becomes. In a neighbouring house lives the one-time partner of her misdeeds and her infidelity, an ineffectual poet who, to all intents and purposes, has abandoned her to her misfortunes, though he still gazes daily at her place of imprisonment through a pair of field-glasses; his father, a scholar who plays a remote, god-like part in the drama; his friend who pays prolonged visits to the place because he has fallen in love with the imprisoned lady and has been accepted by her as an admirer, though not as an actual lover; and a sister who in her turn is hopelessly in love with this visitor.

None of these people, their passions apart for the moment, is truly very remarkable. They are in a curious, dull and rather distasteful sort of way lay figures in a laboriously imagined sexual drama. Such talent for inventing the faintly bizarre and sketching in odd social types as Miss Murdoch has displayed on former occasions is absent. The aura of mystery and romance which all the others have worked up about the central figure herself, their prolonged discussions of the fascination which she and her story are supposed to have on them, are offered to the reader as mere endless advertisement of a product he cannot share; and there is an annoying assumption that what has not been created or brought to life in the reader's imagination can be talked about *ad nauseam*. So too the unfolding of the mystery of the lady's situation is achieved in the early stages by the bare device of allowing the newcomer, Marian, to buttonhole the others, one after another and extract some information from them, rather than by the accumulation of dramatically contrived hints or dramatically effected disclosures.

In one respect at least, however, they can all be said to be truly and astoundingly remarkable; and that is the ease, the bewildering facility with which they all fall in and out of love with each other, changing both their personal allegiances and their broad sexual orientations from day to day, sometimes in the course of the same day, nearly always without prior warning to the reader. This odd phenomenon has been observable in previous novels by Miss Murdoch, but never on such an extraordinary scale. And there is no hint of sexual comedy about all this. Declarations are passionately made, frequently on bended knees, and passionately received, and they are evidently meant. Nor, in spite of all the speech-making and analysis of feeling, is there any really satisfactory indication of the nature of this being 'in love'. It is plainly something more than ordinary sensual attraction, whether or not it is consummated on the foreshore or by the fish-pond; but what they all mean by being 'in love' with each other we expect to be informed more specifically, less muzzily, by a writer of Miss Murdoch's reputation than we expect to be by a writer of common or garden romances.

It is really impossible to believe that such a collection of not very attractive people, verging on middle-age, could be swept by such deep romantic tides of longing for each other, more particularly since they chop and change so often and the tides recede so easily. It is as if we were at one of those drunken parties where declarations of love by almost complete strangers and ordinary people were the order of the night. But there is no hint of satire; far from it indeed. The book ends with no fewer than four violent deaths. Though there has been some exceedingly unsatisfactory talk about God, almost the entire interest resides, as in any ordinary romance, in who gets whom and why, but the permutations and combinations are so endless and apparently meaningless that even the thin interest of ordinary romantic culmination has vanished long before the end.

(*l*) I. COMPTON-BURNETT

A God and his Gifts

Miss Compton-Burnett's new story runs on a minor key and will satisfy only those in whom an acquired taste has become an insatiable appetite. The single death comes late and follows logically from old age and, perhaps, a slight disappointment. Resentment, envy and the will to dominate, the clay which the author can handle with such macabre power, are not in evidence. The passion or disrupting influence under consideration is this time sexual; it is viewed without heat and with regard only to its domestic consequences. These turn out to be not very serious, for the victims who suffer pain and jealousy are gentle people in whom the ashes of humiliation feed the flower of love. The kettle simmers but never boils.

The scene is, of course, a family of the impoverished upper-middle class, possibly late Victorian and certainly not of our own time. The

Egerton family, like its predecessors, is self-contained and its problems no less than its vision are domestic ones. Because of Miss Compton-Burnett's reliance on dialogue in a stage-setting and in view of her reluctance to venture on more narrative than it takes to outline a face or to trace the passage of a patriarch from a chair to a door, this family rather conveniently decides to remain, generation piled upon generation, in one house. From time to time we are reminded of the reason. Financial matters are not all that they might be and income derives mainly from a single source, the 'God' Hereward Egerton. But this is not convincing; even in the good old days sons occasionally braved the outer world in search of a living, especially, one imagines, when their father showed a marked inclination to deflower their brides.

When we first meet him Hereward Egerton, a successful writer with strong blood in his veins, is proposing marriage to Rosa, a tenant on the estate and a strong-minded woman who will have him as a lover but not as a husband. Thereupon he marries poor, kind Ada with the calculated intention of giving her only so much of himself as she will be privileged to receive. Humble, she accepts—and always will.

Soon she faces a double humiliation, Hereward's close relationship with his sister, and his amorous regard for Ada's own sister, Emmeline. Ada, who for once puts her foot down and dispatches Emmeline from the story for twenty-two years, bears Hereward three sons, each different and with a distinctive name of his own, but each inclined, like the rest of the family, to express paradoxical thoughts of a self-examining kind in clipped sentences no more than half a line long. When one of them, Merton, brings home a fiancée for the family's consideration, Hereward, a man of 'full nature', loses no time in fertilizing her behind the scenes. Merton marries the girl and Hereward adopts the baby. But in time the truth can no longer be concealed. Later, Emmeline reappears with a daughter of twenty-two, also sired by Hereward. Finally it is revealed that all along this bread-winner of passion has maintained Rosa in her little cottage on the estate as his rent-free mistress.

Hereward is a proud fellow who never apologizes (like the Man in *Arms and the Man*). He has confidence in his pride and pride in his confidence and he regards his defects—for so they are in domestic terms—as virtues. Take me or leave me, he tells the (invariably) assembled family with each new revelation of fornication. After a good deal of clipped dialogue in which the new relationships created by these misdemeanours are thoroughly exposed, the family invariably decides to take him. His wife, Ada, regards herself as nature's doormat and Hereward shares her opinion. But what is the source of his power? As the bread-winner? As the father of nearly everyone? As a man of feeling and strength?

It seems hardly to matter. In this novel the compulsive force of *A House and its Head* and of *A Father and his Fate* is sadly lacking. To be tolerable, Miss Compton-Burnett's interminable and stylized dialogue must be the vehicle for an emergent underworld of real passion and even of claustrophobic horror. But here neither story, plot nor theme can compensate for an anti-realism which too often verges on the laughably absurd. The author is a ventriloquist with an obsession about families and her characters rarely rise beyond the stature of dummies, or puppets, whose jerky thoughts and confined expectations are imprisoned by their role in the family. On a number of pages one may read ten or fifteen lines devoted solely to a joyful reiteration of family relationships and of their determining role in the emotions. 'You have lost a father'. 'And I a grand-father.' 'But as my wife's niece you will feel also.' 'As your sister's daughter I am not permitted to feel.' And so on. But there is not enough bite, irony, twist, and revelation to transform the gauche into the sinister. And without the sinister Miss Compton-Burnett seems lost.

Were any new writer to submit a manuscript written in this manner a talent of a remarkable kind would be acknowledged but the manuscript rejected. The novice would be told: people don't talk like that and your characters all seem the same. We know why Miss Compton-Burnett is published (and avidly read), for she is a writer of great distinction with a unique approach. But there are times when her equipment breaks down and reveals a quite unforgivable amateurism. For example, in introducing a child of three to the scene she sets herself the problem of making the infantile form of his observations a guise for an insidiously adult content. The result resembles the manner in which Japanese speak English in a film about the American army abroad.

(m) NATHALIE SARRAUTE
Les Fruits d'Or

Mme. Sarraute's new novel contains its own built-in warnings to reviewers, and pertinent they are, too. The subject of her book is another novel, title *Les Fruits d'Or*, and the reactions it arouses among a collection of unidentified reviewers and readers. One should say straight away that the novel *they* have read is not the one *we* are reading, so that we are happily spared the metaphysical complications of being confronted with the perfect fictional circle.

We are not told much about the original *Les Fruits d'Or*, because the actual substance of the book has vanished into a mist of critical commonplaces and prejudices, largely inspired by attitudes that are strictly extra-literary. Faint glimpses of the text can be caught now and again; the author's name is Brehier, there is an episode of a man handing a woman a shawl, another in which an umbrella is left behind (shades of *Howards End*). Typically it is on such trivial, fringe episodes that wholesale critical judgements are made, while any sort of central impact is conspicuously absent.

Mme. Sarraute proves herself here an accurate cartographer of the literary milieu. She produces many 'characters' who give one a pleasant shock of recognition; the man whose personal acquaintance with the author is the key factor in his judgement of the book, the man who picks out the same qualities as a rival and draws precisely opposite conclusions from them, the man determined to classify the author into a literary school, and so on. The portrayals of all these types are exact and economical.

But these of course are only their public faces and Mme. Sarraute, as one would expect, is preoccupied to put them into perspective against their private worlds. Interleaved with the conversation in her novel are the transcriptions of the mental processes that both precede conversation and continue alongside it. The gap between this background cerebration, with its betrayal of the personal animosities and preferences that have nothing to do with the book under discussion, and the eventual spoken judgement, is beautifully observed. Mme. Sarraute's intention is clearly ironic, and she frequently adopts, on behalf of her characters, a style of heroic exaggeration, so that the final verdict emerges as peculiarly mouse-like from a mountain of mental preparation.

Les Fruits d'Or, *our* one that is, has therefore no plot, no real characters, no development. But it says accurate and entertaining things about the aesthetic experience, at that level where Nathalie Sarraute has always chosen to hew away (alongside Ivy Compton-Burnett), that is somewhat below the polite seam of everyday conversation. Her achievement in this book is to show convincingly the iceberg nature of literary judgements, only a tiny fraction of which peep above the surface. They are in fact counters in a different and more serious game, in which person plays person.

(n) ALAIN ROBBE-GRILLET

L'Immortelle

'What is a *ciné-roman*?' asks M. Robbe-Grillet in his introduction to the present work, and naturally does not wait for an answer. What it is in fact, to judge by *L'Immortelle* and its predecessor, *L'Année dernière à Marienbad*, is the script of a film written up somewhat after the fact, with its technical terms reduced to a minimum and with the stage-directions, as it were, amplified so as to convey more vividly to the reader who has not seen the film what the film actually looks like. The only difference between *L'Immortelle* and *L'Année dernière à Marienbad* is that the latter, though slightly changed here and there to conform with the film as shown, was in principle a very detailed description of an imaginary film in M. Robbe-Grillet's mind, which he then handed over to his director, M. Alain Resnais, to realize on the screen, while with *L'Immortelle* what we are given is a precise description of something already in existence, a film imagined and realized by M. Robbe-Grillet himself.

The result is at the same time interesting and boring. Boring in itself, as a would-be self-sufficient literary work, and if anything even more boring than most of M. Robbe-Grillet's novels, since for the obsessive description and redescription we get there of the same room, the same clump of trees or whatever it may be, we have here not only that but a maddening and endless succession of cross-references, so that to find out what the hero is wearing in shot 257 we have to refer back some 109 pages to shot 55, and so on. Interesting, though, in the reflections it suggests on M. Robbe-Grillet's work in general and the relationship between his films and his novels. For what emerges above all from *L'Immortelle* as a book is the cumbrousness and unsuitability of words for what he is trying to do.

Even the most elaborately detailed description of a scene or a person can convey only very inadequately the image in the author's mind (how often does even the most sensitive illustrator hit off exactly a character or scene as the author or the reader has pictured them?), while the film can do it instantly with no difficulty at all; the image is there, unchanging and unchangeable, and that is that. With M. Robbe-Grillet's novels we have, inevitably, never had any reliable yardstick by which we could judge how exactly we were receiving the images in the author's mind.

Even in *L'Année dernière à Marienbad* it was difficult, for though M. Robbe-Grillet spoke with enthusiasm of the uncanny accuracy with which M. Resnais had, in his absence, realized exactly what he had in mind, one could not be sure how far this went. But with *L'Immortelle* we are in quite a different position. The film as it exists, and as it is sketchily but sufficiently represented in this volume by forty stills, is entirely the creation of M. Robbe-Grillet; it is exactly what he sees when he writes his 'ciné-roman', and so from it we can check the accuracy of the impressions we receive from what M. Robbe-Grillet has written. And the extraordinary thing is that whenever, after dutifully visualizing any particular shot from M. Robbe-Grillet's detailed description, we turn to the corresponding still, we are likely to find that, for all the care expended on conveying it to us as exactly as possible in words, it is virtually unrecognizable. As we read, each one of us makes up his own film in his own mind according to the specifications provided by the author, and at the last it proves that any resemblance with the author's own film is purely coincidental.

Moreover the whole business takes so long: even a quite superficial reading of the script (that is, not bothering to check carefully every single cross-reference) takes three or four times as long as watching the film, and gives the reader far less. Not that the film itself is so exciting: the images lack the rich suggestivity of those in *L'Année dernière à Marienbad* and the 'plot' (a French teacher in Istanbul, his head full of romantic notions of Turkey, seems to have an elusive affair with a woman called Leila, or Lâle, or Eliane, or perhaps Lucile, who seems to be playing a double game and seems to be killed in a car crash and then seems to haunt his thoughts until he too dies in a nearly identical crash) is both less teasing and less gripping. But at least the film makes its effect directly upon us: we can recognize at once the correspondences between similar or identical shots, the changes of dress or lighting, and if the recognition is not intellectual at least they have a sort of subliminal effect. In the 'ciné-roman' all this becomes much ado to convey very little. In other words, the script is no substitute for the film, which is just what one would expect. But the book does leave its reader wondering whether M. Robbe-Grillet's novels either were any sufficient substitute for the succession of moving images, the film in fact, which unrolled in his imagination, and of which they are only a stumbling, cumbrous, incomplete description.

(*o*) CYPRIAN EKWENSI

Beautiful Feathers

Cyprian Ekwensi has written another novel about life in Lagos which marks an advance on both *People of the City* and *Jagua Nana*. The characters are more compelling and more rounded, the story is more plausible and better constructed, and if it has its melodramatic side, well, life in Lagos is never far removed from melodrama. There are also important political themes, treated without rant or racialism, but not without that naïve, infectious, impractical enthusiasm that goes with the style of Pan-Africanism described.

The hero, Wilson Iyari, is an Eastern Nigerian, educated in London, who rises to own a chemist's shop, the Independence Pharmacy. He also founds his own political party, the N.M.F.A.M.S. or Nigerian Movement for African and Malagasy Solidarity. He is a notable man in Nigerian politics, but he is despised, deceived and finally abandoned by his wife. It is this that gives Mr. Ekwensi his title, taken from an Ibo proverb: 'the man who is famous in the world but not respected in his own home is like a bird with beautiful feathers, wonderful on the outside but ordinary within.' The theme of the book, and the spring which sets the story in motion, is the conflict between Wilson's private and public life.

But though the book is worth reading for the story, the British reader at any rate is likely to derive more pleasure from incidental attractions. Mr. Ekwensi allows himself to be less than wholly serious about such sacred subjects as African (and, of course, Malagasy) solidarity. He has an admirably dead-pan description of Wilson Iyari's 'peaceful demonstration' which quickly develops into street-fighting, rape, and looting. The first glass broken, symbolically, is that of the Bank of America; immediately after, the mob smashes the window of a bicycle shop and 'a moment later men were mounting new bicycles and riding away into the town.'

The Nigerian Establishment does not get off lightly either. The Prime Minister, indeed, is treated as above the battle and makes a characteristically modest though Olympian appearance; but when it is necessary to bring a minister into the story he is credited with all the vices from publicity-hunting to jobbery. A Nigerian senior civil servant is one of the principal villains. The British Permanent Secretary, on the other hand, is most sympathetically presented:

Independence had not dampened his love for Nigeria, which now prevented him from electing to go back home to England. From master he was now happy to serve, as loyal as a Nigerian, trusted by some, hounded by others but proud to be associated with building a new Africa that had become the centre of interest for the world.

The political novel is not an easy *genre*. Mr. Ekwensi is no Trollope, but the unfamiliarity of his background should bring him readers. He manages skilfully the interaction between his two worlds, the public and the private, and if there is one weak and pointless episode, when Wilson goes to Dakar for an international conference, it is well compensated by a scene which gives a breathing space from city air in rural Benin. This is without doubt Mr. Ekwensi's best novel so far.

(*p*) J. P. DONLEAVY

The Ginger Man

A somewhat expurgated edition of *The Ginger Man* first appeared in England in 1956, on the crest of the 'angry' wave. Mr. Donleavy has been lumped in journalistically with the 'angries' and he has also been described by the editors of an anthology embracing both parties as a link between the 'angries' and the 'beats', a desirable phenomenon if you are going to lump the whole lot in together. How his hero resembles the typical hero of an 'angry' novel, or the typical hero of 'beat' mythology is not now readily apparent, but this is only one of the reflections that may strike a reader on the occasion of the book's republication as a complete and unexpurgated paperback.

Sebastian Dangerfield is an American law student, living in Dublin in the years after the war on the G.I. Bill of Rights. He has a rich father in America and his wife is the daughter of a well-to-do English admiral. If they live in squalor it is because Dangerfield is out of favour with both potential sources of income; because he

N

refuses to accept the responsibilities of marriage, has an expensive
thirst which swallows up the monthly G.I. cheque (how much that
may be we are not told) and has a natural buoyancy of spirit combined with a callousness which enables him to recover his humour
as soon as he is out of the house. Incidentally, some of the squalor is
rather unconvincing—the lavatory pipes that burst through the
kitchen ceiling, covering his wife with ordure when the hero pulls
the chain, the hall door that comes off its hinges are slapstick rather
than revealing detail. Except for his cynicism, his cruelty, his promis-
cuity, his fondness for a 'jar', his violence, his irreverence, and his
generally cheerful resourcefulness in face of debt or lack of money
Dangerfield is not a rebel, against society or anything else.

He likes money and constantly dreams of the clean and silky
pleasures it can buy; he is glad to have the accent and, when dealing
with tradesmen and others, the bearing of a gentleman; there is no
sign of any spiritual despair or ultimate disgust with the way the
world is arranged; he views the prospect of disinheritance with anger
and dismay; has visions of commercial success; and though he cheats
he passes his examinations. He indulges in ferocious bouts of violence,
it is true, when thwarted by his wife at home or by the lower orders,
as he believes them to be, in pubs; the smashing up of the Dublin pub
and the chase through the streets that follows, the orgiastic and
violent party in a Dublin basement, the procession through the
London streets with Dangerfield in kangaroo costume followed by
another bloody battle in a pub are again evidence of Mr. Donleavy
in a crude, unskilful vein of rather sadistic fantasy, but are evidence
of no more than a liking for destruction on the hero's part.

Still, the impression remains that Dangerfield is a rich, or potentially rich, man playing at life and bringing squalor on his head, and
this impression is reinforced by the ambivalent attitude to the Irish
background of his doings; he is both superior, physically and otherwise—it would not be too much to call his impatience and violence a
fascist response to the doings of a lower race—and yet almost totally
dependent on certain Irish tolerances, zests and weaknesses. So
also with his response to women, physical and emotional. He is
dependent on them, yet despises them; capable of momentary
gratitude and fondness, he is incapable of honesty or loyalty; even
his love-making seems absent-minded, as if he was congratulating
himself on the existence of the female sex, money, physical warmth,
and security and various other good things, at a moment when

his consciousness should have been otherwise filled (though this may be simply a literary device on Mr. Donleavy's part to describe the otherwise indescribable); and it seems also, the female being so often the dominant partner, definitely masochistic (though this may be a humorous device to suggest the hero's unfortunate attractions).

To a considerable extent then *The Ginger Man* is a ruthless chronicle of the doings of a rootless and not very interesting person. What remains? Undeniably, freshness and humour. Broad, effective and often delightful use is made of the general Irish background, both in physical description and in particular snatches of detail, though Mr. Donleavy seems, probably for the reasons suggested, exceedingly weak on particular characters and circumstances. There is also Dangerfield's wit, his style and, up to a point, his charm. But *The Ginger Man* is in no way profound, nor does it add up to a comment on living of any particular importance. Though occasionally clumsy, it is freshly and originally done, but it has surely been wrong to suggest that it can bear the weight of any largish statements. It seems a pity that Mr. Donleavy has often in the writing attempted to inflate his hero's attitude to life and the otherwise moderately amusing chronicle of his doings both by a sort of spurious (if comic) poetry and by the suggestion that he represents in some way an illuminating approach towards freedom.

22
RESISTANCE IN PART
FRANCE'S SECRET WAR

IF THE HISTORY of England be ever written by one who has the knowledge and the courage, and both qualities are equally requisite for the undertaking, the world would be more astonished than when reading the Roman annals by Niebuhr. Generally speaking, all the great events have been distorted, most of the important causes concealed, some of the principal characters never appear, and all who figure are so misunderstood and misrepresented, that the result is a complete mystification.

This dictum of Disraeli's applies to the history of many countries and centuries; with particular force to the history of resistance in Europe to Nazi occupation; typically, to the case of France. Many romantic and dramatic tales are already in print about the heroes and heroines of the struggle to set France free, at every level from the jungles of high politics to the hedges and ditches of the French countryside. Romance and drama are fair enough in the context of a clandestine war mounted in a hurry against an implacable enemy and fought on both sides with ardour and ferocity. Yet the fogs of myth have gathered so thick over the fields of French resistance that it may never now be possible to find out who was actually important, or even what actually happened, at the time. Twenty years on, some serious historical analysis has begun. Four recent books purport to forward it, and one at least of them does so. Mr. Thornton, an American, deals mainly with the French capital in the summer of 1944. The three French authors range, at greater length, more widely in space and in time; and their opinions are as different as their aims.

M. Michel's survey is a piece of profound, meticulous scholarship, written with compelling lucidity by a man who has mastered his

---

HENRI MICHEL: *Les courants de pensée de la Résistance.* 842 pp. Paris: Presses Universitaires de France. 32 fr. CHARLES TILLON: *Les F.T.P.* Témoignage pour servir à l'histoire de la Résistance. 686 pp. Paris: Julliard. 27.80 fr. ROBERT ARON: *De Gaulle before Paris.* The liberation of France, June–August 1944. Translated by Humphrey Hare. 312 pp. Putnam. 35s. WILLIS THORNTON: *The Liberation of Paris.* 231 pp. Rupert Hart-Davis. 25s.

subject and has the gift of exposition. Though his title suggests that his study lies in the field of political theory, it is in fact history. For long secretary of the official Commission d'Histoire de la Résistance, he has assembled a vast body of source material—surprisingly vast considering that he quotes German sources hardly at all, that the nature of the secret war must have prevented the recording of much that would have been historically useful, and that so much of what he handles comes from sources unknown. About half of the commission's extensive collection of clandestine newspapers and pamphlets were written under pseudonyms which time and skill have so far failed to unravel. Besides this mass of literature M. Michel has had the use of nearly fifteen hundred *témoignages* by former resisters, some of them historical documents of high importance. His keen intellect has been busy for fifteen years assessing these and more obvious sources. He has now produced an authoritative description of the nature of French resistance, which takes its place at once as the standard work. It suffers, as will be shown, from one important and perhaps critical omission; but to fill this chasm lay in part outside M. Michel's powers, and indeed outside the terms of reference he set himself. His book represents about as complete a picture as we are likely to get from the French side, and from it much subsequent work will derive.

In his view, the kaleidoscopic diversity of resisters can be reduced to five main groups, each of which exercised an important and continuous influence on resistance thought and action; he knows far too much about his subject to claim that his categories comprehend everybody. It is worth setting out what they are.

* * *

First he places France Libre, the politically diverse band of patriots who gathered round the first resister of all when Charles de Gaulle proclaimed from London that one French general at least could distinguish a lost campaign from a lost war. The Free French forces had a distinguished military record, fighting anywhere they could between the Arctic and the desert; their leadership was political rather than military. Some of their bravest people went back into France in plain clothes, as Gaullist agents; and these agents' main problem was to keep de Gaulle and the principal bodies of resisters on the spot in step with each other. M. Michel appreciates the difficulties that beset both sides in the resulting arguments, and explains them with his customary clarity. The main difficulty was this; most leaders in France found they had to give their followers active work to do, or lose them; while most leaders in London and Algiers feared that too much anti-German activity would precipitate ghastly reprisals, or—almost as bad—promote a degree of social chaos from which only the communists could benefit. For de Gaulle saw himself as the trustee of ordered French society, '*la France éternelle*', rather than the instrument by which the vanished republic was to be replaced. This view imposed its own limitations, and most of his immediate followers shared it.

*   *   *

M. Michel equates France Libre with the already familiar category of 'external resistance'. Among the forces of 'internal resistance' he isolates one large tendency, calling it—for want of a better name—Giraudism after the general who came to lead it. Its principal characteristic was a readiness to work along with the Vichy régime; this necessarily placed Giraudists in opposition to Gaullists, who abominated Vichy and all its works. Many Giraudists did valuable work for the Allied intelligence services, as several French memoirs have testified, but General Giraud's own inability to impose himself stultified the whole group's efforts at combat.

Giraudists apart, M. Michel throws all the rest of the spontaneous resistance movements inside France into a single category, to which he devoted more than a third of his long book. For these varied groupings had thinkers in them as well as activists, and as the war progressed they developed a common theory of how France should be run when it was over. This theory added elements of genuine originality to excellent intentions. With a vision of liberty, equality and fraternity infusing economic as well as political life in peacetime, the ordinary clandestine saboteur or courier had something to fight for as well as something to fight against; hence the resilience of many organizations sadly under-trained for the struggle against Himmler's Gestapo or Darnand's Milice. Yet the ordinary resister was also under-trained to deal with unsuspected opponents in liberated France. Many of the aspirations for which men and women gave their lives in the war have never been translated into reality, because politicians and administrators have found the translation too difficult or too inconvenient. The resistance movements cherished the conviction that France's pre-war politicians would not do, but did not throw up enough new men who could survive the war and stay on the rails.

* * *

Two, and only two, of the pre-war political parties survived into the occupation years to play a significant part in resistance: the socialists and the communists, who fill M. Michel's last two categories. The socialists were badly shaken by the troubles of 1940, and long cherished feelings of guilt; so long in fact that most of the sturdy resistance movements were founded without formal socialist support. though they included many individual socialists among their members. Several of these individuals, such as Pierre Brossolette who died in German hands, distinguished themselves; and the socialist leaven worked busily over the whole body of resisters who lay between the extremes of left and right. So busily did it work in fact that the isolation of the socialists in a separate category is the most questionable part of M. Michel's analysis.

Of the nominal left-wingers, the communists, he gives a just and penetrating sketch. In his view, they traced out between 1935 and early 1942 a complete political circle, from embracing the popular front, through divergence, into isolation, and then back with a jerk into embracing a new revivalist popular movement; by the end of 1944 they were already well on their way round the same course for a second time, diverging on their way to isolation. He lays his finger also on just that feature of communists that makes them so abhorrent to others: their unshakeable conviction, however tortuous or variable their leaders' policies, that they and only they are always right. Yet he does not try to hide, much less to deny, the substantial contribution the French communists made—once the German attack on the U.S.S.R. had decided them to join in—to the day-to-day running of the business of resistance, a task for which only they had received any previous organization or training.

M. Michel could have made some use of M. Tillon's book, which came out within a few days of his own at the end of last year. M. Tillon would have been angry, had he had M. Michel's by him as he wrote; but contact with its cool appraisals might have done the hot-headed author of *Les F.T.P.* no harm. M. Tillon is a French revolutionary of standing—he took a prominent part in the mutinies of the French Mediterranean fleet at the end of the Great War and has long sat in the inner councils of the French Communist Party.

During the war he commanded the Francs-Tireurs et Partisans Français, the military wing of the Front National. The Front National was a formidable 'front organization' through which the communists exercised a widespread, often a dominating influence on resistance, severely hampered the Germans, and provided the only serious alternative to de Gaulle's Forces Françaises de l'Intérieur. It was the F.T.P.'s commander who circulated the splendid slogan *A chacun son boche*. His book is subtitled 'Témoignage pour servir à l'histoire de la Résistance'. The reader naturally picks it up in the hope that it will prove a serious contribution to military history.

But M. Tillon is a communist rather than an author. He has written a *témoignage pour servir*, but to serve party rather than history. This long and sometimes hectic tract abounds, evidence or no evidence, with illustrations of the correctness and indeed the necessity of the policies pursued by the French Communist Party at whatever moment is under discussion, and the iniquity of the policies pursued by all non-communist politicians. No doubt for party members present and future this is nourishing stuff. For those outside the closed circle of believers it is a mixture of truth, bombast, and fantasy, through which the undoubted gallantry of the F.T.P.'s rank and file shines steadily. Only a few experts will be able to sift the plentiful wheat from the still more plentiful chaff. The political passages are all cast to suit the doctrines of French communism at the time the book was passed in proof. There is no index. The points of military interest—the strength, distribution, command system, and tactics of the F.T.P.—are hardly touched on at all, except for one operation instruction issued by the author himself at the end of June 1944, which is tucked away in an appendix.

*   *   *

M. Robert Aron's book, which in its French version frequently incurs M. Tillon's invective, tries to be more precise. *De Gaulle before Paris*, a cut-down version of his *Histoire de la Libération de la France*, is frankly Gaullist in sympathy; it aims at describing the triumph of the man in whom all five of M. Michel's main rays of resistance thought found their focus and fulfilment. The book is peppered with minor errors, such as an extra nought on the strength of the Special Air Service troops dropped into Brittany—whose existence is suppressed by M. Tillon, in a slanted quotation from General Eisenhower on the worth of Breton resistance. The translation by Humphrey Hare is reasonable, though it misses the point of one of the best stories in the book; de Gaulle used *reconnaissance*, when two Vichy policemen obeyed a request of his on his first return to France, to mean 'recognition'. There are many such little tales scattered about the book, for M. Aron believes that ordinary readers cannot stomach history unrelieved by anecdote. Some rather jerky alternations result, between discussions of strategy and accounts of the buttons of sub-prefects' uniforms. The general lines of his story are acceptable for those who can accept his leanings.

*   *   *

Mr. Thornton, attacking on a narrower front, penetrates farther in his attempt to communicate the reality of times past. His book is short and clear, well illustrated, and accurate within its limits. Moreover—rare distinction in its field—it is readable without being vulgar. True, there is little in it that will be new to readers of M. Dansette's excellent *Libération de Paris*, but nobody has put M. Dansette into English and the epic bears retelling—three times as many Frenchmen were killed in the streets of Paris as were killed at Valmy. Mr. Thornton retells it well, but with the same lacuna that characterizes all these four books.

For none of them give any account of British participation in resistance; and the one incontrovertible point about resistance, on every front but the eastern, is that without British participation it would have come to nothing. The British nourished it wherever they found it, from Nîmes to Copenhagen, from Bergen to Thessalonika; and without British nourishment in most of occupied Europe the flame of resistance would have gone out. The ladder by which General de Gaulle climbed to power was built as much by the Royal Air Force and the Special Operations Executive as by the population of France, and it is no service to history to leave the R.A.F. and S.O.E. out of the history books. The scattered, partial, and garbled references to them in all the books under review are no substitute for the truth. Mr. Thornton confounds a small part of S.O.E., Buckmaster's section, with the whole. M. Tillon engages in many disputes against the B.C.R.A., the main Gaullist staff co-operating with S.O.E., because it suits him to paint it as crypto-fascist; Buckmaster's agents he ignores. MM. Aron and Michel follow General de Gaulle in treating S.O.E. with reserve and disdain. M. Michel, who takes note of what resisters thought about the combatant powers, should certainly not have overlooked their admiration for the R.A.F. crews who brought them supplies from England. Parachute deliveries of arms and men are treated in all four books like rainstorms—things that just happen: a view nobody concerned with the dangerous tasks of executing them could share for a moment. Such errors may be unavoidable. They are certainly regrettable for they favour the growth of yet more misleading myths.

*   *   *

What in fact has been done on the British side to match the devotion expended by the French, indeed by all the occupied countries, in preparing the history of resistance? Presumably when surviving agents regained allied territory they were cross-questioned about their experiences, and if S.O.E. was like other large headquarters, some staff officers awaiting demobilization wrote up what they could remember of their branches' doings. Again presumably these retrospects are checkable against the texts of radio messages exchanged with occupied Europe; these texts must constitute the main primary source from which the military history of resistance can be written. But where are they? With one or two trumpery exceptions, they have never been made available to qualified inquirers, on the ground that the national interest would not be served by their production. Similar grounds have presumably kept most memoir-writers of the war in Whitehall from referring at all to S.O.E., which must have bulked large there. Participants in S.O.E.'s work have been silenced by the Official Secrets Act: hence the fantasies that mar the work of almost all of them who have wriggled free of the Act's gag. Meanwhile none of them grows any younger, and each year a few more of them die. When at last the passage of years brings home to government how threadbare that cover of 'not in the national interest' has become, and a proper account of Great Britain's vital participation in resistance is drawn up and made public, it will not be before time.

23

HITLER AND HIS GENERALS

IT IS A TRUISM that the vanquished are likely to learn more from their defeat than the victors from their victory. Their histories, also, are often fuller and more reliable. They will naturally contain a human element of buck-passing and self-exculpation, but the catastrophe is there plain for all to see. There is little left to hide, there is everything to be explained; and in any case catastrophes pose more interesting questions for historians than do triumphs. The fifty-year rule, deplorable as it is, is not the only reason why British historians have produced nothing comparable to the reflections of, say, Hans Delbrück on the First World War, or of Friedrich Meinecke on the Second. Defeat might have shaken the academic moles out of their burrows. Victory enabled them to scuttle happily back, leaving it to journalists, official historians and military autobiographers to study the greatest crisis in the history of Europe, if not of the world.

*   *   *

But the trauma inflicted on Germany was too great for German academic historians to remain blind to the need to make a profound examination of the disaster in which they had all been personally

---

Der Zweite Weltkrieg in Bildern und Dokumenten. Edited by Hans-Adolf Jacobsen and Hans Dollinger. Erster Band: Der Europäische Krieg 1939–41. 480 pp. Zweiter Band: Der Weltkrieg, 1941–43. 480 pp. Dritter Band: Sieg ohne Frieden 1944–45. 492 pp. Munich: Kurt Desch. DM. 60 each. *Kriegstagebuch des Oberkommandos der Wehrmacht (Wehrmachtführungsstab) 1940–45.* Volume IV: 1 January 1944–22 Mai 1945. Edited by Percy Ernst Schramm. In two parts. 1,940 pp. Frankfurt am Main: Bernard und Graefe. DM. 118. WALTER WARLIMONT: *Im Hauptquartier der deutschen Wehrmacht. 1939–45.* Grundlagen, Formen, Gestalten. 570 pp. Frankfurt: Bernard und Graefe. DM. 34. GENERAL-OBERST HALDER: *Kriegstagebuch.* Band I. Edited by Hans-Adolf Jacobsen. 391 pp. Stuttgart: Kohlhammer. DM. 56. WALTHER HUBATSCH (Editor): *Hitlers Weisungen für die Kriegführung, 1939–45.* Dokumente des Oberkommandos der Wehrmacht. 330 pp. Frankfurt: Bernard und Graefe. DM. 39. *Hitlers Lagebesprechungen. Die Protokolfragmente seiner Militärischen Konferenzen, 1942–45.* Edited by Helmut Heiber. Stuttgart: Deutsche Verlags-Anstalt.

involved. For a decade or so, while German military archives were in the hands of the victors, their studies had to be, like those of Professor Dehio and Professor Ritter, deep analyses of the development of German society over the past hundred years. War history was left, as it still is in this country, to able journalists such as Walter Goerlitz, retired soldiers like General Tippelskirch, and the personal reminiscences of such generals as Manstein, Kesselring and Guderian. There were no 'official' historians, and there still are none.

But instead the Germans have developed something that we lack in this country, and for which the Cabinet Office Historical Section provides no substitute: a group of academic institutions, part officially and part privately sponsored, which recruit some of the ablest young historians in the country to study and publish the principal documents bearing on the German catastrophe as they become available, and to use them as the raw material for works of scholarship whose thoroughness and sheer bulk put everything produced in this country—the Official Histories alone excepted—to shame.

*   *   *

The Institut für Zeitgeschichte, the Arbeitskreis für Wehrforschung and the Gesellschaft für Auswärtige Politik; working in close co-operation with the Bundesarchiv at Coblenz; enjoying the support of such great publishing houses as Bernard und Graefe, Mittler, and Kohlhammer; employing scholars of the calibre of Hans-Adolf Jacobsen, Walther Hubatsch and Jürgen Rohwer; all this constitutes a scholarly community without parallel elsewhere in Europe and one worthy of the academic traditions of nineteenth-century Germany. In the very existence of such a community Germany's former adversaries can take a legitimate pride. No one who contemplates what the alternative would have been in the event of a German victory, what Reichsministerium with what uniformed, docile officials glorifying the Führer to order—one gets an ugly smell of it from some of the Russian works produced in the Stalin era—can doubt that the total destruction of the Nazi régime was worth every drop of allied and German blood that had to be spilt in achieving it.

For these scholars dodge none of the terrible issues which an honest study of the Second World War must force upon the German people. The remarkable collection of photographs and documents which Dr. Jacobsen has assembled in the three fat, handsome volumes of *Der Zweite Weltkrieg in Bildern und Dokumenten* includes not only pictures of the German Army heroically in action but also pictures of the mass graves, the death-camps, the destruction of the ghettoes and all the rest of the infernal mechanism of the régime for which the German Army fought with such skill and courage, and whose orders it continued loyally to obey.

*   *   *

For the Germans this must be the central problem of the whole war. Why did the Wehrmacht, one of the finest military machines in all recorded history, serve so loyally a régime which its leaders so heartily despised. The German Army prided itself not only on its military skill but also—perhaps to a unique extent—on its 'soldierly honour'. Its leaders retained, at least until the end of 1941, a greater degree of independence than any other body in the state. 'The General Staff', as Hitler himself said, 'is the only Masonic Order that I haven't yet dissolved'; and he declared that 'those gentlemen with the purple stripes down their trousers sometimes seem to me even more revolting than the Jews'. He loathed them as the survivors of an Establishment he longed to destroy; he feared them as potential conspirators and rivals; and he retained a twisted remnant of the front-line soldier's contempt for the Staff. 'And just what has your front-line experience been?' he screamed at General Halder, the last survivor of the great Moltke tradition to serve him. 'Where were you in the First World War? To think of you trying to tell me I don't know about the front!'

Much has been written about this unhappiest of marriages and nothing in English to surpass Sir John Wheeler-Bennett's *The Nemesis of Power*. But with the publication of further documents by the scholarly groups referred to above a fuller picture is now beginning to emerge, not only of this relationship, but also of the entire conduct of the war at its highest level. Most important is the War Diary of the Oberkommando der Wehrmacht, or O.K.W., edited by the survivor of the two staff officers responsible for keeping it, Professor Percy Schramm. Professor Schramm, himself a professional historian, is directly responsible for the last volume, dealing with the years 1944–45, which, following a well-established tradition, is the first to appear; in many ways paralleling Mr. John Ehrman's two Grand Strategy volumes in the British Official History, although Dr. Schramm makes it clear that his work is only material for the historian and not history itself.

The same can be said of the autobiography of General Warlimont. *Im Hauptquartier der deutschen Wehrmacht, 1939–45,* although this is the fullest first-hand study of Hitler's war leadership that has yet been published. General Warlimont, as deputy to General Jodl, occupied a place in the military hierarchy comparable to that of, say, General Hollis in this country. After Keitel and Jodl he was the senior officer in Hitler's personal *maison militaire,* and he is, as a result, the senior survivor. That he did not share the fate of his superior officers shows that the allied tribunals accepted at their face value the protestations of innocence and inability to influence the course of events which recur throughout these memoirs. Historians will be grateful that they did. For General Warlimont's is a solid and scholarly book worthy of the awe-inspiring events he describes; not, like the memoirs of certain British generals, trivial gossip retailed to journalists interested only in maximizing sales.

The same is true of the dry, sparse diary of General Halder, of which only the first volume has so far appeared. Since this deals only with the lightning campaigns of 1939–40, when General Halder was Chief of Staff under General Brauchitsch and not immediately responsible to Hitler himself, it is likely to be of less interest than the second volume which is announced for this year, and which General Warlimont himself freely quotes. This will presumably cover the great controversies of the Russian campaign, Hitler's dismissal of all his senior generals and assumption of direct command of the army, and the nightmare nine months when General Halder worked directly with Hitler as his Chief of Staff. 'If Halder's presentations, in their knowledge and judgement, their style and approach, represented the highest traditions of the General Staff', observes General Warlimont, 'Hitler chose to answer them in the character of a People's Tribune.' General Halder himself wrote in July 1942, at the beginning of the summer offensive, 'No more question of serious work. Neurotic reaction to impressions of the moment and total failure to gauge the structure of command and its possibilities are the chief features of this so-called "leadership" ' (*Führung*). One wonders only how he stood it for as long as he did.

*   *   *

One might be tempted to discount much of General Halder's and General Warlimont's criticisms of Hitler as a military leader simply as professional jealousy of a successful amateur. General Warlimont writes with almost comic indignation of 'Orders given in form that stifled all independent movement—where He Who Knows Best, wholly satisfied with himself, would shift battalions and divisions to and fro, losing entire armies in the process'. But the results speak for themselves and so do the documents. In Hitler's *Weisungen für die Kriegführung*, edited and annotated by Professor Hubatsch, we can trace for ourselves the decline from the crisp and precise statements of aims and methods which characterize the plans for deployment and operations up till the crisis year 1941, when Hitler was still operating by orthodox Staff methods; through the wordy repetitiveness of Directive No. 41, for the 1942 campaign in Russia; to the hysterical appeals for fanatical resistance devoid of any kind of strategic insight, which he launched during the last year of the war. In his Directive for the Battle of Rome, for example, Hitler ordered: 'The struggle must be hard and ruthless, not just against the enemy *but against all units and commanders which are found wanting in this decisive hour*'. An order which was calculated, as General Warlimont remarks, 'to wither any kind of military discipline at its roots'.

Finally, as a clinical record of the atmosphere in Hitler's headquarters from which these crazy orders were issued, we have now a complete edition of all that survives of the *Lagebesprechungen*: the stenographic reports which Hitler ordered to be made of all his staff conferences when he began to suspect, in the autumn of 1942, that his generals were disobeying his orders. A brief selection from this repellent document has already been published by Dr. Felix Gilbert under the title *Hitler Directs his War*; but only this full edition can give the marathon flavour of those dreary ranting monologues in which politics, strategy, philosophic reflection and personal abuse were jumbled together, in which the movement of single divisions was endlessly discussed, in which political and private reminiscence was given free rein and from which, indeed, only one element was missing: any clear strategic concept based on a thorough appreciation of well-authenticated facts, of how the war was to be waged and won. For strategy Hitler substituted intuition, will-power and, towards the end, sheer terror. 'Anyone who speaks to me of peace without victory', he amiably informed his entourage, 'will lose his head, never mind who he is or what his position.'

*　　*　　*

As for his military advisers, Hitler had by 1943 destroyed their hated independence as effectively as that of all the other 'Masonic Orders', and with it all chance that they could win his war. 'Generals have got to obey just like the most junior private . . . ', he laid down; 'I am the leader and everybody must follow unconditionally.' Here was an end to that principle of flexible operational independence on which the whole structure of the Army had rested since the days of Moltke and which was more perhaps than any other element the foundation of its success.

By 1945 every unit in the whole great machine was shackled to the will of a dictator who oscillated between momentary whims and fanatical determination to yield no inch of ground. By his directive of 21 January 1945 Hitler made all commanders down to divisional level personally responsible to himself for all operational decisions, both for withdrawal and for attack. 'His contemptuous formulations', comments General Warlimont bitterly, 'show him openly venting his hatred of the staff officers of the General Staff and their spiritually and ethically rooted independence.' It might be added, however, that after the *Attentat* of 20 July he had some reason to do so.

This peculiar relationship between Hitler and his generals made for a unique command-structure from which it would be unwise to try to draw any conclusions of universal application. When defence organization is discussed in this country the opponents of increased centralization often cite O.K.W. as an example of over-centralized control, which, by separating planning from execution and power from responsibility, fatally diminished the efficiency of the German Armed Forces. But as General Warlimont and Professor Schramm make clear, O.K.W. was not really an operational headquarters. It was Hitler's personal military secretariat, comparable not to the British Chiefs of Staff but rather to the private office which General Ismay ran in London for the Prime Minister.

Hitler appointed Keitel as its head precisely because Blomberg had recommended him as a good *chef de bureau* who was fit for nothing else. Jodl, Blomberg's most intelligent disciple, had at first seen in O.K.W. an organization for centralizing command of the services, and he gladly accepted service with Hitler to achieve this end. In fact, under Hitler's influence it virtually ceased to be a military establishment, as Jodl testified a little pathetically at Nuremberg. It was, he said,

a cross between a monastery and a concentration camp. . . . It was not a military headquarters at all but a civilian one, and we soldiers were there as guests, and it is not easy to be a guest for about five and a half years.

In this atmosphere it was easy to lose touch, not only with the *Stimmung* of the Army—General Warlimont describes with irritation how Jodl always *had his hands in his pockets* at conferences—but also with everything else in the Third Reich, military and civil. Goering ran the Luftwaffe as his private empire. Raeder and Doenitz dealt direct with Hitler over important naval matters, merely keeping O.K.W. informed through their representatives there of what was going on. There was no overall appreciation of the war situation or rational allocation of priorities. The Allied landings in North Africa, for example, came as a complete surprise, and counter-measures had to be improvised in an atmosphere of total confusion.

* * *

As for the Army, Hitler dealt directly with that as well, even before he appointed himself its commander in December 1942. O.K.W. was not consulted at all during the military preparations for the invasions of Austria, Czechoslovakia, Poland, or Russia. The invasion of Denmark and Norway, a three-service operation *par excellence*, was, it is true, planned by a special staff within O.K.W., but this time it was the Army that was left out of consultation: 'better get that on record for the war historians', was General Halder's bitter comment.

The invasion of England was also an O.K.W. responsibility, but one which fell to it largely by default, through Hitler's own lack of enthusiasm for the project. As the war developed, indeed, Hitler increasingly used O.K.W. as a convenient receptacle for matters which were in his view too marginal or too complicated to warrant his own attention. The Baltic, the Mediterranean, the Middle East, relations with allies and satellites, all became O.K.W. responsibilities; not because O.K.W. alone could deal with their far-ranging military-political implications but because they were in Hitler's view secondary—trumpery, almost—in comparison with the struggle on the Russian front. From this last O.K.W. was totally excluded. It was an O.K.H. theatre, and over it Hitler dealt immediately with the Chiefs of Staff to the Army—Halder, Zeitzler, Guderian—until the Russians were at the very gates of Berlin. Only on 25 April 1945 did Jodl achieve an ironical empty triumph, when the armies on the Eastern front, in so far as they still existed, were at last put under O.K.W.'s control.

But during the last two years of the war the development of the Anglo-Saxon threat from south and west was making it impossible

o

for Hitler to regard the O.K.W. theatres any longer as 'secondary'. The collapse of Italy in the summer of 1943 compelled Hitler to give the Mediterranean an overriding priority in order to safeguard the Balkans, over whose security he displayed throughout the war a quite obsessive zeal. Thereafter, watching the allied preparations for 'Overlord' at the end of that year, he admitted: 'The attack in the West, whenever it comes, will decide the outcome of the war.'

Yet he still did not give O.K.W. the authority it needed to allocate resources to these theatres. The only result was a tug-of-war between O.K.W. and O.K.H., between Jodl and Zeitzler, over the rapidly diminishing military resources of the Reich, with himself as the final arbiter. And when Hitler was confronted by problems of priorities which could not be solved by simple calls for fanatical resistance, he showed an indecisiveness and ignorance of strategic principle which deepened the contempt in which the soldiers held his judgement, and embittered still further the hatred which he had always had for them.

*   *   *

Yet it would be quite false to accept the picture, which German soldiers were inclined to paint, of Hitler's interference as being that simply of an ignorant amateur, disrupting plans based on sound military concepts which would inevitably have led to victory. Hitler's interventions in 1940, for example, were usually to support a view being developed within the Army itself, hostile to that of the High Command. His most successful was his sponsoring of Manstein's proposals for invading France through the Ardennes. His most notorious was the famous 'Halt Order' at Dunkirk, which the German generals have depicted as a politically inspired veto on their military plans but which Dr. Jacobsen, in his definitive study of the Dunkirk campaign, has shown to have been a similar intervention in a purely military debate. But in any case these interventions raised no large issue of principle. It was only with the planning and launching of the Russian invasion of 1941 that it became clear that Hitler and his generals had very different views of what war was all about; and in the conflicts that followed it is by no means certain that Hitler was entirely in the wrong.

For Hitler did see, probably more clearly than did the heirs of Moltke and Schlieffen, that war in the twentieth century was not a simple contest between armed forces conducted according to the principles of orthodox strategy which nineteenth-century theorists had derived from studying the Napoleonic Wars. The First World War had shown the bankruptcy of this view. Basically, modern war was a conflict of rival economic systems, which the side with access to the fullest economic resources was virtually bound to win. 'Modern warfare', he laid it down, 'is above all economic warfare, and the demands of economic warfare must be given priority.'

* * *

Not all the triumphs of the Imperial Armies could save the Germany of 1918 from internal collapse, and this must never be allowed to happen again; this is the message which ran through the pages of *Mein Kampf*. The attack on Russia was not simply an assault on the fortress of Bolshevism; it was the essential preliminary to the creation of that New Order which would make the Third Reich self-sufficient and impregnable. The coal of the Donetz basin, the oil of the Caucasus, the grain of the Ukraine, these were the objectives for which Hitler fought, as Ludendorff had fought before him. Deprived of these, and of access to the Baltic, the Soviet Union, he was convinced, would quickly collapse.

To the German General Staff this was the oldest and most dangerous heresy in the whole of military thought: the belief that wars could be won without defeating the enemy armed forces. Warlimont rebukes Hitler because he 'deviated from the first and immutable object of the conduct of war—to eliminate the enemy's vital force—in order to pursue secondary aims'. In the conflict between the generals and Hitler in summer 1941 over whether to aim at Moscow and destroy the armies which would certainly mass to defend it, or to seize first the economic resources without which those armies could no longer fight, we can hear echoes of the old argument so familiar in British military history. Should we attack the enemy's trade, or his fleet? Should we seize his colonies or help our allies destroy his armies? Should we mount a massive surface invasion or devote our resources to attacking his economic structure from the air?

We can follow the course of this controversy over what Jodl rightly discerned to be 'perhaps the hardest [decision] . . . of the present war' in the successive drafts of the Directives for the Russian invasion printed by Professor Hubatsch. We cannot tell for certain which side was right. We only know that the month's delay while the matter was threshed out, added to the late start of the campaign due to the Balkan complications of the spring, made it impossible for the German Army to reach *any* of its objectives before the weather broke. The result was the disaster of 1941, the virtual collapse of the High Command, and that personal intervention by Hitler which, it may be agreed, alone saved the Army from total rout. The next year Hitler was to have no rivals in shaping his strategy round the economic objectives of the Caucasus; but if the absence of the generals made strategic planning easier, it was fatal to strategic execution. Hitler may have saved the German Army in 1941, but he lost it irremediably, by his sheer technical incompetence as a commander, in the campaign of 1942.

There was another and more sinister aspect of the war, however, into which Hitler could certainly claim a deeper insight than any of his military commanders. It was a revolutionary war fought against societies radically alien and hostile to the values which the Nazi Party professed. Military victory was a mere preliminary to social and political transformation, and the Army was only one instrument among many in the hands of the political surgeon. In the pluralistic societies of the west this transformation of the defeated enemy to take his part in the New Order might be gradually carried out behind the façade of a Quisling government. With a rival totalitarian system, sterner measures would be needed. What these measures would be Hitler outlined in a supplement to his Directive for Operation Barbarossa in March 1941. The political aspects of the invasion, he explained through Jodl, were too difficult to be entrusted to the Army. Instead, 'To pave the way for the eventual political administration the Reichsführer S.S. will be given special tasks within the Army area as a mandate from the Führer. These result from the struggle between two diametrically opposed political systems, which must now be conclusively settled'.

There followed the setting up of the Sonderkommandos der Sicherheitspolizei, to carry out the *Sonderaufgaben* or 'special tasks' (we can see them at work in Dr. Jacobsen's horrible photographs) and the issuing of the notorious *Kommissarbefehl*. Hitler carefully explained the whole policy to his senior military commanders at a special meeting on 30 March 1941. No one protested. No one asked any questions. The German military code permitted vigorous and prolonged protest when Hitler dared to violate orthodox principles of strategy: when he declared his intention of violating the fundamental moral and ethical codes which hold human society together, it permitted an acquiescent silence.

General Warlimont gives us the usual assurance that the German Army had no part in these prescribed atrocities, and that when given the chance it fought as cleanly on the Russian front as anywhere else. We can believe him, as we believe the assurance of the defendant that he had no personal part in the murder of the night-watchman during the raid in which he took part, even though he had been told in advance that the murder was to be an intrinsic part of the affair; but he will not expect us, or the Russian people, to be particularly impressed.

This is now past history; though it is easier for us to regard it as such than it is for the peoples on whose territories the atrocities occurred. The political system of Central and Eastern Europe today rests as much upon the freshness of their memories as it does upon the bayonets of the Red Army. Expiation for the German crimes has been exacted and is still being exacted. But the best expiation, that which leads most fully to reconciliation and forgiveness, is to be found in the works of scholars as honest, clear-sighted, and thorough as these, who are prepared both to examine what occurred and explain how it came to occur. In their work, and the respect which it commands among their countrymen, lies our best assurance that we have not been premature in accepting the new Germany as an ally and the new Germans as our friends.

24

THE TRADE OF THE ARMOURER

THE VICKERS STORY

MORAL JUDGEMENTS ARE inherently precarious. In only a few decades what had appeared to be indisputable in the eyes of God and man is rejected by the appeal court of posterity; it is the dissenting opinions which frequently stand. But, as recent events have plainly shown, the pronouncement of moral judgements is likely to remain a popular occupation, not least because the righteous indignation that commonly accompanies their expression is not only pleasurable but generally held to be virtuous as well.

*　　*　　*

Certain sections of British society have always been especially subject to this fairly harmless but not particularly attractive form of self-indulgence. In the 1920s and 1930s a popular target of criticism for such people was the armaments business. The private manufacturer of arms had always attracted some censure, but in the climate that bred appeasement it was natural that disapproval and denunciation should reach a peak in volume and vehemence. It is no coincidence that at the same period the armed forces of the Crown were allowed to fall into a deplorable state both in equipment and manning. The case was usually put with more emotion than logic, and thus fairly easily refuted in detail. But badly argued cases are not always wrong, and even erroneous arguments, when they are based on views widely and passionately held, cannot be ignored.

The stated objections in the private manufacture of armaments were many. If weapons, that is, tools for killing men, are by definition immoral, it can be argued that making or dealing in them is an immoral business. But this basic condemnation does not specifically condemn the private as distinct from the public control of manufacture. It is held, too, that those who deal in socially undesirable pro-

---

J. D. SCOTT: *Vickers: A History*. 416 pp. Weidenfeld & Nicolson. 42s.

ducts become on that account generally less scrupulous than those who deal in beneficial commodities. This is demonstrably not necessarily the case, but it has to be admitted that it tends to be true. It is further maintained that excessive profits are made, but this criticism can be equally levelled at many types of business enterprise that satisfy essential and harmless needs.

More particularly there are the specific charges which were made in 1921 in the Report of the Temporary Mixed Commission on Armaments. The Covenant of the League of Nations had recognized, without specifying them, that grave objections existed to the manufacture by private enterprise of munitions and implements of war. The Mixed Commission summarized these in six accusations; that armaments firms had fomented war scares and persuaded countries to increase armaments; that they had bribed government officials; that they had disseminated false reports to stimulate armaments expenditure; that they had sought to influence public opinion through the control of newspapers; that through international armaments rings they had accentuated the arms race by playing one country off against another; and finally that they had organized international trusts which increased the price which governments paid for armaments. The Mixed Commission never endorsed these accusations in unequivocal terms. But viewed from a position some forty years later it cannot be denied that all these practices have at some time been adopted; but equally certainly no single armaments firm can be firmly proved guilty of them all.

*   *   *

In one respect armament manufacturers have contributed to the unflattering legend that has grown up around them by the secrecy of their proceedings. The path that is worn to the armourer's door by customers is not only due to their better man-trap but to their success in keeping the secret of how it is made. The secrecy of their dealings is in the public mind personified by the late Sir Basil Zaharoff, whose biographies are largely surmise and whose high decorations, awarded by the British and French Governments, seem to demand more explanation than has ever been given yet.

Mr. J. D. Scott's detailed account of the growth of the great firm of Vickers amounts to a partial raising of the curtain of secrecy; some dark corners remain rather obstinately unilluminated. But in so far as it is inescapably an account of virtually all private arms manufacture in Britain since the production of Armstrong's three-pounder rifled field gun in 1855, it is of the highest importance and opens up a field which historians have until now only partially explored. The era it describes is virtually the 100-year period during which warfare was dominated by the rifled gun. Until the Crimean War armament-making had been the business of the Crown, and it must be confessed that it was a conservative and backward business. The Franco-Prussian War and the success of Krupp's steel guns showed the great and latent possibilities of armament development. But even before this, with a moral imperviousness which may be no more than characteristic of nineteenth-century business methods generally, and not peculiar to arms dealing, Armstrongs had supplied both sides in the American Civil War.

*　　*　　*

It was the armoured steel battleship, with rifled guns as the main armament, an extremely expensive and in retrospect a not wholly successful weapon system, which provided private arms manufacture with its heyday. Vickers, first and foremost a steel firm, under the 'optimistic, daring and speculative' direction of Albert Vickers, were alone of all armament firms able to build the largest warships complete—engines, armour, machinery and guns. Moreover, the building of such ships for foreign powers was welcomed by the British Government as providing a reserve capacity for national purposes. How far the development of the armoured warship was a cause of the pre-1914 arms race or how far it was a product of that race is a problem which is possibly unresolvable.

It is nevertheless an important problem, since upon an analogous question hangs nothing less than the fate of western civilization, and in the opinion of many it hangs precariously. But although it is an analogous problem, it is by no means the same one. What in 1934 appeared to some people, and especially to British socialists, a scandal as flagrant as the slave trade can now be seen as an interesting phase in what may be a short-lived aspect of world commerce. The then Mr. Attlee, indeed, compared the arms trade with prostitution; it is not of course entirely clear whether this was done for its emotive effect or because he had made a careful comparison of the organization and conduct of armaments manufacture with that of 'le milieu'. But the implication, seized on by Sir John Simon in debate, that state-sponsored brothels and Royal Ordnance factories should assume entire responsibility in their respective spheres, suggests that emotion had got well ahead of reason. Mr. Scott devotes a short and rather unsatisfying chapter to this fascinating episode in inter-war history. In relation to his main subject he could hardly do more. One is left nevertheless with the nagging thought that if war is too serious a matter to be left to soldiers, armaments may be too dangerous to be left to shareholders, or those whom they nominally control.

* * *

Nevertheless to project directly the experience of the 1930s, however variable or debatable the interpretation of such experience, to the present situation would be to ignore the revolution in armaments which was implicit when the first atomic bomb was exploded. Moreover, the original atomic bombs represented only the mild radical phase of the revolution; the development of the megaton hydrogen bomb has carried the revolution to the extremist stage which usually replaces the first one. Today's supreme weapon, and the immensely complicated systems associated with it, are far too dangerous and expensive for the manufacture to be under the control of anyone but governments themselves, and a vocal section of public opinion holds that they are too dangerous for governments. But the centralization of control of what—for a short time possibly—is the dominant weapon has been accompanied by a tremendous spreading of the interest in armaments generally. This is due both to the increase in volume and to the great diversification of the arms business. In 1932 the four major powers, Britain, France, Russia and the United States, were together spending, in real terms, on armaments only slightly more than they did in 1914. In 1955, in the same terms, the same powers were spending something like twenty times as much, and the trend is still upwards. In such a race nations, not just businesses, are deeply involved. Private manufacture is not confined to those few specialist firms who alone could satisfy the exacting standards of armament manufacture. National prosperity is widely believed to be linked to arms production; the race is far more dangerous because it now has a cheering crowd. The United States, for example, expects to sell, overseas, during the decade 1963–72 at least twice what was sold during the previous decade. It may even be significant that President Kennedy's declaration on 10 June at American University, Washington, that general and complete disarmament was the primary long-range interest, seems to have aroused relatively little enthusiasm in his own country. Some may fear that his political approach was too soft; are there others who fear cancelled contracts?

But apart from the manufacture of arms, the business of selling them has also entered the government field, and it will be for later historians to say whether the methods used have differed widely from those of the old-style armaments kings. All that can be certain is that when business is on so much vaster a scale, if there are undesirable consequences, they will tend to be correspondingly magnified. Lord Grey in 1919—not an easy date for detached judgement—held that the enormous growth of armaments had made war inevitable. Certainly it can be argued that an arms race may stimulate a militant public atmosphere and, further, that the possession of strong armaments can influence a government's readiness to resort to them in a crisis. But while it may have tended to cause war, it cannot be held that competition in armaments invariably does so. Moreover, the nuclear arms revolution has now produced the situation where the possessors of the greatest nuclear arsenals may be the most reluctant to use them; they are too well aware of the consequences. It is curious to reflect that General Staffs, preoccupied with preparations for war, are normally more cautious than their political masters; this again may be because they are more fully alive to the risks and uncertainties of war as a method of achieving political aims.

A history of arms manufacture provokes many more lines of thought than Mr. Scott, with his commissioned task, could be expected to follow up. Why, for example, is national prestige so heavily involved in armaments? This factor, as much as the obvious financial one, seems to block the way to international co-operation in arms production which should have been a major benefit from the North Atlantic Alliance. Is backwardness in design an inherent characteristic of a nationalized arms industry? It was in the past; perhaps it is easier for private industry to sweep their mistakes under the carpet.

*   *   *

Any future writer on this vital subject—and for once the word vital can be used with its full significance—must acknowledge his debt to Mr. Scott for having partially opened a closed door. The era of pre-atomic armaments can already be seen as a well-defined period, a story in many shades of grey, and hanging over the whole subject is the overwhelming question of responsibility. Governments have been forced to become the major partners in the arms industry. Fortunately, at intervals, democratic governments have to rely on popular consent for their continuance; the electorate cannot be treated with the contempt that shareholders have in the past experienced from the autocratic managements of the businesses that they owned. If a social evil is being sustained, it is being sustained by all, and the ultimate sanction, whatever the opinion may be of its effectiveness, is better placed than if it were in fewer hands. Those who protested, in the 1920s and 1930s, often with more vigour than logic against a business which by today's standards was quite small, may have been right. But like many such reformers they may have been right mainly for the wrong reasons.

25

OUT OF BOND

(a) HENRY MILLER

Tropic of Cancer

MR. JOHN CALDER has just brought out the first English edition of *Tropic of Cancer*. Somehow, in the last quarter of the volume, the text has got rather jumbled, although the page-numbering moves serenely on. The censor cannot be accused of interfering or the hand of prudence of wishing to draw a veil, so we must suppose that the proof-reader, drunk with all these swirling words, simply got mixed up and did not notice his mistake. Still, jumbled though it may be, the book is here at last to take its place alongside *Lolita* and *Lady Chatterley's Lover* in the full light of the English day, after a clandestine existence of nearly thirty years.

Tropic of Cancer has a kinship, other than 'outspokenness', with both the above-mentioned works. Like Mr. Nabokov, Mr. Miller goes in for flamboyant picaresque fantasy, so that his hero seems to be rampaging through the English vocabulary at the same time as he is dashing from one episode to the next; the question even arises; is he living a life or disporting himself in language? Like Lawrence, Mr. Miller preaches against modern civilization and takes sex as the mainspring of vitality. But his real connexion now appears to be less with these two than with the Céline of *Voyage au bout de la nuit*, which came out in 1932, two years before *Tropic of Cancer*, and—in spite of the great difference in style—with the Orwell of *Down and Out in London and Paris*, which belongs to the same period.

There must have been something powerfully operative in the

(a) HENRY MILLER: *Tropic of Cancer*. 318 pp. John Calder. 25s.
(b) HENRY MILLER: *Plexus*. The Rosy Crucifixion. 571 pp. Weidenfeld & Nicolson. 30s.
(c) WILLIAM BURROUGHS: *The Naked Lunch*. 226 pp. 15 fr. *The Soft Machine*. 182 pp. 15 fr. *The Ticket That Exploded*. 183 pp. 18 fr. Paris: Olympia Press. WILLIAM BURROUGHS: *Dead Fingers Talk*. 215 pp. John Calder. 25s'

Zeitgeist to make three intelligent and professionally qualified men, a Frenchman, an American and an Englishman, choose to plunge into the lower depths and to write about the underside of civilization. Truth seemed to them to lie not in the rational conduct of everyday affairs, or in the so-called achievements of civilized man, but in slum sick-beds, doss-houses, and brothels, and among prostitutes, alcoholics, and tramps. The trend has continued. The tramps in *Waiting for Godot*, and *The Caretaker* are not unlike Céline, Orwell, and Miller. The Bums and the Beats have added drugs, Zen, and homosexuality to the original mixture, and this does not make them basically different; Kerouac, Trocchi, and Burroughs, instead of appearing to make a fresh start, look like specialized off-shoots of the pre-war trio. And so wide now are the ramifications of this Beat mood that, at last year's Writers' Conference in Edinburgh, the Grand Old Man, the real hero of the occasion for both the people on the platform and the crowd in the auditorium was, precisely, Mr. Henry Miller. With characteristic anarchism he spoke only once, and very briefly, to say that he was no longer interested in literature and had only come to Edinburgh because of the free trip and to look at paintings.

Now that the time has come to judge *Tropic of Cancer* as literature, it is seen to raise some of the same problems as *Voyage au bout de la nuit*. The reader is, at first, exhilarated through being caught up again in a stream of words, which sound so miraculously close to the contemporary spoken idiom. He is rushed helter-skelter into an apparently rich world of eccentrics, interested only in the essential things, food, sex, and art. The obscenity is so compulsive in places that it ceases to be 'realistic' and becomes a litany of energy and horror. The book seems to be cutting very deep into life, to be rejecting everything inauthentic, to be, as it were, a magnificent lyrical outburst by a latter-day Diogenes (Miller himself announces his ambition to paint 'a pre-Socratic being, a creature part goat, part Titan', but Diogenes immediately comes to mind, although he is post-Socratic).

However, in the case of both Céline and Mr. Miller a slight doubt may eventually creep in. Since they always write at the tops of their voices, their lyricism can turn into ranting. They sound as if they were preaching *against* something, and it is not always clear against what exactly: God, civilized society, capitalist exploitation, particular individuals, the Jews, or just the general cussedness of life? The

trouble with irascibility as a literary mode is that it tends to be very
uncertain in aim and to muddle issues instead of clarifying them. Mr.
Miller, having unloaded his bile on to paper, may now be relaxed,
monk-like, and serene, just as Céline, in his last years, was very good
to his cats and a kind of saint to the poor people he could help with
medical advice. But this does not alter the fact that the general tone
of their books may leave one trying to assess, rather uncomfortably,
the degree of truth and the degree of bad temper.

Another limitation common to both is that their subjective fantasy
is so strong as to blur most of the characters in their books, apart
from the central one. Even after two or three readings of *Tropic of
Cancer*, it is not easy to grasp the identity of the men Mr. Miller
consorted with in his Parisian bohemia. When any one of them speaks
at length, he tends to sound exactly like Mr. Miller himself. Some
of the women come to life better—for instance, Germaine, the
vocational prostitute—but others, such as Mona, who is supposed to
be very important to the narrator, never materialize. It is as if the
speed and noise of the writing, instead of revealing the world, were
insulating the author from it. Reading him is rather like being at a
cocktail party and feeling, as the internal sensation of euphoric
excitement increases, that the other people present are becoming
remote and indistinct.

This is, perhaps, just another way of saying that Mr. Miller is not
really a novelist, but an essayist or confessionalist, straining hard to
give his experience an epic quality; and himself uncertain about the
impulses behind his writing. It is not obvious, for instance, why he is
in Paris. Occasionally, there is a paragraph about the beauty of the
Tuileries or about taxi-drivers looking appreciatively at the view
along the Seine, but it does not ring quite true, and may, indeed,
sound mawkishly sentimental, like the sudden, unexpected praise of
Napoleon. The hero's mere presence in Paris may be a Romantic
myth. The action is not taking place in the Paris of the French, since
there is never any contact with the population, apart from waiters
and prostitutes; it is set in the closed mind of an American non-
conformist, and he might be anywhere, as is proved by the great
similarity between *Tropic of Cancer*, *Tropic of Capricorn* and *The
Air-Conditioned Nightmare*. Some of the best episodes may not have
been experienced in France at all; one of the funniest—the description
of the polite, classical concert as seen by the ribald, naïvely self-
confident outcast—could have happened anywhere and might, with

little adjustment, be transferred to *The Horse's Mouth* or *The Catcher in the Rye*.

What comes over, then, is the horror of the underworld in any big city, since the bohemian swamp Mr. Miller is dealing with could be in Berlin, London, or San Francisco. And in the end, for all its show of gusto, *Tropic of Cancer* is a sad book, and perhaps a rather empty one, since it lacks a central core. If society is 'pooped out' as Mr. Miller says, and nothing on the ordinary level makes sense, one might have expected sex, at least, the hero's ceaseless preoccupation, to be built up into some kind of significant experience. Actually, the most telling passages about sex are those which denounce it as a pointless activity, and very amusing some of them are. However, when towards the end of the volume Mr. Miller launches into a meditation about the vagina which is obviously meant to be a major section, he produces not great literature but a flux of words which is both banal and indefinitely extensible:

Out of that dark, unstitched wound, that sink of abominations, that cradle of black-thronged cities where the music of ideas is drowned in cold fat, out of strangled Utopias is born a clown, a being divided between beauty and ugliness, between light and chaos who when he looks down and side-long is Satan himself and he looks upward sees a buttered angel, a snail with wings.

When I look down into that crack I see an equation sign, the world at balance, a world reduced to zero and no trace of remainder. . . .

And so on, for page after page, until we reach the dictum: 'Show me a man who over-elaborates and I will show you a great man.' It is possible to hold a different view and to regret that, in a book as historically important as *Tropic of Cancer*, there is so much verbal cancer.

(*b*) HENRY MILLER

Plexus

Before *Plexus* there was *Sexus* and after it, not surprisingly, came *Nexus*. Of these three auto-novels, as Mr. Henry Miller calls them, *Sexus* 'cannot at the present time be published here' and *Nexus*, which appeared under the Olympia Press imprint in Paris, is 'not available in English-speaking countries or Communist-controlled countries'. So in England we have the middle volume alone of the trilogy called 'The Rosy Crucifixion' and that is a pity, for these auto-novels are largely autobiographical, and characters appear in *Plexus* who have been met in the earlier volume. The books are attempts 'to be and act the man I was', so that the ending of *Nexus* is what Mr. Miller calls 'the break-through', his arrival in Paris and the beginning of the life described in *Tropic of Cancer*. There are other reasons for deploring the absence of the first and third volumes of the trilogy. *Sexus* at first 'shell-shocked' Mr. Lawrence Durrell, so that he accused his old friend Mr. Miller of 'finger-painting in his own excrement rather than producing art', and in *Nexus* the author reveals himself, as he says, as 'something less than zero, something worse than the lowest knave'. In *Plexus* there is no excrementitious finger-painting and Mr. Miller reveals himself only as a bore. His publishers assure us that the volume is 'a complete work of art in itself'. Is it? Is it a work of any literary interest at all? Let us see.

'In her tight-fitting Persian dress, with turban to match, she looked ravishing.' This opening sentence is likely to shock any reader even moderately sensitive about the use of words—not to shell-shock him, but to give him the feeling that he has been hit by a damp pillow. It belongs to the women's page of a daily paper, and not a very good paper at that. '*Spring had come* and she had *donned* a pair of long gloves and a beautiful taupe fur *slung carelessly* about her *full, columnar neck*.' The clichés in this second sentence (or the more glaring ones, for the whole sentence is a cliché), are italicized. Artists do not write like this, not even when their tone is colloquial and their chief concern self-examination or self-revelation. They do not find 'a stunning place to rent', they do not say that a promising boxer is 'on the way to becoming a figure in the world of fisticuffs', they do not call childhood 'the street of early sorrows', they do not talk about 'quiet, grave lads, strangely sombre and reserved'. A great deal of *Plexus* is on this wretched level, and almost none of it is written with distinction. It is the work of a man who has no care or thought for the words he uses. 'It seemed to me that all I had to do was to sit down, turn on the tap, and out it would flow', and that is precisely the effect produced.

*   *   *

Perhaps what the book has to say is of such importance that the atrocious manner of saying it can be forgiven, if not forgotten? That is not the case, even if we are prepared to regard the author's personality with his own reverent seriousness. The 570-odd pages of this book recount in detail Henry Miller's life in New York as manager of a speakeasy, seller of mezzotints and boxes of candies, and in half a dozen other occupations. There are one or two lively comic scenes, in particular those which occur when Miller and his wife go to stay with an earnest statistician, who tries to get Miller to type out his work from a dictaphone, and later to put shingles on the roof. But there are few of these comic interludes. Most of the book is taken up by Hen's (the name by which he is generally known) encounters with his friends, by descriptions of long sessions of drinking and conversation which must have been even drearier to experience than they are to read about, by discussions of what is called in one place 'this weird business of writing'. There is a very long, pointless dream sequence, which reinforces a remark of Mr. Durrell's that Henry Miller takes 'all the data about himself as equally important simply because it happened to him'. The friends who appear and reappear are described with great particularity, yet they have no impact as characters because they all talk in exactly the same way as Hen. Their reality is submerged in his, so that he might just as well be talking to himself. Nor is Mona, she of the full columnar neck, any more real. She is Hen's second wife, she has admirers who give her money, she is convinced of Hen's vocation as a writer, but she is never seen as an individual, she exists only as part of Hen's image. Naturally, *Plexus* contains also meditations about anything that influences Hen or seems to him important—or rather anything that seemed important to him at that time in his development. The last chapter is for the most part given to a panegyric of Spengler, a Spengler who is seen very much as a projection of Henry Miller. The final comment on him reads:

Yes, I was a fortunate man to have found Oswald Spengler at that particular moment in time. In every crucial period of my life I seem to have stumbled upon the very author needed to sustain me. Nietzsche, Dostoevsky, Eli Faure, Spengler: what a quartet! There were others, naturally, who were also important at certain moments, but they never possessed quite the amplitude, quite the grandeur of these four. The four horsemen of my own private Apocalypse! Each one expressing to the full his own unique quality: Nietzsche the iconoclast; Dostoevsky the grand inquisitor; Faure the magician; Spengler the pattern-maker. What a foundation!

In the days to come, when it will seem as if I were entombed, when the very firmament threatens to come crashing down upon my head, I shall be forced to abandon everything except what these spirits implanted in me. I shall be crushed, debased, humiliated. I shall be frustrated in every fibre of

P

my being. I shall even take to howling like a dog. But I shall not be utterly lost!

Anybody who thinks that a criticism of Henry Miller on the basis of *Plexus* is unfair should read a curious work called *The Books in My Life*, published here in 1952. This contains not only a list of 'The Hundred Books Which Influenced Me Most' (they include not only expected classics and books on Zen Buddhism, but *Pitcairn Island*, *Trilby*, *The Three Musketeers* and the works of G. A. Henty), but also articles recommending a variety of authors, from Giono and Krishnamurti to Rider Haggard and Richard Jefferies. The tone of these articles is almost unbelievable or rather it is almost unbelievable that the man who wrote then could be thought to possess a talent for literature. The first of them is called 'They Were Alive and They Spoke to Me'. It is a title that might well be used as promotional material for selling 'inspirational' books by direct mail, and the text might have been designed for the same purpose:

What makes a book live? How often this question arises! The answer, in my opinion, is simple, A book lives through the passionate recommendation of one reader to another. . . . Despite the views of cynics and misanthropes, it is my belief that men will always strive to share their deepest experiences.
Books are one of the few things men cherish deeply. . . .

If it is granted that the bulk of Mr. Miller's writing is cliché-ridden, repetitious, and boring, and preoccupied with himself to the verge of egomania ('I am the hero and the book is myself', he wrote once about *Tropic of Cancer*, and the remark is even truer of his later work), how does it happen that he has ever been taken seriously? To this question there is a double answer. The first part of it rests in the nature of *Tropic of Cancer* and the time at which it was published, the second in the difference between Henry Miller the man and Henry Miller the writer.

*   *   *

In 1934, when it was published in Paris, *Tropic of Cancer* was a revolutionary work. The obscenities in it, the detailed description of sexual acts, the writer's enjoyment of sex and his treatment of it as something often tremendously comic, even the rhapsodic passages deriving from Whitman and Spengler, all were undoubtedly new and seemed possibly important. Put against what was stalely moralistic or narrowly political in the European writing of the time, what

Henry Miller had to say—or rather, the personality he had to express—looked wonderfully fresh and vigorous. The feeling for him was expressed at its most extreme in George Orwell's essay acclaiming Miller as a real man living and suffering compared with what he called the 'nancy boy' Left-wingers of the English intelligentsia. Today the book is no longer a revolutionary document. Several novelists are as outspoken as was Henry Miller in the 1930s, and an awareness of sex as comic or ridiculous is common. But it remains true that *Tropic of Cancer* and one or two of the other books that appeared before the war, in particular *Max and the White Phagocytes* (1938), are very much better than anything Mr. Miller has written since. They are less diffuse and egocentric, and they also exploit much more effectively the brutal comic vein that is Henry Miller's original contribution to literature. The comedy is that of the bum who cocks a snook at a benefactor with one hand while extracting notes from his wallet with the other. The joyful, deliberate outraging of 'good taste' is commonplace today, but few writers have savaged the respectable as successfully as Mr. Miller. Those who called *Tropic of Cancer* an original and startling work in the context of its time have no reason to repent their words.

Such praise is not likely to give satisfaction to Mr. Miller or to his admirers. When Mr. Edmund Wilson wrote about *Tropic of Cancer* four years after the book's publication in Paris saying that it was the most remarkable book to come from the Parisian Left bank expatriates for many years and suggesting that it was neglected, he provoked an indignant reply from its author. Neglected, indeed! 'It may be procured at leading book stores in practically every important city of the world excepting those of America, England, Germany and Russia', he wrote in that tone of a man advertising himself at the top of his voice so often to be heard in his writings, adding that it had 'been reviewed enthusiastically by some of the foremost critics of Europe'. Was it because Mr. Wilson said the characters were cadgers and spongers, and called the hero 'the genuine American bum' that Mr. Miller was annoyed? Very likely, for the burden of his work is that the bum (or this particular bum) is also the sage and saint, doomed to suffer a life that is 'one long rosy crucifixion'.

It is as such a sage and saint that Mr. Miller see himself. Every incident of his life is worth recalling because of this saintliness. Is it possible that we can fail to be interested in 'the fateful day, in the Park Department of Queen's County, N.Y.', when he 'mapped out the whole autobiographical romance [of "The Rosy Crucifixion"] in one sitting'? Shame on us, then—but really Mr. Miller will not be surprised by this lack of interest, for he at once enjoys the knowledge that he is famous, a man praised by some of the foremost critics of Europe, and suffers the bitterness of knowing himself unjustly neglected or misunderstood by those very same critics. This view of him, as a saint whose duty it is to tell the world about himself, is accepted by his friends. When they talk about Henry Miller the artist, they are really referring to Henry Miller the man.

*   *   *

'There he sits, the lone American eagle in his eyrie at Big Sur', Mr. Lawrence Durrell writes to Mr. Alfred Perlès, adding that 'American literature today begins and ends with the meaning of what he has done'. In the correspondence that followed this letter, an attempt by those close friends to create a 'portrait of the artist', some interesting things came through, not least the difference between what his friends find in Henry Miller and the self-portrait drawn in the books. Gentle, loyal, tender, lovable, with a sensibility so finely spun 'that if ever he put a foot wrong it was from sheer nerves', those are some of the characteristics that Mr. Durrell finds in his friend, and that a reader is not likely to discover. The correspondents agree that the master's writing is 'uneven, interspersed with platitudes and long passages of downright bad writing', as Mr. Perlès put it. His philosophy is 'a fantastically digested *pot-pourri* of the literary-philosophic world literature which any half-educated person knows', to quote Mr. Perlès again. The case is almost exactly that made in this review. What justification can there be, then, for taking Henry Miller seriously? Why, simply that 'Henry is no Plato, no Lao-Tzu, no Spinoza, no Nietzsche, no Freud—he is better: he is himself, which very few human beings are able to be, and that's why I maintain that he is a genius though he may not have any genius'. The 'genius' consists in being Henry Miller.

Mr. Miller's own incursion into this correspondence—one knew that the master would not be left out of it—strikes a characteristically humourless note. Mr. Durrell had remarked upon the difficulty of explaining Henry Miller's intentions to the young. Difficulty? What an idea!

As the recipient of thousands of letters, most of them from young people, I get such a different picture. (Could it be that there is this difference in comprehension between the British and the American youth?) At any rate, the young who write do 'get' me to an amazing extent. . . . All the young, and often the old too, are unanimous in writing of the therapeutic value of my work. They were altered. They thank me, bless me, bless me for 'just being', as they often say.

Who is it that the lone American eagle reminds us of in tone on this occasion? Is it not Mr. Godfrey Winn?

It is the belief of Mr. Miller's friends that he had not been justly appreciated as an artist because, in Mr. Durrell's words, 'the books won't get through yet awhile'. The truth is that his reputation has been built upon this very fact. The travel books, bits of fiction, and monologues published in England in the past twenty years were monstrously overpraised because of the feeling that the really important unpublished books justified what was being said about the unimportant published ones. While *Tropic of Cancer* and 'The Rosy Crucifixion' remained unpublished here, it was possible for those who had read the first book years ago and have never seen the trilogy to believe with all the fervour of distant recollection that censorship was depriving us of considerable works of art. Now we have *Tropic of Cancer*, and although it is plainly a book of historical importance, it is just as plainly not a masterpiece: and we have *Plexus*, which should be enough by itself to end this comedy of a reputation based on ignorance. If it does not quite do the trick, let publishers be daring, let the Director of Public Prosecutions be tolerant, let us have *Sexus*, yes, and *Nexus* too, so that tedium may be recognized for what it is.

(c) THE NOVELS OF WILLIAM BURROUGHS

'Now I, William Seward, will unlock my word horde', warns Mr. Burroughs towards the end of *The Naked Lunch*. Struggling upstream through it is not unlike wading through the drains of a big city. The first shock effects are strong as the rash reader plunges in, then a steady nausea follows which hangs around him long after he has fought his way into the fresh air, finally boredom with the endless monotony as he tries to pick up his stinking feet and skip. Look out: here it comes!

From the open bronze mold emerged a transparent green shape criss-crossed with pulsing red veins, liquid screen eyes swept by color flashes—A smell of sewage and decay breathing from years of torture films, orgasm death in his black eyes glinting with the slow fish lust of the swamp mud— Long tendril hands penetrated Bradly's broken body caressing the other being inside through the soft intestines into the pearly genitals rubbing centers of orgasm along his spine up to the neck—Exquisite toothache pain shot through his nerves and his body split down the middle—Sex words exploded to a poisonous color vapor that cut off his breath. . . .

On and on it flows, lapping slowly round what soon becomes a stereotyped debris: ectoplasm, jelly, errand boys, ferris wheels, used contraceptives, centipedes, old photographs, jockstraps, turnstiles, newts, and pubic hairs.

Such is the texture of the grey porridge in which Mr. Burroughs specializes. Three brimming books which he has filled with it for the Olympia Press have already attracted some speculative attention among those who have not read them, partly because of their excellent (though irrelevant) titles, partly because of the respectful admiration of one or two half-stupefied critics, but above all by their blacklisting by the British Customs and the U.S. Mails. Now the author himself has fished out an assortment of lumps from all three, stirring the mixture and topping it up to make a fourth, slightly more hygienic bucketful which can be cast before us swine.

Glug glug. It tastes disgusting, even without the detailed but always callous homosexual scenes and the unspeakable homosexual fantasies—pure verbal masturbation—that figure so largely in the Olympia Press volumes. Yet there are perfectly intelligent supporters of these books who see them as a deliberate indictment of the society we live in: as a satire on the American Way of Life, a great comic saga of the world below the navel, or a nightmare account of the drug addictions through which the author has passed. How far this can be held to make such a diet agreeable or nutritious is another matter, but it is quite true that Mr. Burroughs's writing gives some insight into the world of drugs, both by islets of straight description (as in the opening of *The Naked Lunch*, which is also the opening of the Calder volume) and by suggesting how the imagination and perceptions are affected. It frequently moves into a kind of farcical high gear, the charade-like style that a number of writers have borrowed from Joyce's Nighttown; while *The Ticket That Exploded* is written partly (though by no means predominantly) as a parody of science fiction. On the strength of such qualities it can be argued, as *The*

Saturday Review once put it, that 'the obscenities—if obscenities they are—are inseparable from the total fabric and effect of the moral message'.

But is there a moral message? And how about it if the moral message is itself disgusting? The texture of the passages of farce or satire is in fact very much the same as that of the porridge, even if it is now being chucked around for comic effect; most of them moreover are directed not against the junk world but against the doctors, policemen, psychiatrists and officials with whom the addict and the homosexual have to deal. They are seldom set in the United States, taking place rather in Mexico, Tangier, the Latin American republics or other areas closer associated with the expatriate's than with the American way of life. Nor do the most shocking episodes seem to be put forward in a particularly satirical spirit: like this relatively printable one from *The Naked Lunch*, for instance—

Met Marv in front of the Sagasso with two Arab kids and he said:
'Want to watch these two kids screw each other?'
'Of course. How much?'
'I think they will perform for fifty cents. Hungry, you know.'
'That's the way I like to see them.' Made me feel like a dirty old man but 'Son cosas de la vida' ... —

a comment meaning 'life's like that'. Or take the attitude to the young or relapsed addict, as seen in *The Soft Machine*—

I handed him two nickels under the table. Pushing in a small way to keep up The Habit: INVADE, DAMAGE, OCCUPY. Young faces in blue alcohol flame.

At the very least, such things are too uncritically presented, and because the author gives no flicker of disapproval the reader easily takes the 'moral message' to lie the other way.

In *Dead Fingers Talk* two of the author's farcical quacks are themselves arguing about the question of disgust:

SCHAFER: 'I tell you I can't escape a feeling—well, of *evil* about this.'
BENWAY: 'Balderdash, my boy—We're scientists—Pure scientists. Disinterested research and damned be him who cries "Hold, *too much!*" ...'
SCHAFER: 'Yes, yes, of course—and yet—I can't get that stench out of my lungs.'

There are Benways in the literary laboratory who feel that Mr. Burroughs's characteristic stench is justified by the solemn new 'fold-in' technique by which he claims to compose his books. 'You can cut into Naked Lunch at any intersection point', he says, and again in the same work:

The word cannot be expressed direct . . . It can perhaps be indicated by mosaic of juxtaposition like articles abandoned in a hotel drawer, defined by negatives and absences. . . .

What this amounts to is montage, piecing a book together from disjointed chunks that can be satire or parody or else like the unplanned dribbling and splashing of the action painter. Far from having any 'total fabric' in mind, the author can reshuffle the pieces and make a 'new' book, or the individual chunk can be broken down into phrases and sorted and scattered so that the words come tumbling out in a new order and the already familiar sentences slide out of focus.

This is not a bad way of conveying the mental mists of what Mr. Burroughs terms 'the pick-up frontier, a languid grey area of hiatus miasmic with yawns and gaping goof holes' (a zone he clearly knows well), while the repetitiveness to which it leads is only too natural to an author whose best phrases anyway tend to recur (the subway sweeping by 'with a black blast of iron', for instance), and whose images and adjectives—like 'obsidian'—are often overworked. But it is not always clear whether it is the writing or the writer that is being jumbled, while the air of pretentiousness which surrounds the whole business (aggravated by the author's readings on tape and a ridiculous short film) by no means excuses monotony and impoverishment of style. A yawn is a yawn is a yawn the reader soon comes to feel. The technique is of a piece with the material all right, but only in the sense that without the shocks and the stench there would be nothing much left.

'Montons la pompe à merde', says the old French army song. Well, now it has been mounted here, to produce lunch for the British. Sample menu:

The Clear Camel Piss Soup with boiled Earth Worms

The Filet of Sun-Ripened Sting Ray basted with
Eau de Cologne and garnished with nettles

The After-Birth Suprême de Bœuf cooked in drained crank case oil
served with a piquant sauce of
rotten egg yolks and crushed bed bugs

The Limburger Cheese sugar cured in diabetic urine
doused in Canned Heat Flamboyant

—as one of the supposedly comic chunks in the new house-trained version has it. A delicious prospect, especially considering the second helpings that another sieving-through of the material might produce. If the publishers had deliberately set out to discredit the cause of literary freedom and innovation they could hardly have done it more effectively. Let us hope that they are left to appreciate the probable impact on their own reputation, and indirectly on that of the other authors on their list, without any interfering body turning them into martyrs. Any juryman can vomit, but only one verdict can clear up the mess: that of the book world itself.

*   *   *

This article was followed by a correspondence which ran into 1964 and is far too copious to reprint here. It included a letter from the author himself, published on 23 January 1964, which referred to the second passage quoted on p. 223 and said:

My actual views on the junk industry and the infection of young people with the illness of addiction are well known to any one who reads what I have written on this subject. After many years of addiction to morphine I was cured by the apomorphine treatment developed by a London doctor. Since that time I have written a number of articles urging the use of this treatment since in my experience it is the only treatment that works. Two of these articles have been published in the American edition of *Naked Lunch*.

The moral message of *Dead Fingers Talk* should be quite clear to any reader: Quote Inspector J. Lee of the Nova Police: 'In all my experience as a police officer I have never seen such total fear and degradation on any planet' opus cit page 189 or 'This is war to extermination. Fight cell by cell through bodies and mind screens of the earth' opus cit page 49. Speaking of 'The Board' a cartel that plans to take over and monopolize space I say 'Liars cowards collaborator traitors. Liars who want time for more lies. Cowards who cannot face your "human animals" with the truth. Traitors to all souls everywhere'. Is this a disgusting message or does it just disgust the reviewer who will perhaps ask whether all this is to be taken seriously and I say it is to be taken as seriously as anything else in my work. It is the critic's job to evaluate what a writer is actually saying not to distort and falsify the writer's obvious intention. This job of evaluation was not done by your reviewer whoever he may be.

26

BLOOD AND SOIL

THE LADY OF LOUDUN

FAMOUS MURDER TRIALS light up the years and give a more precise sense of period than the reigns of monarchs or the terms of office of Presidents. The year 1937, as well as being that of the *Expo* which brought Paris the doubtful gift of the Palais de Chaillot, was that of the *affaire* Weidmann, the young German who came to France, succeeded in obtaining a job as a guide to the German Pavilion, murdered five or six people, and was the last person to be publicly executed in France. The Occupation will long be associated with the trial of Georges Arnaud, accused of the murder of his father and his mother, found battered to death in a wing of their chateau in the South-West; it was also the foundation of the reputation of Maître Floriot as the most redoubtable counsel at the Paris Bar. The immediate post-war era, the period of the Provisional Government, belongs uncontestably to the extravagant Dr. Petiot, though his activities with his private gas chamber and human-burning central heating system date to the more favourable circumstances of the Occupation; wars offer undreamt-of opportunities to mass murderers, both on the State and on private-enterprise levels.

*　　*　　*

The Fourth Republic should go without doubt to Marie Besnard— though her final trial took place under the Fifth—*la bonne dame de Loudun*, the lady in black, accused of having poisoned by arsenic eleven, then, more modestly, five of her relatives, among them her husband, her parents, her in-laws, and various aunts and cousins, including an old lady in her ninety-second year, who, Marie not unreasonably suggested, might be taken to have died of old age. There have, it is true, been other *causes célèbres*, and other miscarriages of justice. Dr. Petiot himself claimed to have killed twenty-

MARIE BESNARD: *The Trial of Marie Besnard*. Translated by Denise Folliot. 222 pp. Heinemann. 25s.

226

seven people, which puts him *hors concours*; the Dominici affair made possibly more of a stir, especially in England, in view of the eminence of the principal victim and the horror of Elizabeth Drummond's death; and at one time it was seen by the deputies of the Basses-Alpes as a threat to the department's tourist industry. The case of Madame Chevalier aroused perhaps almost as much attention, and more sympathy—but not for the victim, who was mayor and deputy of Orleans and Under-Secretary of State for Health; Madame Chevalier, who had shot her husband, was acquitted. And there have been plenty of other examples of the over-eagerness displayed both by the French police and by French *juges d'instruction* and *procureurs-généraux* to secure a conviction, in a murder case, at no matter what cost (including the physical and mental torture of the accused and recourse to prison informers, in an effort to produce the much-prized *aveu*). The most notorious of these was the trial of Marguerite Marty before the Perpignan *tribunal criminel*. It was largely thanks to the campaign conducted in the press by Georges Arnaud, who had himself been through the same terrible ordeal, that a retrial was eventually allowed, resulting in Mlle. Marty's acquittal.

*   *   *

Marie Besnard stands out, however, among these pygmies, for one reason because her case went on for such an extraordinarily long time —her first trial was in 1952, her last in 1961; her imprisonment lasted from 1949 to her release on bail in 1954—for another, because so many alleged victims were involved, and, perhaps most of all, because at each of her successive trials the experts, eminent professors, pathologists, chemists, were made to look bigger fools. It was the clash of experts that caught the public fancy and there was an element, too, of macabre comedy in the journeyings, to and fro across France, of intestines, livers, stomach linings, gall-bladders, kidneys, bile ducts, all finally inextricably mixed up in one another's jars—and even these multiplied, twelve left, thirteen returned—in the repeated exhumations and reburials (at the third trial there was even a scale model of Loudun cemetery, a piece of gross extravagance as Marie Besnard saw it, costing as it did 4,500 N.F.). There was general satisfaction at the discomfiture of the ineffable Dr. Beroud and of his unfortunate assistant, M. Médaille. It was unwise, too, to have chosen the first experts from Marseilles—a place which, quite unjustly, suffers from having Fernandel as its best-known citizen and which has been only too successful in selling its own Cannebière image of itself as a manufacture for improbable stories and *galéjades*.

At her first trial Madame Besnard had already been prejudged by an extremely hostile press campaign. Her guilt was taken for granted; on her first appearance in court, at Poitiers, she was hissed and booed, while her extremely able and devoted counsel, the late Maître Gautrat and Maître Hayot, were greeted with cries of *Les Parisiens à la porte*, so strong was the current of Poitevin opinion against her. Even her appearance went against her; the fact that, like so many French peasant women, she habitually wore black—and, goodness knows, she had enough people to mourn to keep her in black for a lifetime—was taken as a sign of hypocrisy, as were her frequent references to her Dear Departed, and the cross that she wore, some felt with undue ostentation. She was short-sighted, wore large and rather thick glasses, which gave her eyes a fishy expression—*l'air glauque, le regard sournois*. She wrote with green ink. And it looked very much as if she had had an affair with a German prisoner of war who had been employed by her as a farm hand; it was to be another ten years before official Franco-German friendship fully flowered.

*   *   *

In her introduction to *The Trial of Marie Besnard* Sybille Bedford suggests that such a miscarriage of justice as this long-drawn-out affair could not have occurred in England, where suspects cannot be held in prison indefinitely while the prosecution rakes up more material against them, subjecting them at the same time to every form of mental torture and where, in murder cases, matters are conducted far more expeditiously. This may well be so; on the other hand, it was partly the very length of her affair that eventually saved the *dame en noir*. One has an uneasy feeling that, in England, and with more efficient experts—Sir Bernard Spilsbury would not have got himself into the sort of position in which the unfortunate Dr. Beroud was to find himself—she might in fact have been condemned the first time, and then hanged; and then someone else would have had to write her trial. It is unwise to use the case to score points off French justice, as compared to our own.

*   *   *

Here then is Marie Besnard's own account of her tribulations, told in simple, direct language, illuminated now and then by an engaging dry humour and by a considerable degree of peasant slyness, and illustrated at frequent intervals by the sort of agricultural and animal metaphors that the leader of the Soviet Government favours in his public declarations, an account that has been very adequately translated in that it preserves much of the original simplicity and crispness. Marie does not believe in beating about the bush, she is crude, direct, unsentimental; with a considerable amount of rural shrewdness, she is not an educated woman, never having got beyond the *certificat d'études primaires*, and her choice of reading would be the horoscope page in *Confidences* or *Nous Deux*. She has certainly never heard of Balzac or even of her near neighbour, Hervé Bazin. In her desire to preserve the earthy, rural vigour of the original, the translator has, however, at times, mis-directed her aim (for instance, 'I had decided to make a clean breast of it' is not the same thing as 'J'avais décidé de tirer la chose au clair'; and one is a bit doubtful whether 'the young man who had made her "jump the gun"' is quite the right expression for a certain situation unfortunate for girls). One can also be grateful to the translator for having resisted the prevailing mode of translating everything; the *procureur général* remains the *procureur général*, we are not served up with such horrors as 'procurator fiscal' or 'process-server'. And the governors and directresses of prisons are given the titles their *pensionnaires* reserve for them: *Monsieur Chef, Madame Chef*.

It is a horrible story, about horrible people (the only pleasant characters in the book are the barristers, two or three very enlightened and human prison governors and directresses, a Salvation Army official, a Bishop, and some of Marie's fellow-prisoners—all of them, incidentally, townsmen and townswomen), in a horrible little market town, the centre of a very rich farming district. The inhabitants of Loudun live off the *rentes* of their land, the *notaires* abound there. Animal health takes precedence over human health; and Marie realizes there must be something up when her sister-in-law, who lives opposite, stops feeding her chickens and rabbits (there was indeed, for she at the time was hanging from the banisters). One is reminded of *The House with Green Shutters*, of *Eugénie Grandet*, of some of Maupassant's short stories, of Hervé Bazin's account of his own dreadful childhood, a little farther to the north, in the damp, fanatical *Craonnais*, and, perhaps, most of all, of a remarkable film by Clouzot, one of those jewels that appeared on the dunghill that was Vichy, *Le Corbeau*, the picture of a small, inbred, airless community in the grip of a writer of anonymous letters—itself essentially a rural and feminine occupation.

Suitably enough, Marie's principal accuser, Madame Pintou, is the postmistress—a person well placed for the acquisition and diffusion of nasty gossip. But she is by no means the only *oiseau noir* in the place. Madame Besnard's other enemies, with the exception of the eccentric Massip, are mostly persons that she or her husband, Léon, had given help to, in one way or another. It is possible, of course, that *la bonne dame* may not have been particularly tactful in the manner in which she administered charity; one does not have the impression that she often did something for nothing and one can be quite sure that she would not let services rendered remain unremembered. But clearly her principal fault, in the eyes of these people, was her wealth; even more, that she apparently got richer and richer as the years went by, and that the one person to profit from each successive death, so many of which occurred in her own comfortable house, was herself. For, in her book, people are always dying, the priest and Maître Demeule, the *notaire*—this is the order Marie puts them in her book, though, in fact, it should be Maître Demeule, the *notaire*, and the priest — are always hurrying to her house, sometimes just in time, sometimes not. Marie is always sending for her mourning, on several occasions two or three days in advance (local gossip, for what it is worth, would have it that she was also in the habit of ordering the coffins in advance too, even as much as a month ahead). One way or another, we are never far from the death bed, plates of cold soup, *pots de chambre*, vomit, death rattles, funeral dinners—both hot and cold—are the accessories of this pretty tale; more often than not, there is someone dying in the big bed upstairs, under the enormous red feathered quilt.

*   *   *

What is it all about? Money, *rentes viagères*, land, wills, houses, farms, furniture. Marie Besnard was—and, happily, is—a wealthy woman; just how wealthy, it is hard to tell. She admits to an annual income of some 400,000 francs, but this could mean anything, as it is not stated whether they are old or new ones. She admits too to owning three farms, with as many *métayers*; and there is an unspecified number of houses, including the local inn, at Loudun, and in the neighbourhood. She now has a house at Châtellerault as well, and has had her Loudun home completely redecorated since her release.

Clearly she was well set up; the frequent visits of Maître Demeule—for whom there is always a bottle of Marie's best—are not merely social. Madame Besnard is constantly buying more land, *pour arrondir son bien*, she has plenty of livestock, one imagines that there would be wads of notes hidden among the sheets and linen, and a *bas de laine* of *napoléons*, there is a full larder and a groaning table; she herself was never happier than when feeding her animals, her husband, the German farm hand and the successive ageing crones in the seventies, eighties or nineties who, at one time or another, are declining upstairs or down.

She was clearly an excellent *ménagère*, her meringues were appreciated far and wide, and it was probably her talents as a cook that laid her open to the suggestion that she had helped her husband, her parents, her in-laws, and so on, on their way to Loudun cemetery. One would imagine that she herself was *une bonne fourchette*, and that she never lost any sleep over anything other than livestock, land and money. Yet she is not just a hard, acquisitive peasant woman, the personification of that sordid cupidity, that brimming stinginess that the Prefects of 1812 attribute so justly to the big farmers who profit by the general calamity to make fortunes out of famine. Certainly, like most farmers, she made money during the Occupation, and she was never short of food. Yet she loves her animals, loves harvest work and the smell of the fields, in prison she was happy when she could work in the kitchen. She liked work, scrubbing, cooking, tidying up.

*   *   *

This is a peasant story all right, and so it is about avarice. Peasants are not nice people—especially rich ones, French peasants are nastier than most, those from the west of France are possibly the nastiest of all, as well as being superstitious, bigoted, reactionary, and brutish. The ancestors of Marie Besnard might have fought for *Christ et Roi*, in the murderous peasant bands of Charette. Their descendants are concerned with more mundane nastinesses. For it would be difficult to imagine a more unpleasant place than Loudun, with everyone watching everyone else, the flicker of a curtain drawn aside, of a shutter suddenly banged, a woman neighbour, prying on her doorstep, who suddenly disappears inside, as if in the presence of a leper, as Marie drives up (the Besnards have an old Peugeot) on her first return from prison, the endless, inane, nagging gossip at the local inn, ricks catching fire, cattle poisoned, a wing of the manor

house burnt (Marie does not have much to say about this, but her
neighbours do), petty affronts, accusations of theft, two young
drunks shouting insults outside Marie's bedroom window. There are
those who speak, and those who do not, *ceux qu'on salue, ceux qu'on
ne salue pas*, those you look through and those you recognize—a
constantly changing pattern of social exchanges, of visits and return
visits, an existence governed by elaborate, mysterious, ancient unspoken rules. Nothing is ever for nothing; everything has to be paid
for, equalled out, so that there will be no ill feelings. Human relationships are on a strictly give-and-take basis. Léon's aunt dies;
here is the scene described by Marie: 'We went to sprinkle holy
water [Marie's most regular form of manual exercise]. As we left
Léon said to his mother: "I did the right thing, I presume she did
too." "What do you mean by that?" "Did she remember me?" "No,
she's left everything to your sister and myself."

"Right, then I shan't go to the funeral" '—and they don't. After
this, there is a period of no talking with the in-laws, 'saying no more
than good morning . . . as we passed them . . . ' and there is still a trace
of resentment at the time of the old man's death: 'we were invited to
the funeral dinner, a cold meal . . . ' The Besnards do not speak to
Léon's sister, who lives in the house opposite. It is the same with
friends: Léon and Marie become very friendly with a retired couple:
'they liked good wine, they liked drinking coffee, they got them at our
house. We liked good cakes (Marie has a sweet tooth) and every Sunday, when they came to tea, they would get a fine cake from Leroux,
the best pastrycook in Loudun, and bring it with them . . . ' The Besnards rent some land to Marie's cousins, the rent is three quintals; 'as
we didn't need it, they used to send us a goose every year at Christmas
and we were quits.'

This is the iron law, the only code that counts, save possibly one
other, that is even stronger: family solidarity. Marie too accepts the
common law, and, speaking of one of the prosecution witnesses,
makes the following very revealing statement:

Garcin, Madame Pintou's son-in-law, . . . stuck up for her. Now he couldn't
do anything else, it was his family. But before, he should have remembered
how I helped him all through the war and occupation, sending him parcels
of clothes and food. . . .

Though, in her account, there is much talk of forgiveness, many
references to the 'dear ones' looking down on her and protecting her,
Marie is not altogether convincing when she drapes herself in such

strenuously Christian attitudes; one can see why her ill-wishers depicted her as hypocritical. She appears indeed more concerned with the forms to be observed at death than attached to her relatives themselves, and so she is particularly outraged at the exhumations, carried out on an almost industrial scale, in Loudun cemetery; her poor Léon is dug up three times, and almost her first visit, after her final release, is to the graveyard. Here she is reassured: 'there were no traces of the damage, the grave was neat, with the chippings tidily arranged between the stone curbs and the five pearl crowns with the crucifix in the middle. . . . ' The family can then rest in peace. Marie, clearly, is more preoccupied with the dead than with the quick. Her relations with the Almighty are close, personal, friendly; there is no doubt that she has a powerful and watchful ally in God. 'God manages things well', she states, charitably, on the subject of one of the female Judases who had turned against her: 'three days later Pascaline was laid on her back with an attack of sciatica, not able to move . . . ' There is further evidence of divine intervention, this time against her principal enemy, Massip; the *châtelain* had left France for Tangier, after having been fined 1,200,000 francs for insulting General de Gaulle: 'See what queer coincidences there are in life', observes *la bonne Marie* gleefully, 'a coffin arrived, bearing his body to his native land! . . . ' Obviously, it does not pay to be on the wrong side. Massip is not the only one. 'Another of those who hunted me, old Toussaint', is not even allowed to have died, he 'croaked', as Marie pleasantly explains to the old boy's grandson, adding: 'Don't bother praying for him, it wouldn't be any use, he's in hell.' It is not really surprising that people found the old girl rather alarming and accused her of having the evil eye.

*　　　*　　　*

Like most books concerned with murder, Marie's memoirs are at times extremely funny. Sometimes the humour is unconscious, more rarely we can hear her own cracked, malicious laughter. There is a fine piece about the inmates of the Petite Roquette: 'A large, clean dormitory with twelve white, roomy beds, and I saw at once that there was a much better type of people than in the place I had come from. My companions were abortionists and women who had had abortions. They were educated and talked agreeably. . . . Number Five was for the élite, and I was lucky to be there. . . . ' When her sister-in-law hangs herself—and again neighbours were quick to point out that she must have been something of a gymnast to have succeeded in tying herself to the banisters—Marie goes with her husband to see the body; it is their first visit to the house on the other side of the street for years: 'My God! when I saw her I thought I'd faint. Even if you haven't much affection for someone, it's terrible to see them hanged.' But she really shared in the fun at the expense of Beroud and Médaille: 'My lawyers proved that they had mixed everything up, muscles and viscera, that they had found an eye in a skeleton. Médaille replied that they had found the eye, but they did not know in which box it had been or whose it was.' It was possibly the straying eye that saved Marie.

Even so, it is mainly with a feeling of relief that we put down this chronicle of petty nastiness, meanness and delation. Relief for the fact that we live in a predominantly urban community, that we are reasonably safe from croaking gossip and from the attentions of those subterranean beings who write anonymous letters; relief for the fact that the word *dénonciateur* is difficult to translate into English. When all is said and done, one is tempted to exclaim: thank God the English yeomanry is dead and gone, along with stocks and ducking stools, Morris dancing, maypoles, milkmaids, *Tess*, fires burning from the beacons, and the whole nightmare band of rural Walpurgia; we have got a lot to thank the Industrial Revolution for. There is nowhere in England quite like Loudun; but can we be so sure that there isn't over the border?

INDEX

This index, in addition to referring to articles and reviews in the present volume, also shows other major reviews of the year which have appeared in the *T.L.S.*
Date references and page numbers *in italic* are to articles and reviews in the *T.L.S.* not reprinted in this volume. Page numbers in parentheses are given only where the reference is not immediately obvious from the article.

235